Ex Líbris

Randy Manning

B212 © APCo

GREAT CAMPAIGNS

THE PETERSBURG CAMPAIGN

GREAT CAMPAIGN SERIES

GREAT CAMPAIGNS

THE PETERSBURG CAMPAIGN

June 1864 - April 1865

John Horn

COMBINED BOOKS
Pennsylvania

PUBLISHER'S NOTE

Combined Books, Inc., is dedicated to publishing books of distinction in history and military history. We are proud of the quality of writing and the quantity of information found in our books. Our books are manufactured with style and durability and are printed on acid-free paper. We like to think of our books as soldiers: not infantry grunts, but well dressed and well equipped avant garde. Our logo reflects our commitment to the modern and yet historic art of bookmaking.

We call ourselves Combined Books because we view the publishing enterprise as a "combined" effort of authors, publishers and readers. And we promise to bridge the gap between us–a gap which is all too seldom closed in contemporary publishing.

We would like to hear from our readers and invite you to write to us at our offices in Pennsylvania with your reactions, queries, comments, even complaints. All of your correspondence will be answered directly by a member of the Editorial Board or by the author.

We encourage all of our readers to purchase our books from their local booksellers, and we hope that you let us know of booksellers in your area that might be interested in carrying our books. If you are unable to find a book in your area, please write to us.

For information, address:
COMBINED BOOKS, INC.
151 East 10th Avenue
Conshohocken, PA 19428

Library of Congress Cataloging-in-Publication Data
Horn, John (John Edward)
The Petersburg campaign : June 1864-April 1865 / by John Horn.
    p.   cm. —(Great campaigns)
    Includes bibliographical references and index.
    ISBN 0-938289-28-4 : $22.95
    1. Petersburg (Va.)—History—Siege, 1864-1865. I. Title. II. Series.
E476.93.H68   1993
973.7'37—dc20   93-13890   CIP
Combined Books Edition   1   2   3   4   5
First published in the USA in 1993 by Combined Books and distributed in North America by Stackpole Books, Inc., 5067 Ritter Road, Mechanicsburg, PA 17055 and internationally by Greenhill Books, Lionel Leventhal Ltd., 1 Russell Gardens, London NW11 9NN
Printed in Hong Kong.

*To Matt and Helen Kelley of Powhatan
County, Virginia*

Acknowledgments

As far as I am concerned, anyone who reads and comments on somebody else's manuscript deserves a medal. If I could, I would pin decorations on (in alphabetical order) Ed Bearss, John Hendron, Bryce Suderow and Andy Trudeau. Scarcely a page of this book failed to benefit from their suggestions and corrections. Any remaining errors are entirely my responsibility.

Reading a manuscript is one thing. Deciphering a microfilm copy of an ancient dairy scrawled in pencil and later retraced in ink is above and beyond the call of duty. Without Bill Zielinski's time and effort, George S. Bernard's war diaries would have remained largely untranscribable. Thanks, again Bill.

Thanks are also due Mrs. Alexander Hamilton for permission to publish the excerpts from Bernard's diaries, and to the staff of the University of Virginia's Alderman Library for their assistance in microfilming.

Stylistic Note

I have generally referred to the various corps, divisions and brigades of both sides by the surnames of their commanders. This was the ordinary practice in the Confederate armies, but not with the Union forces. To distinguish between the official unit names and my own unofficial designations, I have capitalized the unit name in the former case but not in the latter. Some Confederate brigades retained the name of a former commander. Wright's Brigade, for example, was for a short time led by Brigadier General Victor J.B. Girardey. Another, the Texas Brigade, was known by its nickname. A number of Union brigades are also referred to by their nicknames: the *Maryland Brigade* of the *V Corps* and the *Vermont Brigade* of the *VI Corps*.

To further simplify matters several ahistorical conventions have been adopted in this work:

1. The identities of Union units are in *italics*.
2. Union Army corps have been designated with Roman numerals.
3. Times have been rendered on a 24-hour basis.

Contents

Maps

Sidebars

Preface to the Series

*J*onathan Swift termed war "that mad game the world so loves to play." He had a point. Universally condemned, it has nevertheless been almost as universally practiced. For good or ill, war has played a significant role in the shaping of history. Indeed, there is hardly a human institution which has not in some fashion been influenced and molded by war, even as it helped shape and mold war in turn. Yet the study of war has been as remarkably neglected as its practice commonplace. With a few outstanding exceptions, the history of wars and of military operations has until quite recently been largely the province of the inspired patriot or the regimental polemicist. Only in our times have serious, detailed and objective accounts come to be considered the norm in the treatment of military history and related matters.

Yet there still remains a gap in the literature, for there are two types of military history. One type is written from a very serious, highly technical, professional perspective and presupposes that the reader is deeply familiar with the background, technology and general situation. The other is perhaps less dry, but merely lightly reviews the events with the intention of informing and entertaining the layman. The qualitative gap between the last two is vast. Moreover, there are professionals in both the military and academia whose credentials are limited to particular moments in the long, sad history of war, and there are laymen who have more than a passing understanding of the field; and then there is the concerned citizen, interested in understanding the phenomena in an age of unusual violence and unprecedented armaments. It is to bridge the gap between the two types of military history, and to reach the professional and the serious amateur and the concerned citizen alike, that this series, **GREAT CAMPAIGNS**, is designed. Each volume in **GREAT CAMPAIGNS** is thus not merely an account of a particular military operation, but it is a unique reference to the theory and practice of war in the period in question.

The **GREAT CAMPAIGNS** series is a distinctive contribution to the study of war and of military history, which will remain of value for many years to come.

CHAPTER I

War Comes to the Cockade City

By the beginning of May 1864, Petersburg, Virginia, had lost much of the appearance of a peacetime city. Its parks and warehouses now served as hospitals for hordes of sick and wounded. Its former cotton and tobacco factories now turned out munitions for the armed forces of the Confederate States of America. Many of its able-bodied white men had joined those forces and remained absent on duty with them.

But Petersburg's remaining citizens went about their business almost exactly as they had before Virginia's secession on 17 April 1861. The city's predominantly African-American and female labor force went off to work each day in the factories. Farmers from the surrounding countryside still brought their produce to the city's markets. Wedding and funeral processions still outnumbered military columns on the city's streets. Beneath the four-sided clock of the courthouse, citizens resolved their disputes without resort to arms.

Petersburg ought to have long since completed its assumption of the somber aspect of a beleaguered city. The Federals had recognized Petersburg's significance for more than two years. They knew that the city at the falls of the Appomattox River held the key to the Confederate capital at Richmond, 23 miles due north.

Five railroad lines terminated at Petersburg. The Richmond & Petersburg Railroad connected Petersburg with the capital. The Petersburg Railroad, commonly called the Weldon Rail-

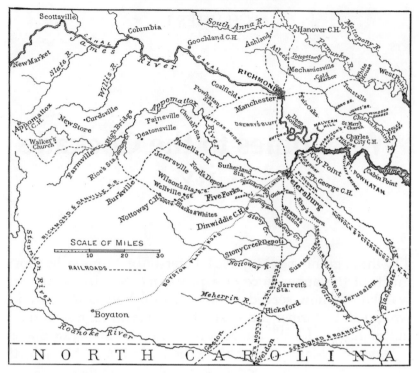

Southern Virginia

road, ran between Petersburg and Weldon, North Carolina. Together, these two railroads provided the only direct rail line between Richmond and the coastal regions of the Carolinas and Georgia. The South Side Railroad linked Petersburg with eastern Tennessee and, at Burke's Station, with the Deep South via the Richmond & Danville Railroad. The City Point branch of the South Side Railroad gave fall line Petersburg access to the deepwater port at City Point. The Norfolk & Petersburg Railroad ran through the bountiful country west of the Blackwater River before entering Northern-occupied territory near Suffolk.

Before launching his Peninsula campaign in March 1862, Major General George B. McClellan considered the alternative of an advance toward Petersburg along the south side of the James River. In July 1862, after the failure of his campaign, he proposed such an advance to his superiors.

The object of the Federal siege from June 1864 to April 1865, Petersburg, Virginia, the Cockade City.

The Confederates did not lag far behind their enemies in recognizing Petersburg's importance and vulnerability. Work on fortifications to protect the city began in the summer of 1862 under the direction of Captain Charles H. Dimmock. Free and slave laborers spent the next year building a chain of low infantry parapets and prominent artillery emplacements 10 miles long. They dug ditches six to eight feet deep and 15 feet wide in front of the breastworks. To provide clear fields of fire from the fortifications, they cut down woods for half a mile. Dragging the felled trees to within a few yards of the ditches, they constructed abatis by sharpening the branches. The huge semi-circle began east of the city on the lower Appomattox River and ended on the upper river west of the city. It protected all of the southern approaches to Petersburg. Fifty-five artillery batteries had consecutive numbers from east to west. Known as the "Dimmock Line," it required 20,000 troops to man properly.

The idea of an advance on the south side of the James River

toward Petersburg resurfaced among the Federals in November and December of 1862. Early in the following year, General Robert E. Lee temporarily detached Lieutenant General James Longstreet and two divisions of his corps from the Army of Northern Virginia to operate Southside. Lee wanted Confederate soldiers there to meet such an advance, which seemed inevitable to him.

In February 1864, one of Major General Ulysses S. Grant's subordinates proposed an advance from Suffolk on Petersburg as a variation of a Grant plan to advance from Suffolk on Weldon, North Carolina.

But fate had so far intervened in favor of Petersburg. In March 1862, the CSS *Virginia* had closed the James River to McClellan. In July and November, the inept Federal general in chief, Major General Henry W. Halleck, had dismissed the notion of an advance on Petersburg as dangerous and impracticable. In December, President Abraham Lincoln shelved the proposed movement on the city. The advance that seemed inevitable to Lee in the spring of 1863 failed to materialize. In the spring of 1864, Grant—newly promoted to lieutenant general—abandoned any notions he had of a seaborne campaign and made his main effort an overland thrust toward Richmond that would cover Washington, D.C.

Though he retained as part of his plan a movement against Lee's communications south of the James, Grant designated the object of this advance as Richmond, not Petersburg. Its path lay through Chesterfield County, south of the James but north of the Appomattox. The plan called for the forces advancing overland to join those moving up the James within 10 days.

Major General Benjamin F. Butler had command of the critical advance up the James. He had little experience as a field commander, but Grant could not remove him with a crucial election coming up in November. This former lawyer and powerful Massachusetts politician, though a Democrat, supported the war.

Butler had two corps commanders with West Point training, but friction between him and them developed before the

The most hated Northern general in the South, Benjamin "Beast" Butler.

campaign even began. Major General William F. "Baldy" Smith, the commander of the *XVIII Corps* from Butler's own Department of Virginia, exhibited the same contentiousness that had marred his relations with most of his previous superiors. Major General Quincy A. Gillmore displayed an irksome slowness in assembling the ragtag X *Corps* from detachments scattered through the Department of the South.

The Confederate War Department recognized the threat to Richmond's back door. Unlike the Federals, the Southerners did not let politics interfere with their dispositions near the James River. On 22 April 1864, General P.G.T. Beauregard received orders to proceed to Weldon and take command of the area stretching from the James to Cape Fear. One of the Confederacy's most able and experienced field commanders, he had long since fallen from favor with President Jefferson Davis and Davis' military adviser, General Braxton Bragg. But with Lee in charge of the Army of Northern Virginia, General Joseph E. Johnston in command of the Army of Tennessee and Bragg in eclipse for having lost the battle of Missionary Ridge the previous November, Davis had nowhere else to turn.

A few days after taking command, Beauregard began reorganizing the Department of North Carolina and Southern Virginia. He wanted to withdraw the Confederate troops threatening the Federal enclaves on North Carolina's coast in order to position those troops to meet the Northern thrust that Southern intelligence indicated would soon come up the James. He also sought reinforcements from his old Department of South Carolina, Georgia & Florida to meet this advance. Petersburg seemed the inevitable objective of such a Union offensive.

On 28 April, the Confederate War Department started ordering troops from Beauregard's old Department of South Carolina, Georgia & Florida to entrain, but directed most of them to Richmond rather than to Beauregard. Permission to withdraw the Confederate troops threatening the Federal enclaves on North Carolina's coast did not come until 4 May.

While forces immediately under Grant began fighting Lee's Army of Northern Virginia in the Wilderness on 5 May 1864, Butler's men landed and took possession of Wilson's Wharf on the north side of the James, Fort Powhatan and City Point on the Southside and the Bermuda Hundred peninsula at the confluence of the James and the Appomattox Rivers. Butler had achieved nearly complete surprise. He had 12 brigades of

General Pierre Gustave Toutant Beauregard led the defense of Petersburg and Richmond in May 1864. This veteran of Fort Sumter, First Bull Run and Shiloh managed to defeat a superior Federal force at Drewry's Bluff and then besieged it at Bermuda Hundred.

infantry on Bermuda Hundred and two more at City Point. The Federals could have walked into Petersburg virtually unopposed if their orders had called for the city's capture.

But Grant's instructions to Butler did not mention Petersburg. They called for Butler to advance on Richmond after he finished fortifying the neck of the Bermuda Hundred peninsula. During the early morning hours of 6 May, it occurred to Butler to forego fortifying and advance boldly toward Richmond. But the inexperienced Butler lacked sufficient confidence in his judgment to override the objections of his West Point educated corps commanders and depart from Grant's orders. His chances of investing Richmond from the south began slipping away.

Before dawn on 6 May, as Butler rejected the idea of an immediate advance on Richmond, Johnson's Tennessee Brigade crossed the James and joined the 450 man garrison of Fort Darling at Drewry's Bluff, seven miles below Richmond. Around noon, Gracie's Alabama Brigade took the place of Johnson's Brigade, which advanced to Ware Bottom Church. These dispositions eliminated the possibility of a rapid investment of Richmond from the south.

Petersburg remained nearly defenseless. Its garrison consisted of a single regiment of Clingman's North Carolina Brigade. Another of Clingman's regiments was en route toward the city from the Blackwater River line. From his headquarters at Weldon, Beauregard expedited the progress of reinforcements northward by rail.

Butler did not launch an advance out of his beachhead until late in the afternoon. He ordered Baldy Smith and Gillmore each to send a brigade toward the Richmond & Petersburg Railroad at Port Walthall Junction. Gillmore failed to cooperate, and Heckman's brigade of Baldy Smith's corps undertook the mission alone.

At 1700, as the weak Federal reconnaissance inched toward the railroad, less than a regiment from Hagood's South Carolina Brigade barred the way. These Southerners had proceeded by rail through Petersburg to Drewry's Bluff before orders sent them back to Port Walthall Junction. The remainder of this regiment and part of another from Hagood's Brigade arrived by rail from the south just before the Federals deployed to attack. The South Carolinians took position in a sunken lane yards east of the railroad and fended off Heckman's feeble thrust.

By midnight, the situation had improved still further for the Confederates. Another regiment and a half of Hagood's men had arrived at Port Walthall Junction. Johnson's, Gracie's and Hagood's Brigades confronted Butler's 12 brigades of Federal foot soldiers in the Bermuda Hundred beachhead,

Quincy Gillmore commanded the X Corps *during Butler's campaign and was blamed by his superior for its failure.*

while part of Clingman's Brigade at Petersburg opposed the two Union infantry brigades at City Point.

On 7 May Barton's Virginia Brigade joined Gracie's Brigade in the entrenchments at Drewry's Bluff. Johnson's Brigade united with Hagood's Brigade at Port Walthall Junction under the command of Brigadier General Bushrod Johnson. The Northerners made a heavier attack on the railroad at the junction at 1000, with three brigades of Gillmore's corps and two of Baldy Smith's brigades under Brigadier General William T.H. Brooks. The Federals gradually pushed the less numerous Confederates back to the railroad, but the resistance of Johnson's command prevented more than minimal damage to the tracks. Johnson's men withdrew to Swift Creek that evening, but the Federals failed to follow.

While Brooks and Johnson battled over the Richmond & Petersburg Railroad, a Union cavalry division under Brigadier General August V. Kautz severed the Weldon Railroad by burning the bridge over Stony Creek, about 20 miles south of Petersburg.

Butler allowed 8 May to pass without taking any offensive action while the battle of Spotsylvania began and Grant sent his cavalry toward Richmond under Major General Philip H. Sheridan. Grant had given Sheridan the mission of forcing a fight with Lee's cavalry, led by Major General James E.B. "Jeb" Stuart.

South of Petersburg, Kautz's cavalry raiders continued to wreak havoc on the Weldon Railroad. They wrecked Jarratt's Depot, about 30 miles south of Petersburg, and burned the bridge over the Nottoway River, between Jarratt's Depot and Stony Creek. Beauregard dispersed the regiments of Wise's Virginia Brigade, which was en route to Petersburg from South Carolina, by posting them to guard the railroad at several points.

Butler's Federals finally reached the Richmond & Petersburg Railroad in strength on the following day. Shortly after sunrise, Baldy Smith's column of five brigades moved on Port Walthall Junction while Gillmore's column of four brigades advanced toward Chester Station. Three Federal brigades remained in the Bermuda Hundred entrenchments. The Northerners demolished the railroad at Port Walthall Junction and Chester Station that morning. In the afternoon, Butler decided to feint toward Petersburg. Baldy Smith's and Gillmore's men skirmished with Johnson's command for the rest of the day along the line of Swift Creek.

While this half-hearted struggle took place, the Confederates in Fort Clifton, at the confluence of Swift Creek and the

Appomattox River, withstood the onslaught of the Union army's gunboats and destroyed one of them. South of the Appomattox, a motley force of Southern cavalry thwarted a probe from City Point toward Petersburg by Brigadier General Edward W. Hinks' division of *United States Colored Troops*. At nightfall, Lewis' Virginia Brigade arrived in Petersburg by rail from the south. Its men had marched around the 10-mile gap the Federal raiders had left in the railroad. Reports of a Union victory in northern Virginia prompted Butler to reject the suggestion of his corps commanders that he transfer his army south of the Appomattox to operate against Petersburg and its rail lines. He elected to return to Grant's original plan and advance toward Richmond.

At daybreak on 10 May, under Major General Robert Ransom, the commander of the Department of Richmond, Barton's and Gracie's Brigades advanced south from Drewry's Bluff toward part of Gillmore's corps. Between Chester Station and Ware Bottom Church, Ransom's men skirmished in sweltering heat with the *67th Ohio* of Howell's brigade. Even though the Ohioans received reinforcements from Drake's brigade, Barton's Virginians captured a cannon from the Northerners at 1100. The arrival of Hawley's brigade brought Ransom to a halt, and he withdrew from the burning woods. After both sides tried with mixed success to rescue their wounded from the flames, Butler ordered his troops back to their Bermuda Hundred position to realign for the prescribed advance on Richmond.

While the battle of Chester Station sputtered along, Hunton's Virginia Brigade crossed from north of the James to Drewry's Bluff. Beauregard himself finally arrived at Petersburg along with Matt Ransom's North Carolina Brigade, William Terry's Virginia Brigade, Wise's Brigade and the remainder of Clingman's Brigade. Major General George E. Pickett, who had conducted Petersburg's defense up to this point with only Johnson's, Hagood's and part of Clingman's Brigades, reported himself sick.

Late in the day, Sheridan's powerful column approached Richmond from the northwest. With the capital threatened

Someone told Grant that Major General Philip Sheridan was "a rather little fellow to handle your cavalry." Grant replied, "You will find him big enough for the purpose before we get through with him."

from two directions, Davis urged Beauregard to alleviate the threat from the south by a prompt attack. Beauregard wisely ignored Davis and concentrated on organizing the seven brigades at Petersburg that finally rendered the city safe.

But Petersburg did not remain well protected for long. Throughout the night, Bragg and Confederate Secretary of War James A. Seddon badgered Beauregard to send reinforcements under Major General Robert F. Hoke from Petersburg to Drewry's Bluff. Bragg and Seddon believed that this would render Richmond safe from both Sheridan and Butler.

Early on the steamy day of 11 May, Sheridan's threat prompted the Confederate high command to return Hunton's Brigade to Richmond. Meanwhile, Colquitt's Georgia Brigade and part of Corse's Virginia Brigade reached Petersburg. At 1000, Hoke and six brigades of infantry moved out from the Cockade City and a seventh brigade followed shortly afterward. The Southerners marched across the front of the quiescent Federals at Bermuda Hundred as if on parade and arrived at Drewry's Bluff at 1700. Their arrival allowed Gracie's Brigade to depart for Richmond.

Panic gripped the capital. North of Richmond, at Yellow Tavern, Sheridan's horse soldiers in a savage fight were besting Stuart's cavalry and Stuart had fallen mortally wounded. During the afternoon, Bragg and Seddon bombarded Beauregard with contradictory orders. His threat to resign restored his superiors to their senses.

Early on 12 May, while the fighting at Spotsylvania's Bloody Angle raged, Butler's army embarked on a demonstration toward Richmond to cover Kautz's departure on what turned into a week-long raid on the Richmond & Danville Railroad. Butler also wanted to prevent Beauregard from sending units to reinforce Lee. Three divisions under Baldy Smith slowly pressed Confederate skirmishers back through the rain-soaked underbrush to Proctor's Creek. Two divisions under Gillmore guarded the army's left and rear.

North of the James, Sheridan's movements prompted the Confederate high command to order Matt Ransom and Barton's, Lewis' and William Terry's Brigades back from Drewry's Bluff to Richmond. At Petersburg, Martin's North Carolina Brigade and the remainder of Corse's Brigade finally arrived.

Before dawn on 13 May, Beauregard sent off the two regiments of Corse's Brigade at Petersburg to protect the Richmond & Danville Railroad bridges from Kautz's raiders. To guard Petersburg, Beauregard left Martin's and Wise's Brigades under the command of Major General William H. C.

Robert F. Hoke engineered the capture of a Union garrison of 3,000 men at Plymouth, North Carolina, in April 1864. His next assignment was with Beauregard in Virginia.

Whiting, whom Beauregard had summoned from Fort Fisher in North Carolina to replace the ailing Pickett. Beauregard himself departed for Drewry's Bluff along with part of Colquitt's Brigade. He marched by way of Chesterfield Court House.

If he had not taken this circuitous route, the Northerners might have captured him. Late in the afternoon, Gillmore's men turned the right of the outer Confederate works at Drewry's Bluff by taking Woodridge's Hill. Hoke's four and a half brigades retreated to the intermediate line of fortifications. Farther east, Baldy Smith's troops crossed Proctor's Creek and halted in front of this line.

Beauregard arrived at Drewry's Bluff before dawn on the rainy morning of 14 May. As soon as he dismounted, he began to plan the destruction of the Union armies in eastern Virginia. He envisioned a Napoleonic battle of the central position. The Southerners would use their interior lines to concentrate against first Butler and then Grant and defeat them in detail. To encompass Butler's destruction, Beauregard thought he would require 15,000 reinforcements. They could either come entirely from Lee's army or include the 5,000 men in Robert Ransom's four brigades at Richmond. Lee would retreat into the Richmond defenses from the Spotsylvania lines while the Richmond, Fredericksburg & Potomac Railroad carried the contingent from his army to the capital. The reinforcements would join Beauregard's 10,000 troops at Drewry's Bluff and attack Butler from the north. Whiting would attack from the south with the 5,000 infantry at Petersburg. The Confederates would cut off Butler from his Bermuda Hundred base and destroy his army. Then Beauregard would take 25,000 men to join Lee and dispose of Grant.

While the Federal skirmishers finished occupying the outer line of fortifications at Drewry's Bluff, Davis and Bragg conferred with Beauregard. The president and his military adviser lacked the nerve for the risks involved in Beauregard's bold and logical plan. For an attack on Butler, Beauregard would get only 5,000 reinforcements—the 5,000 men from the Department of Richmond. To make matters worse, Davis interfered with Beauregard's tactical plan. The president directed Beauregard to order Whiting's men to Drewry's Bluff. Beauregard glumly told Whiting to leave Petersburg on 16 May, contemplating an attack two days later. Dearing's Brigade of cavalry and Walker's South Carolina Brigade received orders to proceed to the Cockade City, which they would guard after Whiting's departure.

Southwest of Petersburg, one of Corse's regiments successfully defended the bridge over Flat Creek, near Chula, against Spear's brigade of Kautz's division. This ensured that Kautz's troopers would inflict only superficial damage on the Confederate railroads.

Federal reconnaissances had revealed a point in the Confederate fortifications vulnerable to assault. At 2100, Butler ordered Baldy Smith to attack on the following day. Smith disliked the idea, but began to prepare. Lack of troops to provide flank protection eventually furnished him with the excuse necessary to persuade Butler to cancel the attack.

While Butler passed to the defensive, Beauregard assumed the offensive. At 0645 on 15 May, the same day as Confederates under Major General John C. Breckinridge at New Market defeated a Union force thrusting up the Shenandoah Valley under Major General Franz Sigel, Bragg learned of Beauregard's intention of attacking on Wednesday 18 May. Davis and Seddon disapproved of the delay. Violating the chain of command, they had Bragg order Whiting to proceed to Drewry's Bluff immediately. Soon afterward, Bragg suggested that Beauregard attack on Monday morning.

Beauregard resolved the administration's mutually exclusive desires by returning to his original plan, but not its timing. The attack would now take place on 16 May. Whiting would not join Beauregard at Drewry's Bluff, but would attack the Federal flank and rear from Petersburg. Confronted with this *fait accompli*, Davis grumbled, but declined to postpone the offensive long enough for Whiting to unite with Beauregard at Drewry's Bluff.

While Sheridan's troopers rested on the other side of the James, Beauregard issued orders for the following day's attack. These orders called for Robert Ransom, the commander of the Department of Richmond, to mass his four brigades on the Confederate left. At dawn, he would attack the Union right and drive the Federals away from the James. Hoke's four brigades would attack in echelon as Robert Ransom's Division swept the Northerners across their fronts. Colquitt's two brigades would remain in reserve. On the other side of the battlefield, Whiting's two and a half brigades of infantry and one brigade of cavalry would advance from Petersburg and cut off Butler's army from Bermuda Hundred.

That night, Corse's two detached regiments arrived via the railroads that they had helped protect from Kautz and rejoined their brigade. Just before dawn on 16 May, the descent of a thick mist compounded the fog of war. At 0500, Robert Ransom's Division struck Butler's unprotected right, Brigadier General Charles A. Heckman's brigade of Smith's corps, and captured Heckman himself. The Confederates drove Heckman's brigade back toward Half-Way House, so called because it stood halfway between Richmond and Petersburg. Disorganization, shortage of ammunition and the arrival of Union reinforcements brought Robert Ransom's Division to a halt. Pitching in at about 0600, Hoke's Division made little headway. Near the Richmond and Petersburg Turnpike, Hagood's and Johnson's Brigades suffered from severe Union fire.

As Hoke advanced, Butler ordered Gillmore to counterattack. While Gillmore responded with glacial slowness, Smith panicked at 0745 and ordered his corps to withdraw to Half-Way House. Gillmore, who had received another order to conform his movements to Smith's, followed at 0900.

Several miles to the south, Whiting's Division failed to press the attack and cut off the Federals from Bermuda Hundred. Its commander, obsessed with Petersburg's vulnerability, lost his nerve and withdrew to the Cockade City.

By 1400, the Federals had consolidated near Half-Way House. An hour and a half later, Butler decided to withdraw his army to Bermuda Hundred. More than 10 days had passed and Grant had not even come close to uniting with Butler. By 2100, Butler's army had returned to the Bermuda Hundred lines.

Despite the limited success of Robert Ransom and the abject failure of Whiting, Beauregard had achieved one of the war's most remarkable successes. With a scratch force assembled mere hours before the battle, at a cost of 3,000 killed, wounded and missing, he inflicted 3,500 casualties on the Northerners and captured five cannon, five flags, 4,000 muskets and a brigadier general. More importantly, he cleared the transportation corridor between Richmond and Petersburg and made it impossible for Grant's forces to invest Richmond from the south when and if those forces reached the James.

On 18 May, after bottling up Butler in the Bermuda Hundred peninsula, Beauregard submitted to the Davis administration a memorandum setting forth another plan involving

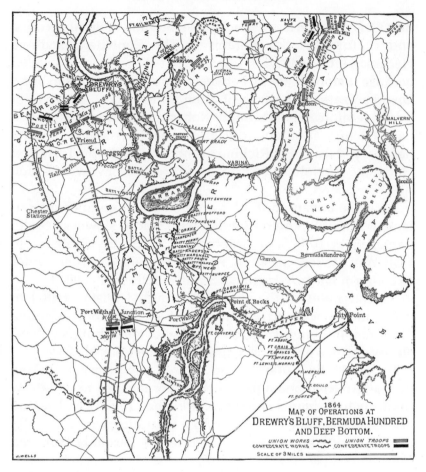

1864
MAP OF OPERATIONS AT
DREWRY'S BLUFF, BERMUDA HUNDRED
AND DEEP BOTTOM.

Lee's army. This plan called for Lee to retreat behind the Chickahominy while Beauregard marched north with 15,000 men to operate on Grant's flank. After Grant's defeat, Beauregard would return to Bermuda Hundred with reinforcements from Lee's army and destroy Butler.

While this plan made its way up the chain of command, Beauregard prepared to destroy Butler using only the troops of the Department of North Carolina and Southern Virginia. Beauregard intended to drive the Federals back to a narrower part of the Bermuda Hundred peninsula, where he could hold them with fewer troops. He would then take the rest of his men and storm Fort Powhatan, about 10 miles down the James from City Point. The erection of Confederate batteries at Fort Powhatan would cut Butler's supply line and render his position untenable.

The memorandum containing the plan involving Lee's army reached Davis on 19 May. Davis used it as justification for ordering Beauregard to send 10,000 reinforcements to Lee immediately. The departure of the 10,000 scuttled Beauregard's plan to destroy the Federals at Bermuda Hundred using only the forces of his own department. But even with those forces reduced, Beauregard attacked as planned on 20 May. At a cost of 800 casualties, he inflicted 702 on the Northerners and succeeded in driving them back to where he could hold them with fewer troops.

Together with his own lack of progress, the defeats of Sigel and Butler depressed Grant. He began to consider withdrawing Butler's army and consolidating it with his own, but Lee's retreat from Spotsylvania caused him to hesitate. If Lee retreated into the Richmond defenses, the force at Bermuda Hundred would be well positioned to participate in operations against the Confederate general's communications. But that contingency did not arise. Lee halted on the North Anna River. On 25 May, Grant ordered Baldy Smith and about 20,000 men to West Point on the York River.

On the following day, Butler considered advancing on Petersburg to keep his army intact. Among the Southerners, who had finally repaired all the damage that Kautz and Butler had done to the railroads, the rumor arose for the first time that Grant intended to transfer his army to the south bank of the James.

By the afternoon of 28 May, Butler had ordered an advance on Petersburg for the following day provided that not enough shipping arrived to transport Smith's reinforced corps to West Point. That evening, the shipping arrived and Butler canceled the advance. Instead of attacking a city protected by a regiment of infantry and a handful of militia, Smith departed for West Point with 16,000 men on 29 May. Intelligence of the transports headed down the James reached Lee on the following day as he neared Cold Harbor. He immediately demanded reinforcements. Beauregard sent Hoke's Division to Lee that night.

In the stalemate that now prevailed on the Bermuda Hundred front, Butler continued to contemplate an advance on Petersburg. On 1 June, he scheduled an attack by infantry and cavalry from City Point for the following morning, but a Confederate reconnaissance in force on his picket line caused him to cancel the plan.

On 3 June, Grant's Overland campaign ended with a bang at the second battle of Cold Harbor. Hurling itself against the supposedly demoralized Army of Northern Virginia, the *Army of the Potomac*, reinforced by Smith's corps, was repulsed with a loss of 7,000 men.

The Bermuda Hundred campaign ended with a whimper on the following day as Beauregard detached Matt Ransom's Brigade to the Department of Richmond. This left him with three brigades of infantry and one of cavalry in addition to a few reservists and militia. He had 5,400 men at Bermuda Hundred and Petersburg to oppose Butler's 10,000 at Bermuda Hundred and City Point. The Federals had lost 6,214 men. The Confederates had lost about 5,000.

The Cockade City lay nearly as defenseless as before the Overland and Bermuda Hundred campaigns had begun.

The Cockade City

A city of more than 18,000 in 1860, Petersburg had its origin in Fort Henry. This fort was erected in 1645 at the falls of the Appomattox River on the river's south bank. Situated near the treaty line between the English settlers and the Indians, Fort Henry soon became a center of exploration and the Indian trade. A short distance downstream from the fort, a village grew up called Petersburg after Peter Jones, the leading Indian trader there in the late 17th century.

In 1700, the Crown opened the area south and southwest of Petersburg to settlement. The area proved so rich an agricultural region that those who settled it referred to it as Eden. The farmers of this area, which extended down into North Carolina, began sending their tobacco to Petersburg for shipment to Great Britain. Bonds of blood and of trade developed until Petersburg became known as half Carolinian.

By 1730, Petersburg had its first tobacco warehouse. Two years later, another tobacco warehouse on the north bank of the Appomattox became the nucleus for another village, this one called Pocahontas. Still another village, Blandford, developed about a mile downstream from Petersburg on the south bank of the river, below Lieutenant's Run. Bristol Parish, which stretched from the James River to the North Carolina border, built a brick church in Blandford in 1735. By the Civil War, the church had become known as Old Blandford Church.

In 1748, the colonial government conferred on Petersburg and Blandford the status of towns. Pocahontas achieved that status in 1752. By the time of the War for Independence, these three towns had among them seven tobacco warehouses and formed a principal center of the tobacco trade in North America. Their bounteous hinterland had already begun furnishing them with a second staple—wheat.

Occupied and devastated during the War for Independence, the three towns rebounded quickly. Another town, Ravenscroft, and suburbs had developed alongside Petersburg, Blandford and Pocahontas by 1784, when the General Assembly incorporated them all into a borough named Petersburg.

Though the export of tobacco and wheat resumed after the War for Independence, Petersburg soon became a center of industry as well as of trade.

Flour-milling, which had begun in colonial times, increased and tobacco manufacturing commenced. The completion of the Upper Appomattox Canal during the first decade of the 19th century expanded Petersburg's agricultural hinterland up the Appomattox Valley all the way to Farmville. When farmers in this expanded hinterland greatly increased their cultivation of cotton around 1825, Petersburg became not only a market for cotton, but a center for manufacturing cotton products. Stimulated by the needs of local factories, an increased demand for agricultural implements and the development of railroads, a substantial iron industry developed in Petersburg by 1840.

The city also became a hub of land transportation. In 1816, the Manchester & Petersburg Turnpike opened and facilitated the passage of wheat and tobacco from Petersburg to the Richmond market. In 1833, the first of the railroads that would make Petersburg a military objective during the Civil War began running. The Petersburg Railroad became known as the Weldon Railroad because it connected Petersburg with Weldon, North Carolina. In 1838, the City Point Railroad commenced operations to City Point and the Richmond & Petersburg Railroad began running to Richmond. The Boydton Plank Road, which stretched to Boydton in Mecklenburg County, opened in 1850, the same year the borough of Petersburg attained the status of a city. The Jerusalem Plank Road, which extended to Jerusalem (modern Courtland) in Southhampton County, opened in 1853. The South Side Railroad commenced operations to Lynchburg in 1854. In 1858, the Norfolk & Petersburg Railroad began running to Norfolk.

The railroads which made Petersburg a hub of transportation also tended to make the city a mere way station on the routes to Richmond, the state capital, and to Norfolk, Virginia's major deepwater port. Petersburg fought grimly to preserve its trade. To prevent passage through the city of commodities that might be sold or processed there, Petersburg refused to allow the railroads which terminated in the city to connect their tracks. Not until 1863, after the evacuation of Norfolk had dramatized the need to join the Richmond & Petersburg Railroad to the Weldon Railroad, did Petersburg relent.

Petersburg was known as the "Cockade City." The name came from the exploits of a company of soldiers from Petersburg during the War of 1812. During the summer of 1812, an infantry company formed in Petersburg called the Petersburg Volunteers. Cockades, or rosettes, ornamented their hats. That autumn, the company marched to Ohio and became part of a force that occupied the present site of Toledo. There the force constructed Fort Meigs. In the spring of 1813, the British and their Indian allies besieged the fort. On 5 May, a detachment of Americans that included the Petersburg Volunteers sortied and broke the siege. The men from Petersburg participated in driving off another enemy force in August.

The Petersburg Volunteers fought with such conspicuous gallantry at Fort Meigs that they earned for their city the sobriquet of "the Cockade City of the Union."

Major Battles Around Petersburg, 1864-1865			
Date	Engagement	Losses U.S.A.	C.S.A.
16 May 1864	Second Drewry's Bluff	3,500	3,000
20 May	Ware Bottom Church	702	800
15-18 June	First Petersburg	10,586	4,000
22-23 June	Jerusalem Plank Road	2,962	700
22-30 June	Wilson-Kautz Raid	1,445	300
27-28 July	First Deep Bottom	488	700
30 July	The Crater	3,798	1,500
14-18 Aug.	Second Deep Bottom	2,901	1,500
18-21 Aug.	Globe Tavern (Weldon RR)	4,279	2,300
25 Aug.	Second Reams Station	2,742	720
28 Sept.-1 Oct.	Fort Harrison	3,327	1,700
29 Sept.-1 Oct.	Peebles Farm	2,889	1,300
7 Oct.	First Darbytown Road	458	700
13 Oct.	Second Darbytown Road	437	50
27 Oct.	Fair Oaks	1,603	100
27 Oct.	Burgess Mill	1,758	1,300
5-7 Feb. 1865	Hatcher's Run	1,539	1,000
25 March	Fort Stedman	2,087	4,000
31 March	White Oak Road	1,867	900
31 March	Dinwiddie Court House	450	600
1 April	Five Forks	750	3,000
2 April	Second Petersburg	3,361	6,500

CHAPTER II

The Battle of Old Men and Young Boys

At Cold Harbor, Grant surveyed the wreckage of his plan. It had proven an almost unmitigated disaster. He had failed to permanently interrupt traffic over the Virginia Central Railroad. He had failed to destroy Lee's army or drive it into the Richmond fortifications. Butler had failed to invest Richmond from the south or hold any of the rail lines leading into the city. The position of Lee's army made it difficult if not impossible for Grant to cross the James River directly into the Bermuda Hundred peninsula, and even if he could, Beauregard barred the way into Chesterfield County. Sigel had been defeated at the battle of New Market, though his successor was proceeding toward Staunton in preparation for a junction with other Federal forces approaching from the west.

At best, Grant and Butler had prevented the Confederates in Virginia from threatening Washington, D.C., or reinforcing Johnston in Georgia. The Federals had also reached a position from which they could directly menace Richmond, but McClellan had gotten that far in 1862 with less than 10 percent of the 63,000 casualties that Grant and Butler had suffered.

The plan had not turned out as Grant had wished, but he made the most of the situation—just as he had after the failure of so many initiatives during the Vicksburg campaign. Rejecting Halleck's advice to invest Richmond from the north to keep Washington covered, Grant adhered as closely as practicable to his original concept. He would swing a little wider,

U.S. Grant (center, standing) with his staff. With Grant occupying Lee north of Richmond, Butler had ample opportunity to seize Richmond and Petersburg with ease. Butler bungled his chance for glory by getting his forces holed up in Bermuda Hundred.

cross lower on the James, capture Petersburg and cut Richmond's rail communications below the Appomattox instead of in Chesterfield County.

Grant reached this decision within hours after the bloody repulse of 3 June. On the following day, while Matt Ransom's Brigade departed Beauregard's fortifications opposite the Federal lines on Bermuda Hundred, the service troops in Butler's Department of Virginia and North Carolina received orders to begin aiding the *Army of the Potomac*. Pontoons dispatched by Grant's engineers arrived off Bermuda Hundred on 6 June. On the same day, Grant informed Butler that the *Army of the Potomac* would soon cross to the Southside.

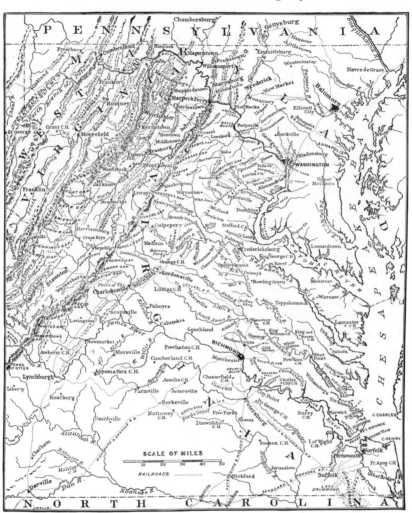

Virginia

Grant also sent two staffers to Bermuda Hundred to get maps and pick the best site for a pontoon bridge.

As did many other Southerners, Beauregard foresaw the crossing. On 7 June he began asking for the return of Matt Ransom's Brigade and Hoke's Division. Preoccupied with the safety of Richmond, the administration and Lee remained deaf to his pleas.

Before the pontoons arrived to facilitate the crossing of the

A Petersburg Soldier's Diary

The 12th Regiment Virginia Infantry was sometimes called the Petersburg Regiment. Six of its 10 companies came from the Cockade City. Company E, the Petersburg Riflemen, was recruited from Petersburg's young professionals and landowners. An unusually high proportion of its men were college educated, and many of them went on to become officers.

George Smith Bernard was born in Culpeper County in 1837. He was educated in the law at the University of Virginia but taught school for a while before opening a law office in Petersburg. He enlisted as a private in the Petersburg Riflemen on 19 April 1861 and left the Cockade City with the Petersburg Battalion for Norfolk on the following day.

Illness felled Bernard in the late summer of 1861 while he was at Norfolk, where the Petersburg Riflemen had become part of the 12th Virginia Infantry. He convalesced at his father's home in Orange County, then resumed teaching in early 1862 at a school near Belfield in Greensville County.

The Southern disasters at Forts Henry and Donelson and at Roanoke Island in early February, 1862, coupled with the rigors of schoolteaching, prompted Bernard to return to the Confederate States Army. In mid-March, he rejoined as 3rd Sergeant of the Meherrin Grays,

---

James River, Grant decided to deal with the unfinished business of wrecking Richmond's principal supply line to the west—the Virginia Central Railroad. On 5 June, he ordered Sheridan to ride with two of his cavalry divisions to Charlottesville. There Sheridan would unite with the army moving up the Shenandoah Valley under Major General David Hunter, Sigel's successor. Grant wanted Sheridan and Hunter to destroy the railroad bridge over the Rivanna River near Charlottesville, wreck the tracks from there to Hanover Junction and then join the *Army of the Potomac.*

Unknown to Grant, Hunter defeated a Confederate force at Piedmont, 12 miles northeast of Staunton, that very day. The defeated Southern force retreated to Waynesborough at Rocka company recruited from Brunswick and Greensville Counties.

A month later, by a quirk of fate, this company was assigned to Bernard's old regiment, the 12th Virginia Infantry, now part of Mahone's Brigade. The Meherrin Grays became the 12th's Company I. Bernard remained with the Meherrin Grays through the battles of First Drewry's Bluff, Seven Pines, French's Farm, Frayser's Farm, Malvern Hill, and Second Manassas. He was wounded in the leg and fell into Federal hands at the Battle of Crampton's Gap on 14 September 1862.

After another convalescence at his father's home in Orange County, Bernard went on light duty as a recruiting officer at Cumberland Court House in early 1863. In April of that year, he returned to the 12th Virginia Infantry. Transferring back to his original company, the Petersburg Riflemen, Bernard resumed the rank of private. Before the fighting reached Petersburg, he participated with the Petersburg Riflemen in the Battles of Chancellorsville, Salem Church, Gettysburg, Second Brandy Station, Bristoe Station, The Wilderness, Spotsylvania, and Cold Harbor.

Bernard had kept diaries before the War. On the day of his enlistment, he began keeping the first of his War Diaries. He was working on War Diary No. 4 when the Army of Northern Virginia reached Petersburg.

Selections from his diaries appear thoughout this book.

---

fish Gap, blocking the way to Charlottesville. Lee learned of this on 6 June, the same day as Hunter occupied Staunton. On 7 June, Lee ordered Breckinridge to Charlottesville, from where he could enter the Shenandoah Valley or dispute a crossing of the Blue Ridge.

Sheridan left Cold Harbor on the same day. Crossing the Pamunkey, he headed west. Lee learned of this movement from Major General Wade Hampton on the morning of 8 June. Hampton suggested that the Confederate cavalry pursue and engage Sheridan. This was the first display of the initiative that would distinguish Hampton during the course of the fighting around Petersburg, and it met with Lee's approval. Lee ordered Hampton to take command of the operation.

South Carolinian Wade Hampton took command of the Cavalry Corps of the Army of Northern Virginia when the legendary Jeb Stuart was mortally wounded at Yellow Tavern on 11 May 1864. He served in the position ably.

As Hampton moved out from Cold Harbor, Federal infantry and cavalry columns from West Virginia united with Hunter at Staunton. At Bermuda Hundred, Butler revived his scheme of 2 June for a raid on Petersburg. Grant saw this, as he did to a degree Sheridan's expedition, as a means of diverting the enemy's attention from the *Army of the Potomac's* crossing of the James. Without thoroughly considering the chances of success or the consequences of failure, Grant approved Butler's plan.

It called for a Union infantry force to dash into Petersburg from the east, while a cavalry force swooped in from the south. Once inside the city, the Federals would burn the Appomattox bridges and the city's public buildings. Against Butler's better judgment, Gillmore commanded the expedition. The forces at Gillmore's disposal consisted of a reinforced brigade of infantry under Colonel Joseph R. Hawley, a detachment of *United States Colored Troops* the size of a small brigade under Hinks and Kautz's cavalry division. These units totaled about 3,000 infantry and 1,500 cavalry. Hawley's brigade would cross the Appomattox from Bermuda Hundred to Spring Hill on a pontoon bridge and then move against Petersburg's eastern defenses. Hinks' men would march from City Point with the same mission. Kautz's troopers would cross the Appomattox on the same bridge as Hawley's men used but swing southwest and strike the city's fortifications on the Jerusalem Plank Road.

The Federal infantry arrived in front of Petersburg's eastern defenses at 0700, as planned. Hawley arrived on the City Point Road, Hinks on the Prince George Court House Road a mile to Hawley's left. Butler had prepared his subordinates to encounter only infantry parapets over which a horse could jump. Gillmore, Hinks and Hawley found the artillery redans which the infantry parapets linked so imposing that none of them saw any chance of an assault succeeding if the Confederates adequately manned the fortifications. And though the works contained only the 46th Virginia, a company of the 23rd South Carolina, a battalion of reservists and a battalion of militia, they looked fully manned to the Federals. Gillmore contented himself with demonstrating and waiting to hear from Kautz.

As so often happened during the course of the Petersburg campaign, geography came to the aid of the Confederates. Though the plan called for Kautz to arrive at his attack

Petersburg's Soldiers

Petersburg's soldiers often fought within sight of their city. Most of the Confederates captured by Kautz on 9 June belonged to the Petersburg militia. Many of these men had received medical discharges from Petersburg companies and batteries that had served in the Army of Northern Virginia. Kautz's prisoners included, for example, Anthony M. Keiley. He had served as a lieutenant with the 12th Virginia's Company E, the Petersburg Riflemen, until a foot wound disabled him.

Graham's Battery, which helped turn back Kautz's advance, also consisted of Petersburg men. It originally belonged to the Petersburg Battalion, officially known as the 4th Battalion, Virginia State Militia, and was officially called the Petersburg Artillery. The Petersburg Battalion left Petersburg to help garrison Norfolk on 20 April 1861. The battalion consisted of Graham's Battery and five companies of infantry—the Petersburg City Guard, the Petersburg Old Grays, the Petersburg New Grays, the Lafayette Guards and the Petersburg Riflemen.

Orders detached Graham's Battery from the rest of the Petersburg Battalion on the following day, 21 April 1861. The battery went on to serve in the Department of North Carolina and Southern Virginia. In the major battles around Petersburg, Graham's Battery fought at Second Drewry's Bluff (16 May 1864), First Petersburg (15-18 June), Globe Tavern (18-21 August), Peebles Farm (30 September-1 October) and Burgess Mill (27 October).

The infantry of the Petersburg Battalion became the nucleus of the 12th Regiment Virginia Infantry, the Petersburg Regiment. At Norfolk, this regiment became part of the brigade of Brigadier General William

position by 0900, first Hawley's rear regiments and then Confederate cavalry pickets delayed the Federal horsemen. But the preponderance of the delay came from the fact that the Union cavalry had more ground to negotiate than expected. Spear's brigade of Kautz's division did not arrive at the fortifications on the Jerusalem Plank Road until 1130.

Kautz's attack provided Petersburg with the supreme moment of its military tradition. About 150 civilians summoned

Mahone, the former president of the Norfolk & Petersburg Railroad. The 12th remained under Mahone for the rest of the war. He served first as its brigadier and later as its division commander. Around Petersburg, the 12th and the rest of Mahone's Brigade fought at the Jerusalem Plank Road (22 June 1864), the Crater (30 July), Globe Tavern (19 August), Second Reams Station (25 August), Burgess Mill (27 October) and Hatcher's Run (6 February 1865).

One of the infantry companies from Petersburg that belonged to the 12th in state service at Norfolk was Lee's Life Guard. In July 1861, when the forces of Virginia became part of the forces of the Confederate States of America, orders designated Lee's Life Guard as Company K, 16th Regiment Virginia Infantry. Like the 12th Virginia Infantry, the 16th belonged to Mahone's Brigade.

During the reorganization of the Confederate army in May 1862, Lee's Life Guard reconstituted itself as a battery of artillery. Its men came mostly from Mahone's Brigade. The battery became known first as Branch's Battery and later as Richard Pegram's Battery. After the Maryland campaign of 1862, orders assigned it to the Department of North Carolina and Southern Virginia.

Pegram's Battery fought at Second Drewry's Bluff and First Petersburg. On 30 July 1864, it occupied Elliott's Salient, unknowingly atop 8,000 pounds of Federal gunpowder. Many of its men perished in the explosion that created the geological feature that gave the battle of the Crater its name. By a quirk of fate, Mahone's Brigade belonged to the force that helped recapture the Crater. In doing so, Mahone's men also retook the guns of their former comrades in Pegram's Battery.

by alarms manned the works on the Jerusalem Plank Road. This force consisted of old men, young boys and invalids commanded by Major Fletcher H. Archer. Archer had served in the Mexican War and later raised the Archer Rifles, Company K of the 12th Regiment Virginia Infantry—the Petersburg Regiment. His ragtag force held off Kautz's initial probes.

A flank movement drove Archer's men back in the early

Union Losses

The total Union losses around Petersburg from 5 May 1864 to 2 April 1865 are estimated as follows:				
Month	Killed	Wounded	Captured or Missing	Total
May 1864	634	3,903	1,678	6,214
June	2,013	9,935	4,621	16,569
July	915	3,808	1,644	6,367
August	876	4,151	5,969	10,996
September	644	3,503	2,871	7,018
October	528	2,946	2,094	5,568
November	57	258	108	423
December	66	278	269	613
January, 1865	13	62	85	160
February	199	1,296	395	1,890
March-April	1,139	7,169	1,952	10,000
Total	7,084	37,309	21,686	65,818

afternoon, about the same time as the Federal infantry withdrew. But the time bought by Archer's force proved fatal to Kautz's advance. On Reservoir Hill, near the city's waterworks, Kautz encountered another line of trenches manned by an even motlier collection of soldiers drawn from the city's hospitals and the provost marshal's jails. The works also contained a battery of artillery—appropriately, the Petersburg Artillery, also known as Graham's Battery. A horse artillery outfit, it had rushed from the other side of the Appomattox and had headed toward Gillmore before turning toward Kautz. As Kautz confronted these works, Graham's Battery opened on his men and more reinforcements arrived—part of

Confederate Losses

The total Confederate losses from 5 May 1864 to 2 April 1865 are estimated as follows:	
Month	Total
May 1864	5,000
June	6,000
July	3,000
August	5,500
September	4,000
October	3,000
November	500
December	500
January, 1865	200
February	1,300
March	6,000
April	9,500
Total	44,500

Dearing's cavalry Brigade. Hearing nothing from Gillmore and realizing that capturing these works would require so much time that still more Southern reinforcements would arrive, Kautz decided to withdraw.

The Federals lost about 60 men and the Confederates about 100 in this skirmish, but it had momentous consequences for the Petersburg campaign. It alerted Beauregard to the city's vulnerability so that he continued pressing for reinforcements until, on 11 June, Bragg reluctantly released Gracie's Brigade from the Department of Richmond. This allowed Beauregard to shift the rest of Wise's Brigade to Petersburg from the Howlett Line, the Confederate fortifications opposite the

Union position on Bermuda Hundred. In the future, the city's attackers would encounter not a single regiment and a few odds and ends but a full brigade, enough to slow down even a substantial force sufficiently for reinforcements to arrive in a repetition of the skirmish's pattern.

The Federal infantry's failure to assault the works infuriated Butler. Though Hinks and Hawley supported Gillmore's decision not to attack, Butler relieved Gillmore of command of the *X Corps*.

CHAPTER III

The Opening Assaults

While the disastrous raid on Petersburg was still in progress, Grant continued to prepare for his crossing of the James River. Halleck received orders to send future reinforcements to Bermuda Hundred. The chief engineer of the *Army of the Potomac* was directed to select and entrench a line behind the Federal position at Cold Harbor. The army would begin its movement to the James by withdrawing to this line.

On 10 June, Major General George G. Meade, the commander of the *Army of the Potomac*, conveyed to Major General Gouverneur K. Warren orders to create a diversion during the river crossing. Warren moved two of his reserve divisions to a position on the New Kent Court House Road four miles from Bottom's Bridge on 11 June. In that position they would be out of sight of the Confederates. Warren's orders called for him to prepare to move the other two divisions of his corps at dark on the following day.

While Warren shifted his reserve divisions, Lee withdrew Lieutenant General Jubal A. Early's Corps from the Confederate front line. Early prepared to march to the defense of the Shenandoah Valley against Hunter, who had disregarded Grant's orders and headed for Lexington instead of Charlottesville.

In a confused fight with Hampton that day, Sheridan secured a lodgment on the Virginia Central at Trevilian's Station. Hampton's forces retreated westward to a position guarding both the road to Charlottesville and the railroad tracks to Gordonsville.

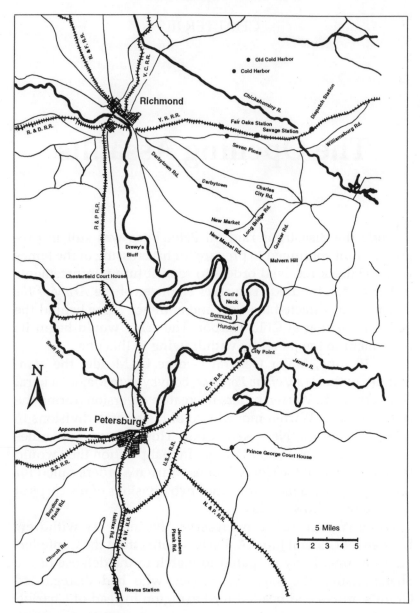

Richmond and Petersburg area.

That night witnessed the completion of the trench line behind the *Army of the Potomac's* Cold Harbor position. The line stretched from Elder Swamp to Allen's millpond.

Sheridan's cavalrymen spent the morning of 12 June ripping up the Virginia Central Railroad around Trevilian's Station. In the afternoon, they attempted to break through Hampton's line toward Gordonsville but were repulsed. Sheridan learned from prisoners of Hunter's departure from Grant's plan. Left in the lurch, Sheridan ordered a retreat. His troopers crossed the North Anna River by way of Carpenter's Ford. Lacking pontoons, Hampton remained on the south bank of the river and paced Sheridan toward White House Landing.

That evening, Lee ordered Early to move out at 0300 the following morning for the Shenandoah Valley by way of Louisa Court House and Charlottesville. Lee instructed Early to unite with Breckinridge and destroy Hunter's force. But Lee did not want Early to stop there. He also desired his lieutenant to move up the Valley, cross the Potomac River and threaten Washington. Such a move might disrupt Grant's campaign as effectively as Major General Thomas "Stonewall" Jackson's operations in the Valley had disrupted McClellan's offensive in the spring of 1862.

While Early received his orders, the *Army of the Potomac* withdrew from its Cold Harbor position. But for delays in the arrival of bridging material, the movement would have taken place earlier. Hancock's and Horatio Wright's corps occupied the rear line of trenches prepared by the chief engineer. Smith's corps headed for White House Landing, where steamers waited to carry it to Bermuda Hundred. Wilson's cavalry division, followed by Warren's reserve divisions and then the rest of Warren's corps, proceeded toward Long Bridge on the Chickahominy River. By a route passing east of Charles City Court House, Burnside's corps marched for Wilcox's Landing, where the crossing of the James would take place. Grant had chosen to cross from Wilcox's Landing to Windmill Point rather than from the vicinity of Malvern Hill to Bermuda

Two Styles of Command

During the Petersburg campaign, the initiatives of subordinate commanders fared far better among the Confederates than under Grant.

In Grant's command, almost all initiative came from the top. Grant decided when and where to take the offensive and usually left the execution of an offensive up to his subordinates. When he meddled with the tactical plan of a subordinate, as at the battle of the Crater in July, disaster resulted. He did not have much better luck when he imposed his own tactical plan on a subordinate, as in the case of Second Deep Bottom in August.

Initiative as displayed by subordinates fared poorly under Grant insofar as it existed at all. No major initiative worked its way up the chain of command except for the Petersburg Mine. Pleasants and his miners conceived and implemented the idea of mining and Burnside built his plan of assault around the mine, but Grant wasted all these efforts by authorizing Meade to alter Burnside's plan of assault.

The only Federal corps commander to display significant initiative on more than one occasion during the Petersburg campaign was Warren. In late June, he proposed cutting loose from the supply base at City Point with most of Grant's command and striking for Burke's Station. The proposal came to nothing, though Grant considered this possibility in March of 1865. On 20 August 1864, at the battle of Globe Tavern, Warren initiated a tactical withdrawal that enabled his men to repulse the Southerners bloodily on the following day. He then incurred the dissatisfaction of Grant and Meade by refusing to counterattack into the same wilderness in which his men had suffered grievous losses on August 18 and 19. Grant wanted subordinates who would do as they

Hundred or City Point to prevent Southern interference, which he feared might result in disaster to his command.

At 0100 on 13 June, Wilson's division crossed the Chickahominy at Long Bridge on a pontoon bridge laid by engineers. His troopers advanced to White Oak Bridge and Riddell's Shop, followed by Warren's corps. As soon as Warren's soldiers relieved the Federal cavalry near White Oak Bridge,

were told without any backtalk. It was Warren's tendency to act on his own initiative that prompted Grant to authorize Sheridan to remove Warren from command of the *V Corps* on 1 April of 1865.

Lee, on the other hand, adopted the initiatives of his subordinates more often than he exercised his own. Hampton originated the plans that resulted in the Confederate victories at Trevilian Station, Samaria Church, First Reams Station, Second Reams Station and Burgess Mill. During the battle of Globe Tavern, Mahone proposed the plan of attack for the ambush of 19 August.

Not all the initiatives of Confederate subordinate commanders met with a favorable reception. The Davis administration frustrated Beauregard's plan to storm Fort Powhatan in May and Lee rejected Beauregard's proposal to attack the left of the exhausted Federal army on 18 June. During December's Apple Jack Raid, A.P. Hill initially rejected Mahone's plan to cut off Warren and then adopted a modified version of it too late to catch the Northerners.

Nor did all the initiatives of Southern subordinates meet with success. Hampton's attack on the Federal right at Second Deep Bottom on 18 August failed to drive the Northerners back into the James River despite initial progress. Mahone's attempt to envelop the Union left on 21 August at the battle of Globe Tavern resulted in disaster.

Lee ordinarily left tactical arrangements to capable subordinates. The exception came at the battle of Globe Tavern, where his insistence on a set piece attack hampered Beauregard and gave the Federals the entire day of 20 August to consolidate their position. In the absence of capable corps commanders, Lee took command himself as at the Darbytown Road on 7 October and at White Oak Road on 31 March.

Wilson pushed out on the Charles City and Darbytown Roads. The Federals drove back Gary's Brigade of Confederate cavalry.

At 0200, while Wilson and Warren advanced, Early's sadly depleted corps moved out for the Shenandoah Valley. The remaining components of Grant's command continued their marches. Everything went as planned except in the case of

Smith's corps, which had the most important task and the right of way over anything in its path. Arriving at White House Landing at daybreak, Smith found insufficient shipping available to transport his men to Bermuda Hundred.

While Smith waited for shipping, Lee discovered that the *Army of the Potomac* had withdrawn from Cold Harbor. The movements of Wilson and Warren had their intended effect. They convinced Lee that Grant was advancing toward Richmond or preparing to cross the James from near Malvern Hill.

Lee at once put his command in motion. Richard Anderson's Corps marched by way of Fair Oaks and Seven Pines across White Oak Swamp, then down the Charles City Road. A.P. Hill's Corps crossed White Oak Swamp lower down and marched on the Charles City Road to Riddell's Shop, where Hill entrenched after a late afternoon skirmish with Wilson and Warren. Anderson's Corps left the Charles City Road in Hill's rear at the Williams house and proceeded to the site of the 1862 battle of Glendale or Frayser's Farm, between Riddell's Shop and Malvern Hill.

Their mission accomplished, Wilson and Warren withdrew in the night to Samaria Church, below Malvern Hill. As they began their withdrawal, Hancock's corps finished arriving at Wilcox's Landing.

By 0715 on 14 June, Smith's men had begun arriving at Bermuda Hundred. Coupled with Grant's crossing of the Chickahominy, the buildup alarmed Beauregard. Again he warned of a movement on Petersburg. But Lee remained convinced that Grant was advancing on Richmond.

Shipping became available for Hancock to begin ferrying his men from Wilcox's Landing to Windmill Point about 1100. Scarcity of ferries and failure to complete landing wharfs and roads delayed his progress.

The other components of the *Army of the Potomac* began arriving at Wyanoke Neck. Wright's corps slogged in first and assumed a defensive position covering the crossing. Burnside's corps came next and waited to cross behind Hancock's corps. By noon, only Warren's corps remained on the road. His men had reached Charles City Court House.

The engineers began construction of the pontoon bridge at 1600 after completing its approaches. The bridge was constructed from each end and built by successive pontoons and rafts. The James was 2,100 feet wide at this point and from 72 to 90 feet deep, with a strong tidal current and a rise and fall of four feet. The engineers required 101 pontoons for the bridge. In mid-channel, the pontoons were anchored to vessels moored above and below. The engineers constructed a draw here for the passage of other vessels.

While the engineers struggled with the James River, McIntosh's brigade of Wilson's division reconnoitered in the direction of White Oak Bridge. Lee remained in the position he had assumed on the previous day.

Smith arrived at Bermuda Hundred around sunset. Reporting to Butler, Smith received orders to march on Petersburg at daylight. Smith's corps continued disembarking throughout the night at Broadway Landing, the southern terminus of a pontoon bridge from Point of Rocks on Bermuda Hundred.

That night Beauregard sent a staff officer to Lee to explain the situation, but no reinforcements resulted. By 2010, the Federals arriving at Bermuda Hundred had been identified as Smith's corps. Beauregard reported this by telegram, again with no results.

At 2200, Hancock's corps had still not finished ferrying the river. Meade ordered Major General Winfield Scott Hancock to move to the City Point Road about a mile east of Petersburg's fortifications as soon as his men received rations. Meade's orders came from Grant, who wanted Hancock to take up a supporting position a mile and a half from the Petersburg entrenchments on the City Point Road while Smith took those entrenchments and then Petersburg two miles beyond. But Grant did not bother to communicate this plan to the two corps commanders, each of whom belonged to a different army. The engineers completed the pontoon bridge at midnight and the Federal artillery and wagon trains started to cross.

As soon as 15 June began, the plan began to unravel. The force assigned to Smith included Kautz's cavalry division,

*Commander of the **II Corps**, Winfield Scott Hancock (seated) with his subordinates (left to right) Francis Barlow, David Birney and John Gibbon.*

2,400 strong, Hinks' black division, 3,700 officers and men and Smith's own corps of about 11,000. Ordered to cross the Appomattox River on Butler's pontoon bridge at 0100 and lead the column, Kautz was delayed. The advance from Broadway did not begin until after daylight.

Back at Windmill Point, the infantry of Hancock's corps and four batteries of its artillery had crossed by 0400. At 0630, three ferryboats were added to his means of crossing and significantly sped up the passage of his artillery and wagons.

But Hancock's infantry remained immobile. The rations Hancock had been told to wait for had not arrived. Hancock bombarded his commander with dispatches about the rations until Meade authorized him to move immediately.

Just then came a report that the rations had arrived. Not until 2100 did Hancock realize that the report was false and order his men to march. But one courier inexplicably failed to deliver this order, and the boat carrying the other grounded. Hancock's 20,000 men did not start marching until 1030.

On the Peninsula, Chapman's brigade of Wilson's division probed toward Malvern Hill and found that the Confederates occupied it in force. Though Lee released Hoke's Division to Beauregard at 1130 in response to Beauregard's frantic pleas for reinforcements, the movements of Wilson's division kept the rest of Lee's army in line of battle between Malvern Hill and Riddell's Shop.

Kautz's cavalrymen encountered enemy skirmishers soon after leaving Broadway Landing. At Baylor's farm, five miles from his starting point and two miles from the Dimmock Line, Kautz encountered rifle pits near the City Point Railroad manned by some of Dearing's dismounted cavalrymen and an artillery battery. A brief delay followed as the unit next in line, Hinks' black division, deployed and took this isolated earthwork, capturing one of the cannon.

Rather than form column again, Hinks deployed by the flank to his assigned position across the Jordan's Point Road while Brooks' division of Smith's corps deployed along the City Point Railroad. The two divisions then advanced a mile and a half, which brought them under the fire of the Confederate artillery. As they arrived at this position, Martindale's division of Smith's corps came up on Brooks' right, between the City Point Railroad and the Appomattox River. Kautz's cavalrymen trotted to their assigned position on the left flank of the infantry, near the Norfolk & Petersburg Railroad.

It was about noon. Hoke's Division had barely begun its 18-mile journey from Drewry's Bluff to Petersburg. Only Wise's Brigade and some militia, less than 3,000 men, held five miles of fortifications from the lower Appomattox almost to the Jerusalem Plank Road. Dearing's 2,000 cavalrymen hovered on the Federal left to keep Beauregard informed of any movement toward the five miles of empty trenches between Wise's right and the upper Appomattox. Smith halted to reconnoiter and form his nearly 15,000 infantry for an assault. Petersburg seemed doomed.

But what Smith saw disconcerted him. Between his men and the enemy entrenchments stretched a low broad valley, cut up by ditches and ravines and swept by the Southern artillery. At Jordan's Hill, where the City Point Railroad entered the works, a salient existed. Brooks' division confronted this salient while on his right Martindale's division faced a line of works withdrawn about 600 yards. Hinks' division, on Brooks' left, opposed works withdrawn about 300 yards. From the works in front of Martindale's and Hinks' divisions, the Confederates had a crossfire of artillery on the ground that Brooks' division would have to cross.

Then there were the fortifications themselves. They consisted of strong redans for artillery connected by infantry parapets with high profiles. All had ditches in front of them. On 3 June at Cold Harbor, Smith's corps had suffered 1,000 casualties in unsuccessful attacks on far less formidable-looking fieldworks. Smith did not intend to lose the rest of his soldiers by hurling them blindly against these. True, the works did not look like they had many infantrymen in them, but there were plenty of cannon, and Smith thought it unlikely that they would be unsupported by foot soldiers. Though Beauregard considered these fortifications poorly designed because of the difficulty in manning them, they had done their work by intimidating Smith on this day.

Wanting to spare his men the sort of repulse they had suffered at Cold Harbor, Smith decided that a reconnaissance was in order and unwisely undertook it himself. Hour after hour passed while Smith performed the duties of a staff officer. Meanwhile Hoke's Division drew nearer and nearer to Petersburg.

So did Hancock's corps. About 1600, a staffer from Grant arrived and informed Smith that the *II Corps* was marching toward him from Windmill Point. Smith immediately sent a dispatch to Hancock requesting him to come up in time to make a night assault in the vicinity of the Norfolk & Petersburg Railroad.

At 1700, Smith finally completed his reconnaissance. He issued orders massing his artillery against the salient facing Brooks' division. Smith wanted to try to carry the works with a heavy skirmish line, which was possible if they were thinly held. He did not want to assault in column under such heavy artillery fire. The infantry formed in accordance with his orders, but Smith's chief of artillery had without authority taken the guns to the rear to water the horses. Another delay ensued.

Shortly before 1730, while Smith's infantry waited for the cannon to return, Hancock was just over a mile from Old Prince George Court House and more than four miles from Smith's left in the vicinity of the Norfolk & Petersburg Railroad. A dispatch reached Hancock from Grant at City Point, directing all haste to be made in getting up to the support of Smith, whom the dispatch said had attacked Petersburg and carried the outer works—a mistake as to the rifle pits carried by Hinks that morning.

This was all news to Hancock. No one had previously troubled to tell him that he was to support Smith in assaulting Petersburg and he had attributed the artillery fire he heard to a raid the country people said Kautz was making.

The *II Corps* commander immediately sent a staff officer to Smith with information of his column's whereabouts and that he was marching to Smith's support as rapidly as possible. Minutes later, Smith's courier arrived with a request for haste, support and a night attack. Hancock turned the head of David Birney's division away from the City Point Railroad and down a country road that led directly to Petersburg. Gibbon's division followed. Hancock ordered Barlow's division, on the road to Old Prince George Court House, to move to Petersburg from there.

Federal observers had noticed Hoke's crossing at Drewry's Bluff. Based on this intelligence, Grant ordered the *Army of the*

Potomac to step up the pace. At 1800, back at Windmill Point, Meade directed Burnside to cross his infantry on the pontoon bridge at once, then march to Harrison's Creek and form on Hancock's left. He also instructed Warren to cross his artillery and wagon trains after Burnside and to begin ferrying his infantry across at daylight on 16 June, pushing his divisions forward as each crossed.

Shortly after 1800, Hancock's staffer reached Smith with word of Hancock's position and that he was coming with all dispatch. At 1830, the head of David Birney's division arrived at a position about a mile in rear of Hinks' division. Leaving instructions for David Birney and Gibbon to advance as soon as they could determine where they were needed, Hancock rode off in search of Smith.

At the inexcusable hour of 1900, before Hancock found him, Smith's heavy skirmish line finally advanced. His artillery opened on the salient in front of Brooks' division which contained Batteries 5 and 6. No reply came from the salient's batteries, which were holding their fire for the lines of battle, but the skirmishers met with a sharp infantry fire. The skirmishers easily carried the works, taking more than 200 prisoners and four cannon.

The lines of battle followed the skirmishers and occupied the works. Brooks' division formed to resist attack. On the right, Martindale's division, and on the left, Hinks' division, attempted to follow up Brooks' success. Martindale's division failed to budge the 59th Virginia from the four redans between the salient and the Appomattox River. But Hinks' division captured Batteries 7 through 11 to the left of the salient, along with another 12 guns. By 2100, a mile and a half of the entrenchments were in Federal hands.

While Hinks' division advanced, the sun set. Hoke's Division began arriving by rail at Petersburg. Hagood's Brigade led and after dark took position in rear of the captured works and between the 59th Virginia and the rest of Wise's Brigade. By the time that Hinks came to a halt, the other three brigades of Hoke's Division had arrived and occupied the ground on Hagood's right.

As daylight waned, so did Smith's nerve. During his reconnaissance, a rumor had reached him that Lee's army was rapidly crossing at Drewry's Bluff. Smith had heard the train whistles in Petersburg all day and he thought that massive reinforcements were arriving. He decided to hold what he had rather than have his troops meet with a disaster in an attempt to reach the vital bridges over the Appomattox. Knowing that Hancock was near at hand, Smith ordered his men into defensive positions. When Hancock finally found Smith, before the cautious general knew the extent of his success, Hancock informed him that two of his divisions were ready to move according to his orders. Smith said nothing about a night attack now. He merely asked that Hancock relieve his infantry in the front line of the captured works.

While Smith remained overly cautious, Beauregard acted decisively. Matt Ransom's Brigade had been released to him late in the afternoon, but he considered this reinforcement inadequate. The time for reasoning had passed. He decided to force the hand of the hostile Davis administration and impose his will on Lee by presenting them with a fait accompli. Beauregard took the daring step of ordering Johnson's Division to withdraw from the Howlett Line, which kept Butler bottled up in Bermuda Hundred. Gracie's Brigade of 1,000 Alabamians remained behind to hold this line until Lee's forces arrived to occupy the trenches. This only released Elliott's Brigade and Johnson's Brigade for the time being, but the former would provide a reserve and the latter would serve to lengthen the right of the Confederate line east of Petersburg.

By 2300, Hancock had finished relieving Smith's men in the captured works. Though it was late and dark, Hancock ordered David Birney and Gibbon to occupy the enemy strongpoints in their fronts. It proved impossible for them to implement this order with their exhausted soldiers in the unfamiliar surroundings.

At 0200 on 16 June, Beauregard notified Lee of the abandonment of the lines facing Bermuda Hundred. By 0400, Lee had moved Pickett's Division of Richard Anderson's Corps to

Drewry's Bluff. Field's Division closely followed Pickett. Kershaw's Division remained at Malvern Hill, A.P. Hill's Corps at Riddell's Shop. Lee was not yet convinced that Grant had crossed the James.

By this time, Johnson's Division had abandoned the Howlett Line. Gracie's Brigade withdrew to the southern bank of Swift Creek. The rest of the division crossed the Appomattox and headed for Beauregard's right, which extended beyond the Norfolk & Petersburg Railroad.

The Federals of the X Corps opposite the Howlett Line noticed movement throughout the night. Alfred Terry's division advanced at daylight, capturing many of the pickets left behind and occupying the Confederate main line. Butler recognized that this had the potential of cutting off Beauregard from reinforcements from Lee, but an uncharacteristically cautious Grant directed Butler not to risk the Bermuda Hundred foothold by interposing.

At Petersburg, the divisions of Gibbon and David Birney sent out reconnaissances in force at daybreak. On the right, Gibbon's *3rd Brigade* made little headway. On the left, Egan's brigade of David Birney's division captured Battery 12 after a stubborn fight with Wise's Brigade. This briefly opened a gaping hole in the Southern line, but Hancock failed to support David Birney's success. Matt Ransom's Brigade arrived just then after an all night march and stopped Federal progress.

The Northerners might still have fought their way into Petersburg that morning. Barlow's division, which had gotten lost on its way to the front, came up on Hancock's left. But Hancock allowed several hours to pass without further action. While the Northerners dozed, Johnson's Brigade ostentatiously marched to the far Southern right. Elliott's Brigade took position in reserve.

At 1000, while Terry's men ripped up three miles of the Richmond & Petersburg Railroad north of the Appomattox, the first of Burnside's soldiers staggered into position on Barlow's left. Many of Burnside's men were too tired to fight and immediately went to sleep. Fifteen minutes later, Grant directed Meade to go to Petersburg and take charge—an order that ought to have issued at least two days earlier. At 1030, Hancock received orders from Grant to take command at Petersburg until Meade arrived and to prepare to assault at 1800.

Back at Wilcox's Landing, Wright drew in Wilson's division. Lee still was unconvinced that the Federals had crossed the river. Hill's Corps remained north of the James along with W.H.F. "Rooney" Lee's Division of cavalry.

At 1315, north of the Appomattox, Pickett's soldiers drove in Alfred Terry's pickets. Discouraged by Grant from exploiting the occupation of the Howlett Line, Butler ordered Terry back to the Federal trenches because the Confederate lines were too long to hold with his small force. The opportunity to cut Beauregard off from Lee was slipping from Grant's grasp.

Meade arrived at Petersburg at 1400 and took command. Within the next hour, Grant finally awoke to the possibilities presented by the capture of the Howlett Line. Grant ordered Wright, whose corps was then crossing the James, to embark two of his divisions for Bermuda Hundred and Point of Rocks. At the same time, Grant directed Butler to try to reverse the Howlett Line, unaware that Butler had abandoned the captured trenches. Butler, who commanded from the rear and did not know the exact position of his men, thought it would be impossible for them to retake and reverse the Howlett Line without reinforcements. Grant notified Butler that reinforcements were en route. At 1745, Butler ordered his soldiers to hold the line of Confederate works nearest their own. His men occupied a position that extended to Clay's farm near the old turnpike.

At 1800, Meade attacked the Confederates at Petersburg. Two brigades of Smith's corps supported Hancock's right and two brigades of Burnside's corps supported Hancock's left. Battery 4 fell into Federal hands on the right. On the left, the Northerners captured Batteries 13 and 14, together with their connecting lines. Heavy fighting stopped at dark, but the Confederates made small counterattacks throughout the night that annoyed the exhausted Federals.

By midnight, Warren's corps had halted a few miles from Petersburg and Neill's division of Wright's corps had finished crossing the James. The vanguard of Wright's other divisions began landing at Point of Rocks and Bermuda Hundred. Only Wilson's cavalrymen remained north of the James, and they began crossing at 0430.

During the night, Potter's division of Burnside's corps stealthily moved through a wooded ravine to within a hundred yards of the Tennesseans of Johnson's Brigade at the Shand house, on the extreme Confederate right. At dawn on 17 June, the Federals swept into the Southern works and took the sleeping Tennesseans by surprise. Potter's men captured four pieces of artillery, a stand of colors, 600 prisoners and 1,500 muskets. A hole a mile wide yawned in the Confederate line, but the Federals could not exploit their success. The slashed timber in the ravine made it difficult for Ledlie's division to follow up Potter's success. Potter's men came to a halt when they encountered the Southerners in a new line stretching from the Appomattox River to Battery 3, and from there along the high ground west of Harrison's Creek to the Norfolk & Petersburg Railroad.

At 1400, Orlando Willcox's division of Burnside's corps attacked this line in front of Battery 14, about a mile north of the redans on the extreme Confederate right. Barlow's division of Hancock's corps supported Willcox's right, but the attack failed. The Confederates blasted it with musketry in front and enfiladed it with artillery from the redans near the Norfolk & Petersburg Railroad.

At 1600, Lee gave Lieutenant General A.P. Hill the option of withdrawing from Riddell's Shop in response to Beauregard's report of a Federal crossing of the James. Hill declined to move.

At Bermuda Hundred, Butler rested the two exhausted divisions of Wright's corps sent to help secure the Howlett Line. At 1730, while Wright's men recuperated, the Confederates of Pickett's and Field's Divisions came under fire from the Federal pickets at Clay's farm. The Southern rank and file responded by storming the Union picket line there despite instructions not to attack. Major General Wright and Brigadier

Union heavy artillery set up in works outside of Petersburg as the siege of the town began.

General Terry found Butler's orders for a counterattack impracticable. The opportunity to interpose between Lee and Beauregard was lost.

Meanwhile, Beauregard continued to make still more difficult the now nearly impossible Federal task of capturing Petersburg. During the day he had his chief engineer lay out a new line on advantageous ground behind a ravine 500 to 1,000 yards in rear of his present position. The line would stretch from near the Jerusalem Plank Road to the Appomattox River.

Near sunset, Ledlie's division of Burnside's corps attacked at the point where Orlando Willcox had failed earlier. The assault was supported on the left by Christ's brigade of Willcox's division and on the right by Barlow's division of Hancock's corps. Farther right, Gibbon and David Birney also advanced.

Gibbon and Birney could do no more than push their entrenchments closer to the Confederate works on the west bank of Harrison's Creek. Barlow's men met with another bloody repulse. But Burnside's soldiers carried part of the Confederate entrenchments after suffering heavy casualties from musketry in front as well as a crossfire of artillery. By the time darkness had fallen, Burnside's troops had captured 100 prisoners and a stand of colors.

But once again, the Federals failed to exploit their success. Burnside's men received only feeble support on their left from Crawford's division of Warren's corps. The Confederates kept Burnside's soldiers under a heavy fire. About 2200, when Ledlie's and Christ's troops had exhausted their ammunition, Gracie's and Matt Ransom's Brigades counterattacked in the moonlight. The Alabamians and North Carolinians routed Burnside's troops from the captured works, taking more than 500 prisoners and restoring the Harrison Creek line.

That night, Hancock's Gettysburg wound reopened and David Birney took command of the *II Corps*. Neill's division of Wright's corps relieved Smith's corps except for Martindale's division. Smith returned to Bermuda Hundred too late to be of any use there. Meade ordered Warren, Burnside and David Birney to attack the Harrison Creek line with strong, well supported columns at 0400 on the following morning. Near the Appomattox, Martindale's division of Smith's corps and Neill's division of Wright's corps would support the attack.

But after midnight, Beauregard withdrew from the Harrison Creek line. His men immediately began entrenching in their new position. While they labored, Lee finally realized that Grant had crossed the James. This realization led to the

Federals sight an artillery piece in their entrenchments outside of Petersburg.

elimination of the last desperate chance the Northerners had of storming Petersburg.

Leaving Pickett's division to hold the Bermuda Hundred lines, Lee immediately sent Kershaw's Division to Petersburg. Field's Division followed at 0300. Hill's Corps began marching to Petersburg via the pontoon bridge at Drewry's Bluff before daybreak. The head of his column started from Malvern Hill, 26 miles from the Cockade City.

At daybreak on 18 June, the Federals attacking Petersburg found the trenches that were their objectives empty. Beauregard's withdrawal served its purpose. Precious time passed while news of the abandoned works ascended the chain of command. From prisoners, Meade learned of the weakness of Beauregard's force. As an engineer, he realized that Beauregard's new works must be inadequate. The general wanted his army to attack before Confederate reinforcements could arrive. He fired off orders for an immediate and simultaneous advance.

But it took time for these orders to make their way back down the chain of command. And it took still more time for the Federals to reconnoiter the new Southern position. To make matters worse, some of these reconnaissances took longer than others.

David Birney's corps, the closest to the Confederates, had

Confederate Arrival in Petersburg

The following selection is taken from Private Bernard's diary:

Entrenchments of Wilcox's farm, one mile south of Petersburg Sunday, June, 19 '64

Yesterday afternoon about 5 o'clock we reached this place after a most severe march of 26 or 27 miles coming from within 3 miles of Malvern Hill. We crossed the James at Chaffin's Bluff on a pontoon bridge. Struck the turnpike near the Halfway house on R.&P.R.R. & marched through Petersburg. As we marched up Sycamore Street it was difficult to realize that we were within range of the enemy's shells & that we were marching to take position in line of battle. The great number of ladies that greeted us along the streets made us feel more as though we were going to participate in some festivity. Reaching a body of woods near this point we bivouacked until about 2 o'clock this morning when we took position in the breastworks. Last night the City of Petersburg sent us out some refreshments. A huge barrel of coffee & a large quantity of crackers. Our ration of late has been so good & abundant I rather think we live quite as well as the citizens. Everything pretty quiet this morning. A little shelling has been going on this morning on our left. Yesterday afternoon the enemy threw several shells into the city.

to advance only about 300 yards from the Hare House before encountering opposition. Burnside's corps, on David Birney's left, had to move forward nearly a mile before it found enemy outposts in the Norfolk & Petersburg Railroad cut and a ravine. To the left of Burnside's corps, Warren's corps had still farther to go. Deep ravines and the curving, deep railroad cut, enfiladed from the north, hindered his advance.

While all this time passed, the final Federal chance of storming Petersburg slipped away. At 0730, Kershaw's Division crossed the Appomattox and relieved Johnson's Division. Two hours later, Field's Division arrived and took position on Kershaw's right.

By this time, Meade had observed the different conditions facing the several corps. He realized that his order for a simultaneous attack could not be implemented unless his

Federal skirmishers take pot shots at enemy trenches from an advanced picket post outside of Petersburg.

corps commanders were given a specific hour for their advance. Meade selected high noon as the hour for the assault. Only David Birney's corps met the deadline. Gibbon's division attacked twice on the right of the Prince George Court House road, but the Confederates repulsed both attacks with heavy losses.

Burnside's men had to drive the Southerners out of the railroad cut in front of them before they could assault the Confederate entrenchments. Warren's corps had to cross a large expanse of open ground swept by Confederate artillery. Both of these corps failed to get into position on time to attack simultaneously with David Birney's corps. Finding it impossible to effect cooperation, Meade gave up on it. He ordered assaults by all his corps—with their whole force, at all hazards, and as soon as possible.

Before these attacks took place, A.P. Hill's Corps began arriving. In its van marched the 12th Virginia Infantry, the Petersburg Regiment. The Cockade City went wild as its citizens mobbed their friends and relatives in the 12th.

Eventually, all of Meade's corps attacked. They went in late that afternoon, one at a time. David Birney's corps again struck first. Mott's division, supported by one of Gibbon's brigades, attacked on the left of the Prince George Court House Road. Barlow's Division advanced on Mott's left. Hoke's Division repulsed David Birney's attack with heavy losses, including the most severe of the war by a single regiment in the 1st Maine Heavy Artillery.

To David Birney's right, Martindale's division advanced and captured some rifle pits but did not assault the main Southern line. On David Birney's left, Potter's and Orlando Willcox's divisions of Burnside's corps drove the Southerners from the Norfolk & Petersburg Railroad cut. Assaulting the Confederate main line, Burnside's soldiers accomplished nothing more than to establish themselves within a hundred yards of Kershaw's Division.

Still farther left, some of Warren's men made it to within 20 feet of the works held by Field's Division. Otherwise, Warren's corps suffered severe losses for little gain.

Toward evening, Meade belatedly received intelligence that Lee was reinforcing Beauregard. Satisfied that further assaults would achieve no useful end, Grant ordered his soldiers to get under cover and rest. The trenches they dug for themselves and the works erected by the Confederates on this front remained substantially the same to the end of the campaign.

As Mahone's Division of Hill's Corps took position on the right of Field's Division, Beauregard proposed an attack on the Federal left. Lee, aware that his soldiers were exhausted, rejected Beauregard's plan. The opening assaults on Petersburg had come to an end. The Federals had lost 10,586 men. The Confederates, usually protected by fortifications, had lost about 4,000.

United States Colored Troops

More than 180,000 *United States Colored Troops* served in the Union Army during the Civil War. More of them saw combat around Petersburg than in any other campaign.

Hinks' black division of Smith's corps successfully assaulted the Dimmock Line east of Petersburg on 15 June 1864. Ferrero's African-American division of Burnside's corps unsuccessfully attempted to capture Cemetery Hill at the disastrous battle of the Crater on 30 July. One of Ferrero's black soldiers won the Medal of Honor. William Birney's *Independent Brigade* of black troops stormed a line of Southern rifle pits on the Kingsland Road on 14 August, the first day of the second battle of Deep Bottom. One of that brigade's regiments, the *9th Regiment United States Colored Troops*, was the last Federal unit driven from the captured Confederate breastworks on the Darbytown Road on 16 August. Paine's (formerly Hinks') African-American division of David Birney's (formerly Smith's) corps assaulted and occupied New Market Heights on 29 September. Soldiers of the division won 13 Medals of Honor to attest to their gallantry. Later that same day, William Birney's *Inde-*pendent Brigade* of black troops unsuccessfully assaulted Fort Gilmer. On 27 October, Holman's brigade of Hinks' old African-American division attacked on the Nine Mile Road and captured a battery, but relinquished it to a Confederate counterattack.

All but one of these actions occurred under Butler. Unlike Grant, who considered black soldiers fit for little more than digging ditches, Butler believed they could fight and assigned them key roles. Burnside also believed in their fighting ability and assigned them the lead role in the battle of the Crater, only to have Grant and Meade order him to give that role to used up white troops—with disastrous results.

Relations between black soldiers and the Southerners constituted one of the ugliest aspects of the Petersburg campaign. The Confederate Congress had made black soldiers caught in Federal uniform, as well as their white officers, subject to summary execution. The black troops knew this and, besides drastically reducing straggling among them, it made them fight more desperately. The African-American troops were also mindful of the Fort Pillow and Poison Spring

Massacres of April 1864, and they wanted revenge.

The first of the war crimes that occurred around Petersburg took place on 15 June. Hinks' African-American troops bayoneted Southern prisoners captured in that day's successful assault on the Dimmock Line until white troops of Smith's corps intervened to protect the Confederates.

At the battle of the Crater, soldiers of Ferrero's black division cried "No quarter!" as they surged out of the Crater toward Cemetery Hill. Mahone's Southerners met them head on and neither gave nor asked quarter in driving the Federals back. Berserk Confederates murdered many African-American prisoners that day.

Second Deep Bottom was the Petersburg campaign's first major action between Southerners and African-American troops in which no prisoners were murdered. The *7th* and *9th Regiments United States Colored Troops* refrained from murdering their Southern prisoners on 14 August. The North Carolinians of Lane's Brigade murdered none of their black prisoners on 16 August. This did not mean that the malice of the Southerners toward the African-American troops had dissipated. Confederates from the Deep South re-

garded Lane's men as soft for allowing their black prisoners to live. The North Carolinians took consolation in the belief that they had killed droves of African-American troops fair and square. In fact, very few African-American troops perished on 16 August. Almost all of the Union dead were white. But Second Deep Bottom was fought in unbearable heat, which turned the bodies black overnight. In the morning it seemed to the North Carolinians that they had annihilated an entire army of black troops. Lane's men gloated over their supposed achievement at meetings and in memoirs for decades to come.

Paine's division committed no atrocities at New Market Heights on 29 September, but later that day the Texas Brigade murdered prisoners from William Birney's *Independent Brigade* of black troops after their unsuccessful assault on Fort Gilmer.

Neither side murdered prisoners on 27 October. That was the last significant combat around Petersburg in which African-American troops were engaged. On 3 December, the *Army of the James* was reorganized into two corps, the *XXIV* and the *XXV*. The army's white troops went into the *XXIV Corps*. Into the *XXV* went the army's African-

American troops as well as those of the *Army of the Potomac*. Late in December, Butler departed Virginia on an unsuccessful expedition to Fort Fisher on the North Carolina coast. The expedition's failure provided Grant with an opportunity to sack Butler, whose utility had vanished after the November election. Ord, the new commander of the *Army of the James*, shared Grant's disdainful view of African-American troops. William Birney's African-American division of the *XXV Corps* remained onlookers on 2 April 1865, as the white soldiers of the *XXIV Corps* stormed Fort Gregg with heavy loss of life.

The Confederates gave the *United States Colored Troops* the highest accolade available. In February 1865, the Southern soldiers in Lee's command voted overwhelmingly to admit to their ranks free blacks and slaves. Recruitment had barely begun when the Confederacy collapsed.

Anatomy of Failure

The Union lost an excellent chance of forcing the Southerners to abandon Richmond—and perhaps of ending the war—on 15 June 1864. Baldy Smith bears most of the responsibility for this failure. As at the second battle of Drewry's Bluff, he lost his nerve and thousands of men would pay with their lives for every hour he wasted reconnoitering for an attack that he might just as easily have ordered upon his arrival.

When Hancock arrived, Smith ought to have undertaken the night attack that he had suggested. Night attacks were risky business, but he certainly knew the ground by that time—and he knew that his soldiers faced weak opposition. Instead, Smith merely asked Hancock to relieve his men. Hancock initially assumed an aggressive posture. He ordered Gibbon and David Birney to push out and take the points of opposition in their fronts. But the ground was unfamiliar, and the men were exhausted. Hancock's orders could not be executed.

Beauregard took his first great step toward saving Petersburg when he pulled Johnson's Division out of the Howlett Line and put one of its brigades on Hoke's right and another in reserve. This left Petersburg's communications with Richmond open to the Federals at Bermuda Hundred but increased the difficulty faced by the leaderless Union forces confronting the defenders of the Cockade City. For this leaderlessness, Grant bears the responsibility. He failed to provide an alternative if Smith did not take Petersburg at first lunge. The crossing of the James River seems to have absorbed all the energy of Grant and his staff. They appear to have assumed that the occupation of the Cockade City would be assured by a successful crossing and gave no thought to what action would be appropriate if they encountered serious opposition.

Grant also bears the responsibility for Butler's failure to interfere with Lee's progress towards Petersburg. Grant's uncharacteristic caution in the face of Butler's initiative allowed the Confederates to drive Butler back into his Bermuda Hundred bottle. Hoke's crossing at Drewry's Bluff on the previous day had unnerved the entire Federal chain of command, including the usually imperturbable Grant. It appeared that Lee was at hand and the Northerners had no desire to absorb one of his devastating counterattacks.

Another chance to take the

Cockade City slipped away on the morning of 16 June. After Hancock's daylight probes, the Federals remained inactive while Johnson's Division reinforced the Confederate lines south of the Appomattox. Grant did not put Hancock in charge of the troops in front of Petersburg until 1030, by which time Johnson's men had dug in and it was probably too late to take the city. To make matters worse, Grant did not order an attack until 1800 and Hancock displayed the lack of initiative that characterized him for the rest of the campaign. As a result, the tired Southerners had a good rest. Their counterattacks that night fooled no one about their strength, but they wore out the Federal rank and file.

By the time Meade arrived, at 1400 on 16 June, the best chances of taking Petersburg had vanished. Grant's failure to have Butler oppose Lee in Chesterfield County made Meade's task of retrieving the Southside failures of Smith and Grant nearly impossible. Meade might have increased his chances of success by sending troops toward the Jerusalem Plank Road, but Dearing's Brigade would have alerted Beauregard to such a movement, which in any event could not have been completed before the morning of 17 June. Such a maneuver would hardly have forced Beauregard to abandon the Cockade City. He would merely have extended his right another mile, which would have only thinned his existing lines by 20 percent.

Beauregard displayed great generalship in this battle for the second time when he withdrew from the Harrison Creek line in the early morning hours of 18 June. This stratagem threw Meade's army into such confusion that it would have almost certainly bought Petersburg another day regardless of whether Beauregard received reinforcements from Lee. The arrival of Field's and Kershaw's Divisions eliminated whatever infinitesimal chance of success remained to the Federals. Beauregard had the right idea when he advocated a counterattack on the Federal left, but the long, hot march from Malvern Hill had utterly exhausted Hill's Corps.

Once Smith failed in the initial attempt to take Petersburg and Beauregard deployed Johnson in its defense, the Federals had little chance of taking the Cockade City by assault. Meade became a scapegoat for mistakes made before he arrived.

Beauregard's defense of Petersburg in June at least equals in brilliance his feats of May. It ranks among the great defenses of the war.

CHAPTER IV

War Against the Railroads

While Grant's men beat their heads against Beauregard's brick wall at Petersburg, another Confederate city in Virginia escaped Federal occupation. Hunter reached Lynchburg on 17 June to find that Breckinridge's Division and part of Early's Corps had arrived ahead of him. On the following day, Hunter's forces skirmished with the Southerners while Early transported the balance of his corps to Lynchburg from Charlottesville on the Orange and Alexandria Railroad.

On 19 June, Hunter withdrew from in front of Lynchburg on account of a lack of ammunition. His fateful decision to retreat by way of Salem and Lewisburg left the Shenandoah Valley open and enabled Early to mount the threat to Washington suggested by Lee. At Petersburg, while the rest of Grant's command rested, Brigadier General Robert Potter observed that the salient opposite him, on the other side of Poor Creek, was vulnerable to mining. North of the Pamunkey River, Sheridan continued his slow retreat to White House Landing. Hampton, on the Pamunkey's south side, continued to shadow Sheridan.

Grant began rearranging his dispositions. That night the two divisions of Horatio Wright's corps at Bermuda Hundred returned to the south side of the Appomattox. Grant also selected Deep Bottom below Bailey's Creek as the site for a pontoon bridge to the Peninsula from Jones Neck on Bermuda Hundred. This would allow him to operate directly against Richmond and play upon Lee's fears for its safety.

Hampton reached White House Landing on 20 June, ahead

Union Strength			
According to the official returns, "the present for duty equipped" strength of the Union armies operating against Petersburg and Richmond from June 1864 to April 1865 was as follows:			
Date	Cavalry	Artillery	Infantry	Total
---	---	---	---	---
30 June	14,177	9,383	86,702	110,262
20 July	13,981	10,167	70,841	92,989
31 July	8,936	9,995	62,562	81,493
31 Aug.	6,358	7,846	45,963	60,167
30 Sept.	7,122	10,182	66,818	84,122
31 Oct.	6,295	8,011	76,637	90,943
30 Nov.	8,698	10,294	77,387	96,379
31 Dec.	10,059	9,719	92,141	111,919
31 Jan.	10,920	11,037	99,214	121,171
28 Feb.	9,994	9,701	98,457	118,152
20 March	9,743	10,961	104,338	125,042
31 March	17,616	9,390	106,180	133,186

of Sheridan. Though the Confederate cavalry skirmished with the Federals at this base, the presence of gunboats deterred an outright attack.

On the next day, Foster's brigade of the *X Corps* crossed the James River on the newly constructed pontoon bridge at Deep Bottom. Lee hurried Cooke's and Davis' Brigades of Heth's Division back to the Peninsula to reinforce the Department of Richmond, now under Lieutenant General Richard S. Ewell— Robert Ransom had been transferred to Lynchburg to serve under Early.

Sheridan arrived at White House Landing. Hampton withdrew but continued to display the initiative which would put

Confederate Strength			
According to the official returns, the present for duty force of the Confederate armies defending Petersburg and Richmond from June 1864 to April 1865 was as follows:			
Date	Cavalry	Artillery	Infantry	Total
30 June 1864	10,593	7,989	44,652	63,234
10 July	10,073	7,921	43,617	61,611
31 Aug.	8,129	7,414	34,486	50,029
10 Sept.	8,355	7,214	32,869	48,438
20 Oct.	6,791	5,793	35,889	48,473
31 Oct.	6,988	6,639	38,102	51,729
10 Nov.	7,072	6,775	40,186	54,033
30 Nov.	7,810	8,133	47,404	63,347
20 Dec.	7,745	7,105	56,664	71,514
10 Jan.	7,044	6,987	48,045	62,076
31 Jan. 1865	5,535	6,711	46,551	58,797
10 Feb.	3,992	6,233	45,510	55,735
1 March	6,711	6,233	45,349	58,293

him in a class by himself among the subordinate commanders of both armies. He submitted a plan for destroying Sheridan on the foreseeable march from White House Landing to the James.

At Petersburg, Grant decided to extend his partial investment from the Appomattox below the city to the Appomattox above. This would have forced Petersburg's evacuation because the Federals would have threatened Lee's line of retreat.

Smith's corps came back south of the Appomattox. Together with Warren's and Burnside's corps, Smith's corps stretched to hold the line from the Jerusalem Plank Road to the river. This freed David Birney's and Horatio Wright's corps. In the lead, David Birney's corps struggled through the three miles of intervening swamps and thickets toward the Weldon Railroad. The Confederate cavalrymen of Barringer's Brigade turned back this Federal reconnaissance just short of the tracks. That night Meade ordered David Birney's corps to extend from the Jerusalem Plank Road with Wright's corps on its left, drive the Southerners back into the works and invest Petersburg to the Weldon Railroad, all on the following day. On the day after that, Wright's corps would extend the investment to the South Side Railroad and the upper Appomattox.

To increase the pressure on the Confederates, Grant was sending the cavalry divisions of Wilson and Kautz under Brigadier General James H. Wilson on a raid against the Confederate railroads fanning out south and west of Petersburg. Meade emphasized to Wilson the importance of destroying High Bridge, which conveyed the South Side Railroad over the Appomattox near Farmville, and Staunton River Bridge, which carried the Richmond & Danville over the Roanoke (Staunton) near Clover. Major General Andrew A. Humphreys, Meade's chief of staff, led Wilson to believe that the Federals would have control of the southern approaches to Petersburg by the time Wilson returned and that Sheridan would keep Hampton occupied north of the James. His mind at ease, Wilson set out at 0200 on the morning of 22 June.

The Federal horsemen crossed the Weldon Railroad at Reams Station, 10 miles south of Petersburg. They burned the station and ripped up a short stretch of track before the Confederate cavalrymen of Barringer's Brigade came down from their headquarters at Globe Tavern, four miles north up the tracks. Passing through Dinwiddie Court House with Barringer's men in pursuit, the Federals reached the South Side Railroad at Sixteen Mile Turnout in the afternoon.

Back at Petersburg, David Birney's and Horatio Wright's corps moved out that morning for the Weldon Railroad. They had orders to conform their movements to one another. This meant that Wright's corps had to constantly shift to its right—while still advancing—as David Birney's *II Corps* swung up like a door to the Confederate fortification.

This proved impossible in the uncharted thickets between the Jerusalem Plank Road and the Weldon Railroad. After the delays became unendurable, Meade lost his patience and ordered the two corps to move without reference to one another. This speeded matters up but created a gap between the two corps.

The *II Corps* advanced with its right pivoting on the Jerusalem Plank Road. Gibbon's division, on the right, got into position first and was reinforced by a battery of four cannon. Mott's division went into position on Gibbon's left and began entrenching. Barlow's division took position on the far left short of the Weldon Railroad and put two brigades perpendicular to the corps front as flank guards. Without a pivot or point of reference, Wright's corps floundered through the brambles a mile to the southeast.

Lee knew that the Weldon Railroad was too long and exposed to be successfully defended, but he did not want to give it up without a fight. That morning, as David Birney's skirmishers advanced toward the Confederate front, Lee directed A.P. Hill to drive them back. Hill went out with the divisions of Wilcox and Mahone to accomplish this task.

Wilcox and Hill had little more idea of their whereabouts than did David Birney and Horatio Wright. Hill could conceive of no more effective maneuver than placing Wilcox's Division in the same position Barringer's Brigade had occupied on the previous day—interposed between Wright's corps and the Weldon Railroad.

But Mahone knew every inch of the ground around Petersburg. He had surveyed the area while chief engineer for the Norfolk & Petersburg Railroad, of which he subsequently became president. Finding the gap between the two Federal corps, he led Ambrose Wright's Georgia Brigade, Sanders' Alabama Brigade and his own old Virginia Brigade under Colonel David A. Weisiger up the ravine that leads into the present Wilcox Lake. This concealed Mahone's movement into David Birney's left rear. Mahone formed his battle line on

A Confederate general who distinguished himself during the Petersburg campaign, William Mahone. His victories on the Jerusalem Plank Road, at the Crater and at Globe Tavern on 19 August inflicted heavy casualties on the Yankees, and included thousands of captured.

the Johnson farm. He put Sanders on the left, Ambrose Wright on the right and Weisiger's Brigade en echelon behind Ambrose Wright. A section of Dement's Maryland Battery accompanied the formation.

At about 1700, while Wilcox's Division was skirmishing with Horatio Wright's corps, Mahone led his men into the woods east of the Johnson farm and requested Cadmus Wilcox to advance on his right. Only yards into the woods, Sanders' men hit the refused left of Barlow's division. At first the Alabamians encountered stiff resistance. Barlow, a survivor of Mahone's devastating flank attack against the *II Corps* on 6 May in the Wilderness (a part of Longstreet's onslaught against the Federal left there), instantly sent his reserve brigade under Nelson A. Miles back to man the trenches on the Jerusalem Plank Road.

This move proved fortunate for the Northerners in the long run, but disastrous in the short term. The Federal left crumbled as Confederates Ambrose Wright and Weisiger swept into its rear. Within five minutes, Barlow's division bolted. "It was run or be gobbled," a Federal soldier said. As Mahone's battle lines pushed east, the Confederates scooped up prisoners and battle flags. Meanwhile, in typical Southern fashion, the Confederates that remained in the trenches attacked sequentially as the flank attack approached their front.

To Barlow's right stood Mott's veteran division. This division was the consolidation of the divisions that Major General Gershom Mott and David Birney had led in the Wilderness. It reacted to Mahone's ambush here as the division Mott commanded in the Wilderness had reacted to the enemy flank attack on the morning of 6 May. Knowing they were enfiladed, Mott's soldiers glumly headed for the rear in some semblance of order but without stopping to oppose the Confederates.

The departure of Mott's division with scarcely a shot left Gibbon's men unaware of the approaching danger. The first that many of them knew of Mahone's attack was the appearance of Confederates in their rear demanding their surrender. Hit from both sides, Gibbon's division disintegrated. Several

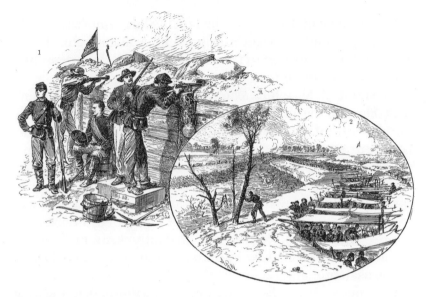

The siege of Petersburg. 1. (Left) Sharpshooters of the XVIII Corps.
2. (Right) Rifle pits of the V Corps.

battle flags, the four cannon, and a large number of Federals
fell into Southern hands.

Mahone's attack broke down under the weight of Northern
prisoners. A few men of Weisiger's Brigade attacked the
entrenchments along the Jerusalem Plank Road, but Miles'
brigade and the fugitives who clustered around it repulsed
the Confederates. Mahone thought that he might have rolled
up the entire Federal army if Cadmus Wilcox had come to his
assistance in time to storm these trenches. But Wilcox did not
arrive with two of his brigades for another half hour. By that
time the Confederates had reversed the captured breastworks
and the Federals had recovered from their panic. Mahone, the
alumnus of Virginia Military Institute, vented his wrath on
Wilcox, a West Pointer.

The shaken Northerners failed to mount a counterattack
until after dark. It struck the front of Nathaniel Harris'
Mississippi Brigade, which had moved up to occupy the
captured position. The Mississippians blasted the Federals
with the Southern equivalent of repeaters—each man fired off

several captured muskets in addition to his own. The Northerners recoiled, and now the fight took on another, grisly, aspect of the Wilderness. The woods, without rain since 3 June, caught fire, and the night resounded with the screams of wounded unable to outdistance the advancing flames.

While Hill's Corps trounced the Federals south of Petersburg, Sheridan broke up the Union base at White House Landing and headed for the James, escorting a wagon train. He intended to cross to Bermuda Hundred on the pontoon bridge from Deep Bottom. Hampton gathered his forces near Malvern Hill, between Sheridan and his destination, and waited to pounce.

Meanwhile, on the South Side Railroad, Wilson's men tore up the tracks west of Sixteen Mile Turnout and destroyed Ford's Station. Harassment by Rooney Lee's troopers prevented the Northern horsemen from doing a proper job. This entailed pulling up the rails and ties, piling up the ties with the rails atop, setting the ties afire, wrapping the rails around trees when the rails grew red hot in the center and then digging six-foot trenches across the roadbed for good measure. Wilson's men merely gathered fence rails, set them lengthwise along the tracks and lighted them, hoping that this would ignite the ties. If the ties caught fire, they would warp the rails, necessitating a trip to the rolling mill to straighten them. If the ties did not catch fire, no damage was done. Luckily for the Federals, the long dry spell meant that the ties ordinarily caught fire.

Early in the morning hours of 23 June, Mahone's men evacuated the works they had captured from David Birney's corps. The Confederates took with them many flags, four guns and more than 1,600 prisoners. The once elite Union *II Corps* had suffered its most humiliating defeat to date. The Southerners lost about 400 men.

While Mahone's men evacuated the trenches, Wilson ordered Kautz's division ahead to Burke's Station, where the South Side Railroad crossed the Richmond & Danville tracks. Kautz moved out at 0300 and followed the Cox Road, which

Federals draw fire for entertainment during a lull in the Petersburg fighting.

went straight toward Burke's Station, rather than the railroad, which arced to the south.

Wilson's men followed the railroad, tearing up the tracks. But at noon, at Nottoway Court House, they met Dearing's Brigade and a battery of horse artillery. Rooney Lee had hurried these units along the road that formed the chord of the arc described by the railroad. The Confederates had interposed between Wilson and Kautz.

Dearing's troopers attacked Chapman's brigade, Wilson's lead formation. At first, the Southerners drove the Federals. But when reinforcements from McIntosh's brigade arrived, the tide turned. The Northerners drove back Dearing's men. Only the arrival of the 1st North Carolina Cavalry of Barringer's Brigade in the nick of time saved the Confederate artillery. As the rest of Barringer's Brigade came up, the fighting slackened to a skirmish that lasted until after dark.

The fight at Nottoway Court House, though drawn, had profound consequences. It saved High Bridge, the destruction of which was one of Wilson's principal objectives. Wilson ordered Kautz, who had torn up the track in all directions from Burke's Station, to abandon the projected attack on High Bridge and head down the Richmond & Danville Railroad to Staunton River Bridge. Had Wilson destroyed High Bridge, the South Side Railroad would have been cut for months.

While Rooney Lee and his men saved High Bridge, Mahone and his soldiers prevented the Federals from establishing the first of the conditions precedent to Wilson's safe return—extending their investment of Petersburg to the upper Appomattox. A.P. Hill was a profound disappointment as a corps commander, inept in battle and subject to fits of illness at critical moments. But he knew an outstanding division commander when he saw one, and today he gave Mahone a free hand.

Though the Union *II Corps* remained near the Jerusalem Plank Road licking its wounds, Horatio Wright's corps advanced to the Weldon Railroad near Globe Tavern, six miles south of Petersburg. A.P. Hill ordered Mahone to drive the Northerners back. Mahone marched down the Halifax Road in the broiling heat. The sight of his dust cloud alone alarmed Wright, the cautious commander of the *VI Corps*.

During the afternoon, Mahone's skirmishers felt around the angle of the refused Union left, where a work party from the *Vermont Brigade* of the *VI Corps* was tearing up the railroad. Shortly before dusk, Mahone struck. Nathaniel Harris' and Ambrose Wright's Brigades drove back the Northerners in the thickets to the right of the work party. Perry's Florida Brigade cut into the open field behind the work party's left and gobbled up 483 Vermonters after killing and wounding about 100 more. Hill's Corps lost fewer than 300 men. For the second day in a row, three Confederate brigades had whipped three Union divisions—an ominous sign. Ambrose Wright withdrew three miles to the Jerusalem Plank Road and entrenched. Mahone had ensured that the Federals would not extend their investment of the Cockade City to the upper Appomattox. In two days, at a cost of about 700 Southern casualties, Hill's Corps had inflicted 2,982 on the Northerners.

On the following day, Hampton thwarted the establishment

Action on the Jerusalem Plank Road

The following selection is taken from the diary of Private Bernard:

Entrenchments Wilcox's Farm, Friday afternoon June 24, 1864

For several days past I have neglected to write in this book rather from want of inclination than absence of any worthy of interest. From Sunday afternoon until Wednesday morning everything was pretty quiet. We remained quietly in the trenches & were visited by many of our citizen friends who brought out with many little good things to eat & drink. Many of our boys, as might have been expected, ran the blockade into town and on Tuesday evening 50 men from the brigade were granted regular permits by order of Gen. Mahone and by division to visit Petersburg allowing them to go in at 6 P.M. & return at 8 o'clock next morning. The men pledging themselves to return to their command immediately in the event of an attack from the enemy. I was fortunate to be one of those fifty and went into town spending however more pleasant a time than I anticipated, in consequence of the absence of friends & relatives whom I was very anxious to see. Wednesday our brigade, Wright's & Saunders (Wilcox's old brigade) were moved outside of our breastworks & put in position in a line perpendicular to the line of the breastworks & along the edge of the woods just in front of our position. Here we encountered the enemy who seemed to have moved there that morning or the night before. The fire to which our brigade was exposed was very severe as we moved by the right flank to get into position on the right of Wright's

of the second condition precedent to a safe return for Wilson. Sheridan had crossed the Chickahominy at Jones Bridge and hoped to sneak the wagon train from White House Landing to Bermuda Hundred by turning west at Charles City Court House. He sent David Gregg's division to seize Samaria Church, held by Wilson's division 10 days earlier.

The Confederate cavalry wrecked Sheridan's plan. Hampton's Division struck David Gregg's front and Fitzhugh Lee's Division hit his right. The Northerners buckled and skedaddled all the way back to Charles City Court House. Like Grant two weeks earlier, Sheridan gave up hope of crossing directly

brigade. One man of our reg't (Hall Co C) was severely wd here. Getting into position Wright & perhaps Saunders also moved forward with a yell, our brigade moving at the same time but rather I think behind Wright. The enemy were soon put on the run & continued to give way until they were driven fully 3/4 of a mile back to their breastworks & then out of them, which we occupied & from which we repulsed attempts to assault us firing upon the enemy heavy volleys, almost every man having two or three guns. Suffice it now to say that this repulse is considered a most brilliant one that resulted in the capture of 1742 prisoners, 4 pieces of artillery & 24 or 5 stands of colors (5 of the latter by our brigade), with a loss of perhaps only 300 or 400 on our part. We killed a great many of the enemy. The loss in our reg't was only 2 wd and very slight in the other reg'ts of our brigade. About midnight we fell back to our old positions leaving the skirmishers at the yankee works until day, this enabling our men to collect 1500 or 2000 stand of arms & bring off many hundreds of the wd, yankee & confederate.

Next day (Thursday) our division went a long march down the Weldon R.R. and entrenching, the enemy skirmished with them & captured about 500 prisoners. Our reg't was engaged in the skirmish. I myself was fortunate enough to miss this tramp, going to Petersburg on surgeon's certification to have a tooth extracted. Today we have been under marching orders since early this morning, but everything is quiet now. We heard heavy cannonading with some musketry down about the river this morning. We have heard there was an unsuccessful attempt on part of Gen. Hoke with 400 men to capture an important position of our old entrenchments.

from the Peninsula to Bermuda Hundred and resigned himself to crossing downriver. This would take more time and put him farther out of position to protect the returning troopers of Wilson and Kautz. It would also free Hampton and his men to operate against Wilson.

Early that morning, Kautz headed southwest on the Richmond & Danville Railroad, setting fire to fence rails piled on the ties as he went. Wilson disengaged from Rooney Lee at Nottoway Court House and rode toward a rendezvous with Kautz. Barringer's Brigade dogged Wilson's column in the blistering heat.

At Petersburg, columns of unfortunate Federal captives passing through the city on their way to prison camps received insults and scorn from the people of the city. The bag of prisoners suggested to Lee that the Federals were on the verge of collapse. He ordered Beauregard to storm the Union lines between the City Point Road and the Appomattox River. Swinging to the right, Beauregard's force would then seize the Hare House Hill—the future site of Fort Stedman—and roll up the Northern lines to the Norfolk and Petersburg Railroad.

But the plan called for cooperation between two divisions from different departments. The division commanders, Hoke and Major General Charles W. Field, misunderstood their respective roles. Supported by artillery from across the Appomattox, Hoke advanced only Hagood's Brigade instead of his entire division. With Hagood's Brigade, Hoke merely occupied the enemy's entrenched picket line instead of attacking the Federal main line. Field's Division, awaiting such an attack, did not move to the support of Hagood's Brigade. Northern fire pinned down Hagood's South Carolinians and about 200 of them surrendered. The Federals lost fewer than a dozen men.

Grant mounted no counterattack. He had realized from the stampede of David Birney's *II Corps* two days earlier that the Northern soldiers were exhausted. He allowed them to rest.

By this time, the notion that the salient opposite Potter's division could be reduced by a mine had occurred independently to one of Potter's subordinates, Lieutenant Colonel Henry Pleasants of the *48th Pennsylvania*. A mining engineer in command of a regiment of coal miners, Pleasants approached Potter with the idea. Potter put it in writing and sent it up the chain of command to Major General Ambrose E. Burnside. Thinking no harm could come from beginning the mine, Burnside authorized Potter's men to proceed and resolved to take the matter to Meade.

The miners commenced their work at noon on 25 June. Burnside notified Meade of Pleasants' initiative at 1445. Meade approved of it wholeheartedly. Like Burnside, he thought it best to keep the men occupied.

While Sheridan's column plodded down the James to Douthard's Landing, Wilson and Kautz arrived at Staunton River Bridge, about 75 miles southwest of Petersburg. A scratch force of 938 militia and men on leave defended the vital span. About half of the Confederate infantry occupied masked rifle pits on the river's north bank. Half a dozen cannon on the south bank supported the men in the rifle pits. Only one of the Southern artillery pieces had the range to duel effectively with Wilson's 12 cannon and four mountain howitzers.

Late in the afternoon, Kautz's tired but unbloodied troopers drew the task of attacking the bridge. Again and again, losing more men to sunstroke than to Confederate fire, Kautz's soldiers plodded forward through the bottom land on both sides of the Richmond & Danville's embankment. Again and again, Southern fire drove the Federals back.

Barringer's Brigade arrived behind the Northerners and attacked their rear while Kautz attacked the bridge. The attacks of both sides failed, but the presence of the North Carolinians in Wilson's rear convinced him that the time had come to depart. At midnight, his men staggered off to the southeast.

Wilson had now failed to destroy either of his principal objectives. Like the destruction of High Bridge, the destruction of Staunton River Bridge would have required months to repair.

By daybreak on 26 June, Wilson's vanguard had reached Wyliesburg. There his exhausted troopers halted and boiled coffee. Luckily for the Federals, the Confederates were scarcely capable of pursuing. Fatigued by the fighting and the terrible heat, only 300 men of Barringer's Brigade remained on Wilson's trail. That same morning, Sheridan reached Douthard's Landing and began ferrying across the James. Hampton's and Fitzhugh Lee's Divisions withdrew to Drewry's Bluff. On the Southside, Lee ordered Chambliss' Brigade of Rooney Lee's Division to Stony Creek to intercept Wilson on his return. Wilson's troopers plodded through Christiansburg and Greensborough to Buckhorn Creek in Mecklenburg County.

Early on the morning of 27 June, Wilson's raiders broke camp. Crossing the Meherrin River at Saffold's Bridge, they reached the Boydton Plank Road at Great Creek in Brunswick County. Passing through Lawrenceville, they rode on to Poplar Mountain in Greensville County and headed for Double Bridges, near the mouth of Hardwood Creek on the Nottoway River. Many men were so tired that they fell asleep in the saddle. The more energetic plundered the bounteous countryside, previously unravaged by war. The slave population joined the column, seeking to follow the Northern cavalrymen to freedom.

At Douthard's Landing, Sheridan finished ferrying his wagons and soldiers across the James. He received orders from Meade to take position on the Union left, near the Jerusalem Plank Road. Meade issued these orders in preparation for Wilson's return.

Lee also prepared for Wilson's return. Hampton's Division received orders to join Chambliss' Brigade at Stony Creek. Fitzhugh Lee's Division remained at Drewry's Bluff. Hampton arrived at Stony Creek at noon, just as Wilson reached Double Bridges. Wilson received false intelligence that only a small garrison occupied Stony Creek, two miles off the road from Double Bridges to Prince George Court House. Wilson thought that he was home free and headed up the road.

By 1230, Hampton had sent out scouts to locate Wilson and ascertain what route he was taking back to the Federal lines. While Hampton waited for the scouts to report, he again displayed his initiative. He suggested that Lee send infantry and artillery to Reams Station, halfway between Petersburg and Stony Creek. This would force Wilson to swing out as far as Jarratt's Station, 30 miles from Petersburg, or Belfield, 40 miles from the Cockade City, to cross the Weldon Railroad.

Shortly afterward, Hampton's scouts found Wilson. Hampton immediately sent a message to Lee asking him to send Fitzhugh Lee's Division of cavalry to Reams Station as well. Hampton informed Lee he would attack Wilson at Sapony

Church, where the road from Double Bridges to Prince George Court House crossed the road to Dinwiddie Court House from Stony Creek.

Chambliss' Brigade led Hampton's column and met Wilson late in the afternoon, soon after crossing Sapony Creek. The Virginians drove the surprised Federals from the old church and pushed them some distance beyond. McIntosh's brigade counterattacked and pressed Chambliss' Brigade back to the church. Hampton reinforced Chambliss first with Rosser's Brigade, then with Young's Brigade and finally with 200 infantry of the Holcombe Legion. A stalemate developed that lasted until 2200.

Finding his way blocked, Wilson at that hour attempted to evade Hampton by taking the Old Stage Road to Petersburg. The Old Stage Road ran right past Reams Station.

Kautz's division departed Sapony Church first with Spears' brigade in the lead. Wilson was not ready to disengage his own division until daylight on 29 June. To Kautz's surprise, his men struck infantry pickets when they arrived at Reams Station at 0700. Lee had sent Mahone there with Perry's and Sanders' Brigades.

The Confederate infantry responded by knocking Kautz's troopers back on their heels. Reinforcing his lead brigade, Kautz counterattacked and captured about 60 of Mahone's soldiers. The exhausted Federals erected breastworks and waited for Wilson's division to arrive. Some of Kautz's men had scarcely been able to stay awake during the skirmish.

Wilson had serious difficulty withdrawing at Sapony Church. McIntosh's brigade made the break successfully, but Hampton's attack pinned down Chapman's brigade, the rear guard, before it could disengage. Chambliss' Brigade, Young's Brigade and the Holcombe Legion held Chapman's front while Butler's and Rosser's Brigades struck Chapman's left. The Southern maneuver cut Chapman's brigade off from McIntosh's brigade. Chapman and his men only made it to the Old Stage Road by using rural lanes and going cross country. They then followed McIntosh's brigade to Reams Station.

Hampton stopped his pursuit when he ascertained Wilson's direction. Assuming that Lee had covered Reams Station, Hampton deployed his men to block the crossings of the Weldon Railroad to the south.

Wilson reached Reams Station in mid-morning. There he learned for the first time of the Union infantry's failure to extend its lines to the Weldon Railroad. Leaving Kautz to hold the Depot Road, Wilson prepared to force a passage to Globe Tavern along the Old Stage Road with McIntosh's brigade.

The discovery that Confederate infantry barred his path put an end to that notion. Wilson sent off a courier to Meade with a message describing the plight of the raiders. Then Wilson issued all his ammunition and destroyed his wagons and caissons in preparation for an unimpeded retreat to the Nottoway.

After losing half his escort, the courier made his way from Wilson to the Federal left on the Jerusalem Plank Road and arrived at 1030. Apprised of Wilson's predicament, Meade reacted slowly and indecisively. Not until noon did he order a division of Horatio Wright's corps to Reams Station to be followed by the rest of Wright's corps and Sheridan's cavalry.

By then it was far too late. While Meade issued his orders, Wilson started to pull out, but again the Confederates were too fast for him. Mahone's infantry pinned down Kautz's division while Fitzhugh Lee and his men enveloped McIntosh's brigade on the Northern left. The Confederates cut McIntosh's brigade in two, blocking the right half and Kautz's division from the Old Stage Road.

Kautz's division and the eastern portion of McIntosh's brigade headed for the *Army of the Potomac*'s lines cross-country. The exhausted, panic stricken troopers abandoned their artillery and their stolen silverware and kicked free of the slaves who sought to ride their stirrups to freedom. Every man was his own general, and this force disintegrated as the Federals floundered through the swamps and thickets. Hampton's brigades on the Weldon Railroad chopped up some of these groups as they tried to break out of the trap.

Fitzhugh Lee pursued the fragment under Wilson down the Stage Road. The Northern troopers in Wilson's column also

Exhausted Federal troopers come into Federal lines after escaping entrapment by the enemy during the Wilson-Kautz raid. At the expense of 1,445 casualties and 16 cannon, two Federal divisions destroyed around 60 miles of track on the Weldon railroad.

abandoned artillery, slaves and booty. Fitzhugh Lee's pursuit ended at Stony Creek, where the Northerners crossed the rickety bridge in a panic. The Federals remained in headlong flight for Double Bridges. Without notifying Hampton of the direction of Wilson's column, Fitzhugh Lee and Mahone returned to Petersburg encumbered with prisoners and trophies.

Late in the afternoon, long after any chance of saving Wilson and Kautz had passed, Horatio Wright's soldiers arrived at Reams Station. There Wright's corps erected breastworks that would give rise to controversy two months after the second battle of Reams Station in August.

While his subordinates mauled Kautz's command, Hampton waited at Stony Creek for word of Wilson's whereabouts, knowing that Wilson was retreating toward the Nottoway River. Fitzhugh Lee's failure to communicate with Hampton saved Wilson's column, which recrossed the Nottoway at 2200

Civilian visitors are entertained in the Petersburg entrenchments.
As the siege continued, both sides built miles of fortifications.

at Double Bridges. Wilson then headed for Jarratt's Station, pausing for rest two miles short of the station at 0200 for two hours. His men crossed the Weldon Railroad at Jarratt's Station at dawn, encountering only Confederate pickets. The Federals then continued riding east.

Hampton had no word from Fitzhugh Lee until 0900 on 30 June, and then it was only an intercepted order to the Stony Creek garrison commander to cut off the Federals at Jarratt's Station. Five miles short of Jarratt's Station, Hampton learned that Wilson had already passed through that place. Wilson recrossed the Nottoway River at Peter's Bridge at 1300 with Hampton two hours behind him. Resting until 1830, Wilson's force reached Blunt's Bridge on the Blackwater River late that night. The Federals rebuilt the bridge and crossed by 0615 on 1 July. Spooked by rumors, they reached Chipoak Creek the next day.

Thus ended the last of the disasters that constituted Grant's second offensive. Mahone had smashed the attempt of the Northern infantry to extend its investment of Petersburg to the upper Appomattox. Rooney Lee had prevented the Union cavalry from destroying either of its principal objectives— High Bridge on the South Side Railroad and Staunton River Bridge on the Richmond and Danville. He also kept the Northern horse soldiers from doing a proper job of destroying the tracks. Hampton, after besting Sheridan at Samaria Church, went on to distinguish himself by the initiative he showed in planning Wilson's undoing, which might have been more thorough but for Fitzhugh Lee's error of omission. The Southern cavalry and Mahone lost fewer than 200 men at the first battle of Reams Station while inflicting losses about five times that number on Wilson, four-fifths of them prisoners. The Confederates also captured 12 cannon and four mountain howitzers. Wilson's raid cost the Federals 1,445 casualties while inflicting on the Confederates only about 300.

Wilson's raid failed to force the Confederates to evacuate Richmond. Least damaged by Wilson but most vulnerable to Federal depredations, the Weldon Railroad would return to operation in early July. The South Side Railroad remained intact from Lynchburg to just short of Burke's Station, the Richmond & Danville from just north of Burke's Station to the capital. Because of Hunter's departure from Grant's plan and Hampton's victory over Sheridan at the battle of Trevilian's Station, the damage to the Virginia Central Railroad caused by Hunter and Sheridan in early June had been repaired by 29 June, when locomotives resumed running again from Staunton to Richmond. These lines carried the supplies which fed Lee's army during the weeks that would be required to repair the damage to the tracks east and south of Burke's Station.

Despite the fearfully disproportionate losses suffered during the operations of late June, the fortunes of Grant's command and the Union had not yet reached their nadir. While Early hurtled toward Washington, Burnside's corps burrowed towards Petersburg.

CHAPTER V

The Battle of the Crater

While the army groups of Grant and Lee attempted to recuperate above ground, Pleasants' miners struggled toward Petersburg below the surface. By 2 July 1864, they had tunneled 250 feet. But on that day, they hit quicksand and mining slowed.

The mine had grown into a major operation. Pleasants' command included a sawmill and a sandbag factory. Such a vast undertaking could not escape detection for long. When the Northern miners hit the quicksand, the Southerners were already detailing men to train for countermining.

In the Shenandoah Valley, Early reached Winchester that same day. The Federals knew less of his approach than the Confederates did of Pleasants' mine. Grant thought that Early had rejoined Lee.

On 3 July, Grant asked his subordinates whether any of them thought a successful assault could be made on their fronts. He wanted to take the offensive again at Petersburg. He particularly wanted to break out of the Bermuda Hundred bottleneck and invest Richmond from the south, as he had originally planned. Meade queried Warren and Burnside as ordered by Grant. Warren, as usual, was pessimistic, but Burnside thought a successful assault could be made on his front if the mine were utilized.

Unfortunately, Meade read Burnside's answer as demanding control of the operation and became indignant at the imagined presumption. His pique was aggravated by the fact that the guileless Burnside was senior to him. After putting

Commander of the IX Corps, *Ambrose Burnside.*

Burnside in his place, Meade ordered his chief engineer and chief artillerist to examine the mine site's potential for a successful assault. Grant ordered his own chief engineer to make the same examination. Meanwhile, Burnside decided to give the lead in any assault to his black division. He ordered its commander, Brigadier General Edward Ferrero, to reconnoiter and formulate a plan of attack.

Rumors that Grant would launch an Independence Day assault to capture Petersburg on the anniversary of Vicksburg's fall put the Confederates in a state of alarm. But

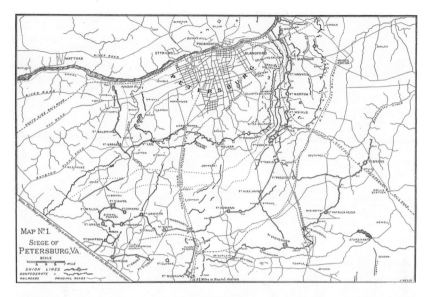

MAP N°1.
SIEGE OF
PETERSBURG, VA.
SCALE
UNION LINES
CONFEDERATE
RAILROADS   PRINCIPAL ROADS

Independence Day at Petersburg passed with nothing more than the usual sniping and shelling.

In the Shenandoah Valley, Early burst back into the Federal field of vision like a fireworks display. At the Valley's lower end, his lean ragged soldiers drove the Northerners into Harper's Ferry. Halleck's cautious warning to Grant that crossing the James River would leave Washington uncovered began to look prophetic. The capital was defended only by heavy artillerists and rear echelon troops.

On 5 July, Early's threat to Washington began to have the effect intended by Lee—one similar to that produced by Stonewall Jackson's threat to Washington in 1862. As Early began crossing the Potomac at Shepherdstown, Grant ordered Ricketts' division of Horatio Wright's corps to Baltimore along with all of his army group's dismounted cavalrymen.

Meade received lukewarm reports from his chief engineer and chief artillerist on the prospect of a successful assault at the site of the mine. The problem was that Rives Salient, where the new Confederate works joined the old Dimmock Line near the Jerusalem Plank Road, flanked Elliott's Salient, under which the mine was directed. Meade's staff thought Rives Salient would have to be reduced by regular approaches

Jubal Early's raids north of the Potomac and campaigns in the Shenandoah Valley influenced events around Petersburg. It took an army under Philip Sheridan to rid the Federals of Early's command.

before the explosion of the mine beneath Elliott's Salient would lead to a successful assault there. Grant's chief engineer independently came to the same conclusion. But neither

Grant or Meade ordered the mining stopped nor the site of the mine moved.

Ricketts' division and the dismounted cavalrymen, in all 9,000 men, embarked for Baltimore on 6 July. Lee's strategy in sending Early to threaten Washington continued to bear fruit on 9 July. Early routed Ricketts' division and the rest of the motley Federal force that opposed him at the battle of the Monocacy in Maryland. As a result, Grant ordered to Washington the remaining two divisions of Wright's corps and diverted to Washington a division of the *XIX Corps* on its way to City Point from Louisiana, where it had participated in the disastrous Red River campaign. The loss of these units undermined Grant's plans for an assault at Petersburg on 18 or 19 July.

Siege operations against Rives Salient began on 10 July, the same day as the Confederates began countermining. About this time, Ferrero presented Burnside with a plan for the assault subsequent to the explosion of the mine. The plan called for the two brigades of the African-American division to advance in parallel columns. One regiment of each brigade would sweep down the trenches to the right and left while the remainder of the division headed for the crest behind Elliott's Salient.

On the next day, Early's tired soldiers staggered into view of Washington. The two remaining divisions of Wright's *VI Corps* and the rerouted division of the *XIX Corps* arrived before Early could mount an attack against the militia and rear echelon troops guarding the capital.

Seeing that he could not successfully assault Washington, Early headed back to the Potomac on 12 July. An attack mounted by Wright met only a Southern rear guard. South of Petersburg, the Confederates had finished repairing the Weldon Railroad and it resumed operation.

Two days later, only a small gap remained on the South Side Railroad between Burke's Station and Petersburg. Just four more days would elapse before the railroad resumed running between those two points. But the Southerners still had 25 miles of the Richmond & Danville Railroad to return to operation. And Grant contemplated sending his cavalry to wreck the Weldon Railroad down to Hicksford and then destroy the Richmond & Danville Railroad south of Staunton River Bridge.

On 16 July, Early returned to the Shenandoah Valley. Grant expected Early to return to Petersburg as Jackson had gone to Richmond before the Seven Days Battles in 1862. To strike at Petersburg before Early arrived, Grant sought the return of the *VI* and *XIX Corps* from Washington.

Burnside's men had completed the main gallery of their mine by 17 July. It extended 510 feet, a length thought impossible by Meade's chief engineer. The Northern miners had also become aware of Confederate countermining.

Foster's Brigade expanded the Federal bridgehead at Deep Bottom to the lower side of Bailey's Creek on 21 July. On the following day, construction began on a second pontoon bridge at Deep Bottom. This one linked Jones Neck to the Peninsula downstream from the mouth of Bailey's Creek.

Grant wanted the Virginia Central Railroad wrecked from Charlottesville to Gordonsville, and he was willing to leave Wright's corps in the Shenandoah Valley if it could be employed to that purpose. But on 23 July, Wright returned the *VI Corps* to Washington after leaving Early at Strasburg. This convinced Grant that Wright's corps belonged back at Petersburg. Grant thought that Early was returning to Petersburg to allow Lee to detach men to Georgia for the defense of Atlanta.

Burnside's mine was ready for loading that day. Each of the two lateral chambers stretched 75 feet from the main gallery. But springs near the mine's head made it necessary to load the mine with gunpowder as close to the planned firing as possible. The staffs of Grant and Meade had examined the sites of proposed attacks near Ware Bottom Church and Port Walthall on Bermuda Hundred as well as at Elliott's Salient at Petersburg. They considered the site of the mine at Elliott's Salient the most promising location for a successful assault. Meade did not agree. He made it clear that he thought the odds favored failure in an assault at the site of the mine.

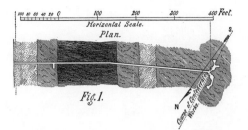

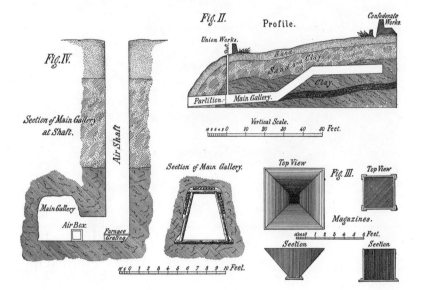

Details of the Petersburg mine construction.

On 24 July, Grant ordered Wright's corps back to Petersburg. Grant wanted to explode the mine either as the preliminary to an assault or as a diversion that would allow Sheridan's cavalrymen to get off cleanly on a raid that would take them as far as Hicksford on the Weldon Railroad.

The increased level of Federal activity at Deep Bottom prompted Lee to order Kershaw's Division to the Peninsula. Kershaw's four brigades joined Fulton's (formerly Johnson's) Brigade of the Department of Richmond and Lane's and McGowan's Brigades of Cadmus Wilcox's Division.

Fearful that Halleck would persuade Lincoln to raise the siege of Petersburg because of the threat Early posed to

Union soldiers carrying powder to the mine while under enemy fire.

Washington, Grant wanted to compel Lee to recall troops from Early. By 25 July, Grant had formulated a plan for another offensive. It would commence with a demonstration on the Peninsula by the *II Corps* and the cavalry, both under Hancock. Grant hoped that Hancock's forces would capture Richmond or wreck the Virginia Central Railroad. He expected that they would at least divert enough troops from Petersburg that an assault following the explosion of the mine might succeed. The mine explosion would in turn at least allow Sheridan to get away cleanly for a raid on the Weldon Railroad. Overriding Meade's objections, Grant ordered the mine charged.

Meade did not fear the numbers of opposing Confederates so much as he was concerned about their artillery, which the diversion on the Peninsula would not affect. He also wanted the *II Corps* present in case the Confederates counterattacked the *Army of the Potomac*'s left, which he thought vulnerable. Grant agreed to return the *II Corps* to Petersburg if it failed to attain its most ambitious objectives on the Peninsula.

Late that night, Butler gave Grant intelligence of the increase in Confederate forces on the Peninsula around Deep Bottom. Grant must have realized that the chances of achieving the more ambitious goals of his Peninsula diversion were slim.

On 26 July, Burnside submitted to Meade Ferrero's plan for an assault following the explosion of 12,000 pounds of powder in the mine. Burnside intended for Ferrero's division, consisting of *United States Colored Troops*, to lead the attack. These soldiers had guarded the *Army of the Potomac*'s wagon trains from the Rapidan to the James River and were far fresher than the white troops of Burnside's other three divisions.

Meade immediately began meddling with Burnside's plan. Instead of giving Burnside the 12,000 pounds of powder that he wanted, Meade furnished only 8,000 pounds. The affable Burnside carried on without protest, but he delayed charging the mine. That would have to wait until the last possible minute so that dampness would not seep into the gunpowder.

Early's movements in the Shenandoah Valley drew Wright away from Washington and prevented his return to Petersburg. Grant ordered to Washington the portion of the *XIX Corps* that had not yet arrived at Petersburg. He began planning a meeting with President Lincoln at Fort Monroe to discuss the best manner of dealing with Early.

Hancock's corps commenced its march to Deep Bottom at 1600. The soldiers began crossing the Appomattox on the pontoon bridge at Point of Rocks at 2130. Barlow's division, at the head of the column, reached the lower pontoon bridge on Jones Neck at 0245 on 27 July. Most of Hancock's corps had crossed the James by 0615 followed by Sheridan's cavalrymen. With Gibbon on the left, Barlow in the center and Mott on the right, Hancock's corps advanced against a line of

Troops of Barlow's division capture a Confederate battery near the New Market Road on 27 July.

Confederate rifle pits on a crest overlooking the New Market Road. The Federals captured the rifle pits and a battery of four cannon.

The *II Corps* continued to advance northward, towards the Long Bridge Road. At 0720, a Southern battery opened fire on the Union right. Mott's division chased the guns away, but Hancock realized that any chance of surprise had been lost. Instead of unleashing Sheridan's cavalry around the Confederate left, Hancock wheeled the *II Corps* into position on the east bank of Bailey's Creek. Gibbon's division held a line near the New Market Road, Barlow's division occupied the ground on Gibbon's right and Mott's division was near Fussell's Mill. Sheridan's cavalry rode to the high ground on Mott's right, overlooking the millpond.

The Confederates manned formidable works on the west bank of Bailey's Creek. The angle formed by their refused left was at Fussell's Mill, where Bailey's Creek flowed through a steep-sided ravine. A successful attack seemed out of the question to Hancock and the Federals spent the rest of the day reconnoitering.

Despite Hancock's failure to get beyond Bailey's Creek, General Lee reacted as Grant had hoped. Heth's Division of infantry and Rooney Lee's Division of cavalry were dispatched from Petersburg to the Peninsula. Lee also sent Lieutenant General Richard H. Anderson to take command at Deep Bottom. In the Department of Richmond, Ewell called out the local troops to assist in manning the trenches.

Though Grant agreed with Hancock that the likelihood of success was small, Grant still wanted Hancock to try to turn the Confederate left and roll it up all the way to Chaffin's Bluff. On the morning of 28 July, Grant reinforced Hancock with Birge's brigade of the *XIX Corps*—the only portion of that corps not at Washington. This brigade relieved Gibbon's division at the crossing of the New Market Road. Hancock ordered Sheridan to explore the possibility of an advance up the Darbytown Road or the Charles City Road.

But Sheridan found the Southerners heavily reinforced. Not only was a Northern attack unlikely, but the Federals had to go on the defensive. At 1000, Lane's and McGowan's Brigades of Cadmus Wilcox's Division and Kershaw's Old Brigade of Kershaw's Division assaulted Sheridan's right. The Federal troopers and their repeating rifles blasted the Southerners with Sheridan's men taking nearly 200 prisoners and several colors, though the Confederates captured a cannon from David Gregg's mounted division on the Charles City Road.

Hancock redeployed his troops to prevent the Southerners from cutting him off from the lower pontoon bridge at Deep Bottom. Gibbon's division took position on the Long Bridge Road. The cavalry moved to the New Market Road. Meanwhile, soldiers of Foster's Brigade crossed Bailey's Creek to garrison the lower bridgehead.

That afternoon, Grant was satisfied that Hancock had attracted to himself a large portion of Lee's command and decided to proceed with the plan of assault based on the mine at Petersburg. He ordered Hancock to send Mott's division to Petersburg that night to relieve the *XVIII Corps* in the trenches so that the *XVIII Corps* could take position to support Burnside's assault. Mott's division departed the Peninsula at 2000, recrossing the James on the lower Deep Bottom pontoon bridge.

The Confederates were still sending men from Petersburg to the Peninsula. After dark, Field's Division of infantry and Fitzhugh Lee's Division of cavalry departed the Cockade City to cross the James at Drewry's Bluff. This left only three divisions of Southern infantry at Petersburg and a single cavalry division to picket the Confederate right.

Meanwhile, Meade continued to interfere with Burnside's plan of assault. That morning, Meade insisted so vehemently that the assault column must press on to the crest behind Elliott's Salient that Burnside abandoned the notion of sending one regiment from each of his lead brigades right and left down the line of Southern trenches. Meade also objected to Burnside placing the black troops in the lead because of their inexperience and because of the political ramifications should they be slaughtered. But Burnside refused to yield on this point. The white troops of his corps were used up and too experienced not to take cover immediately if they came under fire. Meade agreed to submit the question to Grant and promised to return with Grant's answer that night.

Meade did not return until the following morning, less than 24 hours before the planned assault. Grant had decided in favor of Meade and against Burnside. Driven to despair by the meddling of his superiors, Burnside resorted to the unmilitary expedient of having the commanders of his white divisions draw lots to see which would replace Ferrero's black division at the head of the assault column. The lot fell to Ledlie's division, the freshest but worst led. Grant was aware of Burnside's method of selection and its result but declined to replace Ledlie's division because of the demoralizing effect of all the previous meddling.

No combat took place at Deep Bottom that day. Grant ordered the II Corps and the cavalry Southside. The first battle of Deep Bottom had cost the Confederates about 700 casualties, while Northern losses amounted to 488. Hancock's infantrymen moved out at dark. By 2315, they had crossed the

James at Jones Neck. They marched all night to get into position at Petersburg to support the *XVIII Corps*. The cavalry proceeded toward Lee's Mill, a position on the extreme Federal left. From there, the horsemen could easily strike the Weldon Railroad.

In the early morning hours of 30 July, the Federal army stood poised to exploit the mine explosion. Directly opposite Elliott's Salient waited the jaded veterans of Ledlie's division, with Potter's division on their right, Orlando Willcox's division on their left and the African-American division in reserve. Burnside had his bags packed, ready to enter Petersburg.

The *XVIII Corps*, with Turner's division of the *X Corps* attached, stood ready to support on Burnside's right. Major General Edward O.C. Ord had taken command of the *XVIII Corps* after Grant sacked Baldy Smith earlier in the month for creating dissension. The reserves of Warren's corps stood ready to support on Burnside's left and Hancock's tired men staggered into a supporting position behind Ord's command. Still farther to the rear, the Northern army's engineers waited with pontoons in case the Confederates managed to destroy the crossings of the Appomattox. Grant's plan called for his men to cross that river, uncork Butler from his Bermuda Hundred bottle and invest Richmond from the south as originally intended.

Opposite the Federals, the Confederates slept on their arms as they had for many nights. Though their sappers had not located a Northern mine, they knew the Federals were tunneling. The Southerners rose before dawn every day as they always did when enemy surprise tactics seemed imminent.

Pleasants lit the fuses at 0315. He expected the mine to explode 15 minutes later. Nothing had happened by 0415. Volunteers found that the powder train had gone out at the splices and the fuses were relit shortly afterward. The mine finally exploded at 0444.

The tremendous explosion annihilated Richard Pegram's Battery, the 18th South Carolina and half of the 17th South Carolina, blowing a hole in the earth 150 feet long, 60 feet

The Petersburg mine explosion was an awe inspiring sight for soldiers on both sides. Built by coal miners from Schuylkill County, Pennsylvania, the mine's galleries held a four ton charge of powder.

wide and 25 feet deep, with a rim 12 feet high. It frightened large numbers of soldiers on both sides, who took to their heels. Five minutes elapsed before Ledlie's shaken soldiers advanced.

It took the Northerners another five minutes to clear away the abatis that Meade had ordered leveled but that Burnside had allowed to remain lest he sacrifice the element of surprise. Ledlie's soldiers then filed into the Crater.

Inside, many of Ledlie's men fell out to gawk at and dig out half buried Confederates. The broken ground itself broke up Ledlie's formations. Those of his men who made it through

Scattered bodies of South Carolinians and broken artillery pieces of Richard Pegram's battery are the aftermath of the mine explosion. A gap 150 feet long, 60 feet wide and 25 feet deep now existed in the Confederate line.

the sand and clay to the opposite end of the Crater suffered further disorder in climbing over the rim. As the lead regiments formed to rush the crest near the Jerusalem Plank Road, scattering fire from the network of pits, bombproofs and traverses on either side of the Crater drove them to ground before they had advanced 100 yards. Groups of Ledlie's soldiers drove into the network of trenches extending north and south from the Crater. Hand-to-hand fighting began.

As Ledlie's division advanced, Hartranft's brigade of Orlando Willcox's division went forward on its left and Simon Griffin's brigade of Potter's division advanced on its right. These brigades and part of Bliss' brigade, which followed Simon Griffin's brigade, entered the trenches to the right and

Union troops charge the Crater. The success of the attack appeared likely as the Confederates had been caught off guard by the explosion. But the Yankee attack became confused and the enemy counterattacked.

left of the Crater. The trenches were soon cleared of Confederates for several hundred yards in each direction.

But already the crossfire of the Southern artillery was channeling Federal reinforcements toward the Crater. There no order prevailed. It was too packed with Union soldiers separated from their commands. Passing through this mob, new formations entering the Crater lost cohesion.

By 0630, Meade had become impatient. He ordered an advance to the crest behind the Crater without regard for threats to the flanks. Potter's men made several charges, but failed to take the crest. Burnside then ordered forward the black division.

On the other side of the crest, Lee instructed Mahone to send two brigades from his division to plug the gap in the Confederate line. Mahone accompanied Weisiger's Brigade and Ambrose Wright's Brigade as they moved by a route that kept them out of sight of the Federals. The remainder of

The Confederate counter-attack at the Crater. Union troops became stuck in the Crater while under heavy fire from the Confederates. The hole became a killing ground.

Mahone's Division extended itself to cover the spaces vacated.

By the time Ferrero's African-American division advanced, the crossfire of Confederate artillery had become vicious. Southern cannon had also opened up from the top of the crest. The small arms fire from the trenches had increased dramatically. Part of Sigfried's black brigade retained sufficient order to charge into the rifle pits to the right. The hail of Southern lead drove the rest of Sigfried's men back into the Crater. There they became intermingled with the white soldiers, whose density prevented portions of Potter's and Willcox's divisions from advancing.

On Burnside's left, Warren exchanged dispatches with Meade's headquarters instead of attacking a two-gun battery that appeared vulnerable. On the right, Ord's men had difficulty advancing because of the traffic jam around the Crater.

Next in line behind Sigfried, Thomas' African-American brigade made its way through the Crater. The *31st United*

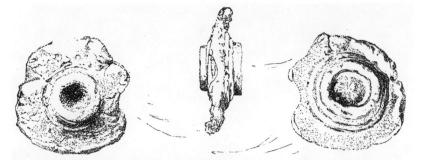

An oddity of war. The result of two bullets smashed together when they collided head on during the battle for the Crater.

States Colored Troops was in the lead and mounted the brigade's first threat to the crest. Southern fire from the swale 200 yards behind the Crater front blasted the 31st before it could advance. Shortly before 0900, the rest of Thomas' brigade stepped out of the captured trench just beyond the Crater and began forming for the charge.

Unfortunately for Thomas' troops, Mahone's leading brigade had just arrived and formed its line in the swale beyond the captured trench. Observing the numerous Northern battle flags in the Crater, Mahone ordered Sanders' Brigade to join him.

The brigade in the swale was Weisiger's Brigade, which Mahone had previously commanded. Its men were Virginians, half of them from Petersburg itself and almost all the rest from the other cities and counties of Southside. They had begun their march angry at the Federals. Like most of Lee's soldiers, they considered mine warfare unfair. On the way to the Crater, Confederates heading to the rear told Weisiger's men that the enemy were blacks who were giving no quarter. This drove the Virginians berserk. In common with most other Southern fighting men, they held the enemy's employment of African-American troops to be even more unfair than the use of mining.

Weisiger's Virginians had reason to be even more sensitive on this point than the average Confederate soldier. There were a number of Weisiger's men with relatives who had been slain

The disaster of the mine behind them, these black troops engage in drill. The **United States Colored Troops** *served ably throughout the Petersburg campaign, but their heroic sacrifices often went unrecognized by Grant and Meade.*

in or had helped suppress Nat Turner's Rebellion of 1831, 40 miles down the Jerusalem Plank Road in Southampton County—Mahone's birthplace. Most had gone to war because Lincoln's call for 75,000 volunteers in 1861 was viewed as just a bigger version of John Brown's raid. And they knew that Brown's intent had been to raise a slave insurrection beside which Nat Turner's would have paled into insignificance.

These Southsiders saw themselves as standing between their friends and relatives in Petersburg and havoc of the same sort as Nat Turner had loosed on their kin in Southampton County. "Revenge must have fired every heart and strung

The Mine

The following selection is taken from the diary of Private Bernard:

Sunday July 31 '64

Yesterday witnessed a bloody drama around Petersburg, perhaps as bloody as any affair of the war, Fort Pillow not excepted. At this point about 1/2 mile southeast of the old Blandford Church, the enemy exploded a mine under a fort in our works, blowing up 4 pieces of Pegram's Artillery with 2 Lieutenants, Lt. Hamlin & Chandler and 22 men together with 5 companies of the 18th SC Reg't of Elliot's Brigade, whereupon they immediately rushed upon & captured that portion of our works and about 200 yds of the works to the left of the exploded portion. This occurred soon after sunrise, soon after which our brigade & Wright's, which occupied the extreme right of our line, were put in motion for this point approaching it cautiously by the military roads recently constructed. We were not long in learning our brigade would be assigned the task of capturing the works, supported by Wright's. Arriving at the works, fortunately just at the moment we were about to charge the enemy were also about to charge, when seizing our advantage & rising with a yell we rushed forward & got into the works, about 100 yds distant, receiving but little fire from the enemy, who turned out to be negroes! The scene now baffles description. But little quarter was shown them. My heart sickened at deeds I saw done. Our brigade not driving the enemy from the inner portions of the exploded mine, Saunders & Wright's brigades finished the work. I have never seen such slaughter in any battlefield. Our reg't lost 27 Kd & Wd, the majority of whom were killed & among them Emmet Butts, of our company. Put Stith, of our company, was wounded. Col. Weisiger, commanding the brigade, was wounded. From what I have seen the enemy's loss could not have been less than 5 to 700 killed, to say nothing of those wounded and between 500 & 1000 prisoners. Ours probably did not exceed 400 killed, wounded or missing. Negotiations under a flag of truce are now pending. Probably Grant wants to bury the dead between the lines. Permission was granted today to water his wounded. I observed several citizens from the enemy's lines take part in this act of humanity. They were probably members of the sanitary committee. I also saw a woman standing in the Yankee breastworks. We indulge a hope that our brigade will be relieved tonight & return to its quiet position on the right.

Confederate troops lounge about in works rebuilt in the Crater. The failed attack cost the Federals 3,798 men for no purpose as all ground initially gained was lost to the Confederate counterattack.

every arm with nerves of steel for the herculean task of blood," wrote one of Weisiger's officers.

Before Thomas' troops could finish forming, Weisiger's Brigade was ordered forward by its officers. With the Virginians charged the regiment and a half of Ambrose Wright's Brigade that had formed on its right and the Carolinians from Elliott's and Clingman's Brigades who had fallen in among Mahone's soldiers. The Southern onslaught overwhelmed Thomas' brigade. The black soldiers who stood their ground died. The panic of the rest drove a wave of Federals out of the Crater and across the fireswept no man's land between the Union and Confederate trenches. This wave of fugitives in turn threw into disorder Turner's division as it advanced to the north of the Crater. The Virginians took the trench network north of the Crater in merciless hand-to-hand fighting. Ambrose Wright's men recoiled in the face of the withering fire from the Crater itself.

By 0930, Meade had suspended the assault and ordered the evacuation of the Crater. Unfortunately for the Federals holding that position, the Southern crossfire on no man's land had become so fierce that only the panic stricken would hazard the storm of Confederate lead. Burnside hoped that his men could hold on until nightfall and then retreat under cover of darkness.

The Federals in the Crater still had enough fight in them to blast a charge by the rest of Wright's Brigade shortly afterward. Two of Pegram's cannon dug out and manned by Northerners assisted in repulsing this charge. For two hours afterward, while Sanders' Brigade approached, a stalemate prevailed. The day's terrible heat and the accurate fire of the Southern mortars made life hell for the Federals in the Crater.

Shortly after noon, Sanders' Alabamians lifted their hats on their ramrods. After a volley from the men in the Crater riddled them, the Alabamians leaped over the rim. Another massacre ensued. The Southerners slew white and black alike without mercy for 15 minutes before their blood lust was sated. Such African-American prisoners as made it safely to the Confederate rear owed their lives to the fact that slaughter-minded Southerners could not kill them fast enough. By 1300, the Confederates had recovered all the ground and cannon lost, plus 16 flags and 1,100 prisoners. In all, the Federals had suffered 3,798 casualties. Southern losses totaled about 1,500.

Shortly afterward, Meade brought charges against Burnside, who testified at a court of inquiry packed with Meade's supporters and then went on leave. Predictably, the court of inquiry censured Burnside along with Brigadier General James Ledlie, Ferrero, Brigadier General Orlando B. Willcox and Colonel Zenas R. Bliss. Burnside was never again assigned to duty. Ledlie, who had spent the entire battle drunk in a bombproof behind Union lines, was relieved of command. The other three disgraced officers remained in their positions.

Grant and Meade, who had caused the disaster by their interference with Burnside's plan, of course, went undisciplined by the Court of Inquiry. But in early 1865, the Joint Congressional Committee on the Conduct of the War vindicated Burnside and condemned Meade for changing the plan of attack.

The finding did Burnside little good. He resigned, and the war ended, shortly afterward.

A Tale of Two Craters

Grant and his staff performed strategic wonders at the beginning and at the end of the Petersburg campaign. The *Army of the Potomac*'s crossing of the James River, in June of 1864 at the campaign's beginning, was a great coup. The concealment of Ord's crossing of the James with three divisions of the *Army of the James*, in March of 1865 at the end of the campaign, was one of the war's most important strategic achievements.

But Grant and his staff were also capable of some of the war's most egregious sins of omission. In June 1864, they failed to provide for practically any contingencies once the *Army of the Potomac* had crossed the James. The result was a failure to take Petersburg at that time.

In August of 1864, Grant ordered Hancock's corps to steal a march on the Confederates by disembarking directly from steamers to the shore at Deep Bottom. But Grant and his staff had failed to inform themselves of the difference between the James and the western rivers with which they were familiar. Such a landing would have been possible on the western rivers with the assistance of nothing more than gangplanks. But the

James was subject to the action of the tides, and a landing at Deep Bottom required the use of either lighters or wharves. As a consequence, the landing took so long despite herculean efforts by Hancock that the element of surprise was lost and Hancock failed to flank the Confederates from their line behind Bailey's Creek.

A sin of omission by Grant and his staff that ranks with those of June and August occurred in July. Grant and his staff had more experience with mine warfare than any other group of men at Petersburg. At the siege of Vicksburg, Grant's army had exploded two mines beneath the Confederate fortifications. More significantly, Grant had followed up one of the explosions with an assault. This explosion had taken place on 25 June 1863, after lead miners from Grant's army dug a tunnel beneath a fortification known as the Third Louisiana Redan. Around 2,200 pounds of gunpowder opened a crater 50 feet across and 12 feet deep. Grant's assault column easily entered the crater, but his men had great difficulty climbing up its sides to come to grips with the Confederates in a secondary line behind the Great Redoubt. Its force absorbed by the crater itself, the attack stalled. The Federals held the crater, but nothing more, and they abandoned it on 26 June. They completed and exploded another mine beneath the redan on 1 July, but did not follow it up with an assault.

From their experience with mine warfare at Vicksburg, Grant and his staff knew or ought to have known of the tendency of the crater formed by a mine explosion to absorb the momentum of an assault. Yet they did not lift a finger to help Burnside with the problem of passing his men through the crater quickly enough and in good enough order to storm secondary Confederate positions before the Southerners could react. Maybe Grant and his staff officers thought that Burnside was aware of the problems that a crater formed by a mine explosion posed for an assaulting force. Two divisions of Burnside's corps had been sent from Kentucky to reinforce Grant at Vicksburg prior to the explosion of the Vicksburg mines. Though Burnside himself had been absent, the two divisions were under the command of Major General John G. Parke, Burnside's chief of staff at Petersburg. But as Parke and his men were posted at Oak Ridge, 12 miles northeast of the siege

lines, they would have known little of what happened on 25 June and 1 July.

More likely, the attitude of Grant and his staffers toward mine warfare remained as sour as it had been at the end of the siege of Vicksburg. They had merely tolerated the Petersburg mine during its construction and they remained so skeptical about the prospects of success of an assault following up a mine explosion that they never even thought of assisting Burnside with traffic control. Burnside's assault, they probably figured, would at best provide a diversion that would help Sheridan and his cavalry get away safely for a raid on the Weldon Railroad.

But the mine assault came so close to success that they realized an extraordinary opportunity had been missed. It also failed so miserably that a court of inquiry was required to apportion blame. The court of inquiry found five causes of failure. Among them was, "The halting of the troops in the crater instead of going forward...." Naturally, neither Grant nor any member of his staff were among the officers found answerable for the "want of success" that the court of inquiry believed should have resulted. Nor were Meade nor any of his staff, which included Major James C. Duane.

Meade's chief engineer, Duane was also an expert on mining operations. It was he who had pronounced it impossible—somewhat prematurely, it turned out—to dig a mine as long as Burnside proposed. Duane had written a manual for military engineers on the subject of mining. In it, he had listed about 40 pieces of equipment essential to such operations. His department did not provide a single one of these to Pleasants.

This probably came as no surprise to Burnside. Duane had also been McClellan's chief engineer. In that capacity, Duane led Burnside to the wrong ford on Antietam Creek on 17 September 1862. The delay in capturing Burnside's Bridge that day substantially detracted from the reputation that Burnside had made for himself during his earlier coastal campaigns in North Carolina. Duane had also had a hand in delaying the delivery of pontoons to Burnside during his Fredericksburg campaign. Burnside's plan of campaign was premised on the prompt delivery of the pontoons. The campaign's disastrous failure made him an object of scorn and derision within the *Army of the Potomac*.

The battle of the Crater, of course, ended Burnside's military career.

CHAPTER VI

The Destruction of the Weldon Railroad

Despite the disastrous failure of the mine assault, Grant let only a few hours pass before he tried again to strike the Southerners a blow. Receiving intelligence that the Confederates on the Peninsula had not yet begun to come back to the Southside, he ordered Meade to send Sheridan's cavalry and a corps of infantry to wreck the Weldon Railroad all the way down to Hicksford. But before the Federals could move, the Southerners began returning from the Peninsula. Grant suspended the order for the raid.

Then news came from the north that hit the Federals like the mine explosion had struck the Confederates. Early's forces had crossed the Potomac again and his cavalry had burned Chambersburg, Pennsylvania. Departing for a conference planned for 31 July 1864 with President Lincoln at Fort Monroe, Grant ordered his command's siege artillery returned to Broadway Landing and a division of cavalry sent to City Point for transportation to Washington. He warned Meade that two corps might have to be sent north, which would allow Lee to shift more forces to the Shenandoah Valley or to Atlanta. It appeared that abandoning the siege of Petersburg was not out of the question.

This was the Union's darkest hour. Gold soared to unprecedented heights on the New York Stock Exchange. Republicans despaired of Lincoln's prospects of reelection as Grant's grand strategic plan appeared to have failed. He was stalled

Construction of the Dutch Gap Canal by Butler's men. The canal was intended to allow Federal gunboats to bypass enemy batteries on the James River. Not successful during the war, it provided a ship channel to Richmond after hostilities had ended.

outside Petersburg and Sherman was stalemated on the Atlanta approaches while the Confederates were on the move in the lower Shenandoah Valley.

Fortunately for the Union, Lincoln and Grant decided to transfer only two divisions of cavalry and an infantry division of the *XIX Corps* from Petersburg to Washington. An equally important decision they reached was to unite the four departments responsible for the defense of the Shenandoah Valley and to put Sheridan in charge of the new Middle Military Division. Grant went north in person to effect the necessary changes at the president's insistence, because the War Department and Halleck occasionally declined to transmit Grant's more aggressive orders.

Lee soon received intelligence of the Federal troop movements. Fearing that the Northerners would overwhelm Early, Lee ordered Richard Anderson to take Kershaw's Division of infantry and Fitzhugh Lee's Division of cavalry to Culpeper Court House and threaten the rear of any Union force advancing toward Early from Washington.

A Confederate bomb went off at City Point on 9 August blowing up a barge and killing 43. Grant himself was nearly a victim of the explosion.

At Deep Bottom, Lieutenant Colonel John C. Pemberton prepared to bring the Federal pontoon bridges under the fire of mortars and howitzers. A lieutenant general when he surrendered Vicksburg to Grant a year earlier, Pemberton served at his present rank because no unit that merited a higher-ranked officer would serve under him.

Nearby, Butler commenced the excavation of the Dutch Gap

Canal. Intended to allow Federal gunboats on the James River to bypass the Confederate batteries on the Howlett Line, this project produced the modern ship channel to Richmond—but not until after the war had ended.

Grant returned to City Point in time to nearly fall victim to a Confederate time-bomb that blew up an ammunition barge on 9 August. Two days later, Lee finally designated Hampton to be commander of the Army of Northern Virginia's Cavalry Corps. Hampton received orders to take his division to Culpeper Court House and assume command of the Confederate cavalry in northern Virginia. Field's Division of infantry was put under marching orders for that destination as well.

Hampton's arrival in northern Virginia would have put three of the Army of Northern Virginia's four corps commanders there, a situation that would have required the presence of a full general. Confederate forces there would have totaled three divisions of cavalry and six of infantry, as opposed to the equivalent of two divisions of cavalry and six of infantry at Petersburg. Lee was shifting his forces northward as gradually as he had in early June 1863, after the Chancellorsville campaign.

Grant received exaggerated reports of Lee's troop movements. An entire Southern corps was said to have left for northern Virginia. With this knowledge, Grant determined to launch another offensive to take advantage of the Confederate weakness at Petersburg and Richmond or at least force the Southerners to recall troops from northern Virginia. He decided to employ the same basic plan as he had at the end of July, a Peninsula thrust at Richmond and a dash onto the Virginia Central Railroad that at least would draw Confederate forces from Petersburg, followed by a Southside drive toward the Weldon Railroad. But there were some changes in the plan's details. Hancock, who would command again on the Peninsula, would have two divisions from David Birney's *X Corps* in addition to his own *II Corps*, but only a single division of cavalry. The *II Corps* would board transports at City Point and the steamboats would head down the James on 13 August before turning upriver at midnight and disembarking at Deep Bottom by daybreak on 14 August. Warren's *V Corps* would make the attack on the Weldon Railroad.

The plan immediately started unraveling. In the fierce heat, *II Corps* soldiers began dropping from sunstroke on the 13 August march to City Point. They spent a sleepless night on board the steamers, tormented by mosquitoes. To make matters worse, Grant's plan assumed that a landing from deep water steamers on a tidal river could be effected as easily as one from vessels of shallow draft on tideless western rivers. This assumption proved false. Despite heroic efforts by Hancock, insufficient time remained to remedy the inactivity of Grant's staff. Only a few wharves could be built, and the landing immediately fell behind schedule. One of the ships even went aground.

Hancock's tactical plan called for David Birney's corps to demonstrate against New Market Heights employing the upper Deep Bottom bridgehead as a springboard while the *II Corps* moved up and to the east of Bailey's Creek and turned the Confederate left. David Birney's corps, despite numerous cases of sunstroke among his men, scored an initial success. His soldiers drove in the Confederate pickets on the Kingsland Road, rendering the position of Pemberton's guns untenable.

The tired soldiers of the *II Corps* lagged badly in the suffocating heat. Hundreds fell out by the roadsides, and many died. Hancock had to halt David Birney's corps while Barlow led his own division and Gibbon's into position to turn the Southern left.

Barlow's men did not run into Confederates in their path until they encountered Southerners holding rifle pits on the Darbytown Road, just north of the Long Bridge Road, around noon. The Confederates belonged to the 7th South Carolina Cavalry of Gary's Brigade. Barlow's men had advanced so slowly that the Southerners had time to shift a section of the 3rd Richmond Howitzers to Mitchell Fussell's farm. It took three feeble attacks by successive brigades of Barlow's division to drive the Confederate cavalrymen behind Bailey's Creek. By that time, George Anderson's Georgia Brigade had arrived and made the Confederate line impregnable at this point. Barlow resumed the march up Bailey's Creek.

Late in the day, his men arrived in position near Fussell's Mill and its pond. Macy's brigade of Gibbon's division attacked across Bailey's Creek, which formed a veritable canyon here. Though a few Northerners made it up the vine-covered bank into the thinly held Confederate works, the arriving portions of George Anderson's and Gary's Brigades drove the Federals back. Barlow abandoned the offensive.

While Barlow's attack failed, David Birney's soldiers reaped the harvest of their successful advance near Four Mile Creek that morning by taking possession of Pemberton's horseless, stranded guns. On the far right, David Gregg's cavalrymen captured a few pickets of the Hampton Legion at Fisher's farm on the Charles City Road.

Grant's plan had fallen short of its most ambitious objectives. But it succeeded in preventing Lee from sending more men to northern Virginia as Lee diverted Hampton's Division to Deep Bottom and canceled the marching orders of Field's Division. It also weakened the Confederate position at Petersburg. Lee ordered the infantrymen of Ambrose Wright's and Sanders' Brigades of Mahone's Division and the cavalrymen of Rooney Lee's Division to Deep Bottom from Petersburg. This was less of a reaction than the July thrust on the Peninsula had prompted, but it was still substantial.

No hope of surprise remained on the Peninsula, but Grant wanted to give the Confederates time to shift their forces to Deep Bottom. He ordered Hancock to resume the attack on the following day. Hancock adhered to his original plan of turning the Southern left. To accomplish this, he sent David Birney's corps on a night march in the rain through the unrelenting heat. A third of David Birney's men fell by the wayside. Those who arrived near Fussell's Mill on the morning of 15 August collapsed.

Hancock ordered David Birney to advance westward, but Birney could hear firing to his right. He was in the same sort of wooded terrain as prevailed near the Jerusalem Plank Road, where his command had fallen prey to a devastating

Confederate ambush, and he did not intend to fall victim to another such attack. Instead of advancing to the west, he sent an attached brigade of the *II Corps* to reconnoiter to the north.

This force did not discover any Confederates in ambush. It only tipped the scales in favor of the Union in the ongoing skirmish between Northern and Southern cavalry on the Charles City Road. But by the time Birney learned this, the shadows were getting long. In response to Hancock's progressively sharper prods, David Birney ordered Osborn's and William Birney's brigades of his own corps to advance. The unfamiliar terrain proved as deadly as the Confederates. The two brigades stumbled into one another in the woods and exchanged fire. All the killed and wounded wore blue.

This fiasco ended the day's fighting. Disgusted, Hancock prepared to attack on the following morning, 16 August, with a plan that called for two thrusts at daybreak. On the Charles City Road, David Gregg's cavalrymen supported by Miles' brigade of Barlow's division would push toward the Confederate left rear. Above Fussell's Mill, David Birney's corps—reinforced by Craig's brigade of the *II Corps*—would attempt to pierce the Southern fortifications.

The force on the Charles City Road broke through the picket line of the 13th Virginia Cavalry at Fisher's Run. The Federals killed Brigadier General John R. Chambliss and drove his brigade back to White's Tavern, where the rest of Rooney Lee's Division stiffened resistance. If David Birney's infantry had pierced the Confederate lines above Fussell's Mill at the time of David Gregg's breakthrough on the Charles City Road, the Southerners might have had to retreat to one of the many lines prepared by slave labor nearer to Richmond. Mahone's men had not yet arrived on the Peninsula, and McGowan's and Lane's Brigades of Cadmus Wilcox's Division were still near the James.

Instead, the Federals paid the price for Birney's failure to advance westward on the previous day. Alfred Terry's reinforced division, spearheading the attack, lurched into the unknown at dawn and halted a few minutes later upon encountering Fussell's mill pond. Terry reformed his division and looped around to his right. At 1000, his advance stalled again in the face of a deep ravine. By this time, Confederate resistance was solidifying on the Charles City Road. Reforming his division yet again, Terry advanced for the third time. At noon, his men paused opposite the weakest point in the Confederate lines, about half a mile north of Fussell's Mill. Here a thicket protected the advance of the Federal column. Beyond the thicket were only 30 yards of slashing to cross before the column would strike the Southern works.

Out on the Charles City Road, the tide of battle was already turning. With the infantry of the Texas Brigade on the right and Gary's cavalrymen on the left, Rooney Lee's Division launched an attack against David Gregg and Miles. Hampton's Division arrived about this time and headed off to turn the Federal right. David Gregg and Miles commenced a fighting retreat, leapfrogging their commands eastward in a relatively orderly fashion.

Not until then did Terry's force attack above Fussell's Mill. Pond's brigade of Terry's division led the assault. Its men got blasted by a single volley before they vaulted into the Confederate works. Pond's fought hand to hand with the Georgians of Ambrose Wright's Brigade for a few minutes before the Georgians broke. Their commander, Brigadier General Victor J. B. Girardey, tried to rally them. Promoted only days before from a captain on Mahone's staff for heroism at the Crater, Girardey fell with a flag in his hand and a bullet through his head.

The attack pierced the Southern line as the Confederates were sidling to their left to accommodate Mahone's men. Early that morning, McGowan's and Lane's Brigades of Wilcox's Division under Brigadier General James Conner proceeded to the far left, between the Darbytown and Charles City Roads. The five regiments of George Anderson's Brigade were scattered all around the breach created by the Pond's Brigade, which cut Field off from his left. Field ordered John Gregg, in command of Field's Division on the Southern right, to send reinforcements. Lee found himself reduced to the

The destruction of the Weldon Railroad. Federals pulled up track and ties, building fires with the latter to heat the iron rails. These were then bent into the Maltese Cross, the symbol of the V Corps.

status of a provost guard, forcing retreating soldiers to show their wounds.

Pond's brigade disintegrated in pursuit of Girardey's Georgians. Hawley's brigade moved west through the hole in the Confederate lines and came to a halt in front of a portion of Anderson's Brigade. The 15th and 48th Alabama of Law's Brigade halted Craig's Federals as they sought to roll up the Confederate line to the south. A series of Confederate counterattacks drove the Northerners back into the captured works before William Birney's division, positioned too far back by brother David Birney, could exploit the breakthrough. One of William Birney's brigades charged the Confederate lines and disintegrated under fire from its front and flank.

An hour passed while more Southern reinforcements arrived. The Northerners caught their breath, and were reinforced only by a single regiment, the *9th United States Colored Troops*. Several Northern formations went to the rear.

At 1400, the Confederates resumed the attack, Field's men from the south and Conner's men from the north. After a fierce struggle, the Southerners drove the exhausted Federals from the works. Miles' brigade returned from the Charles City Road just in time to cover the retreat. To David Gregg, it had appeared that he could spare Miles. The Federal line had stabilized on the Charles City Road at Fisher's farm, west of Fisher's Run. But after Miles departed, the Confederates struck. The Texas Brigade and Gary's cavalrymen cut the

Federals off from the Charles City Road and drove them into White Oak Swamp.

That night Lee ordered to Deep Bottom Nathaniel Harris' Brigade of Mahone's Division from Petersburg and a scratch brigade from Pickett's Division at Bermuda Hundred. Grant tried to lure the Confederates into attacking at Deep Bottom on the following morning, 17 August, by feigning a with-drawal. The Southerners did not rise to the bait and the day passed without any large-scale fighting.

When Grant received intelligence that indicated a thrust toward the Weldon Railroad would succeed, he ordered Meade to unleash Warren. The *V Corps* began its march toward the Weldon Railroad on the morning of 18 August. The Federal infantry brushed aside cavalry pickets of Dearing's Brigade and reached the tracks in the Globe Tavern clearing at noon. The destruction of the railroad began immediately. The Northerners stacked the ties, set them on fire, heated the rails over the fires, and then twisted the rails into Maltese Crosses, the emblem of the *V Corps*. Ayres' division headed up the tracks toward Petersburg, with Hayes' brigade in the lead and Crawford's division on its right. The advance took the North-erners into a belt of woods about 500 yards wide.

Hancock's men had lured three brigades of infantry away from Petersburg to Deep Bottom. To counterattack Warren's corps on the Weldon Railroad, Beauregard at first could spare only Davis' and Walker's Brigades of Heth's Division. Heth attacked in mid-afternoon.

Heth's men overlapped the flanks of the lead Federal brigade as it emerged from the woods into the cornfield of the Davis farm, where the Vaughan Road intersected the Weldon Railroad and the Halifax Road. Hayes' brigade bolted, creat-ing a gap between the two brigades in echelon behind its flanks. The Southerners entered the gap under cover of the woods and put to flight the *Maryland Brigade* west of the railroad and Lyle's brigade of Crawford's division east of the railroad. It took three more Federal brigades and overwhelm-ing artillery support to halt the Confederates at the southern edge of the woods. Heth's men retired to Davis' farm, having inflicted against three times their number three times the casualties they suffered. There they were joined by Colquitt's Brigade, belatedly scrounged up by Beauregard. The Federals cautiously advanced to the northern edge of the wooded belt.

Shortly after Heth attacked Southside, Hampton struck on the Peninsula. He acted, as usual, pursuant to a plan of his own, approved by Lee, which called for a flank attack on Hancock's right. Rooney Lee's Division would drive east on the Charles City Road against David Gregg's front. Hampton's Division under Brigadier General Matthew C. Butler would burst into the Federal cavalry's rear at Riddell's Shop after crossing White Oak Swamp. When the pincer movement of the Confederate cavalry had destroyed David Gregg's division, the Southern infantry would pitch in and roll up the Northern line above Fussell's Mill.

The Confederate troops were in position at 1100. But a guide misled Hampton, who did not arrive to give the signal for the attack until 1700. The onslaught of the Confederate cavalry cut all lines of communication between David Gregg's horsemen and the Federal main body except for a wood road. Butler's Division penetrated deeply into the Union rear. But when McGowan's, Lane's and Harris' Brigades advanced, the Federal infantry held except for a momentary panic in Foster's brigade. Hampton retreated with about 150 prisoners.

Having finally effected a lodgement on the Weldon Railroad that had withstood Confederate attack, Grant and Meade began shifting men back from the Peninsula to improve their grip. Late that evening, Mott's division left Deep Bottom for Southside. Meade realized that after a long night march in the rain, the division would not arrive at Globe Tavern in condition to be of any help on the following day. In a masterful piece of staff work, he arranged for Mott's division to relieve two small divisions of Parke's IX Corps. Parke's two divisions would take the place of Mott's division at Globe Tavern.

While the Federals tightened their grip on the Weldon Railroad, a plan made its way up the Confederate chain of command. The plan came from Mahone, who had distinguished himself on the Jerusalem Plank Road, at First Reams Station and at the Crater. A.P. Hill forwarded the plan to Beauregard, who gave it his approval. It called for Heth to attack southward along the Weldon Railroad while Mahone led a force through the woods between Warren's corps and the Jerusalem Plank Road and struck the *V Corps'* right. Mahone correctly reasoned that Warren's right had to be in the air since not enough time had yet passed for Warren to have properly linked up with the main Union position at Fort Davis.

But while Beauregard gave the plan his approval, he could not give it sufficient force. Heth had only the same two brigades with which he had struck on the previous day and Beauregard could release to Mahone no more than Colquitt's and Clingman's Brigades of Hoke's Division in addition to Weisiger's Brigade from Mahone's own division. Mahone protested, but the cupboard was bare. Grant's feint on the Peninsula paid another dividend.

Warren's right did indeed hang in the air. Throughout the morning of the 19th, Warren struggled to establish a picket line between the right of Crawford's division on the Johnson Road and Fort Davis on the Jerusalem Plank Road. Mott's division relieved White's and Orlando Willcox's divisions of Parke's corps in the soggy trenches. Willcox's division staggered into the Globe Tavern clearing at noon.

Shortly afterward, Mahone led his men up the same ravine that had conveyed them to victory over the Federal *II Corps* on 22 June. The Confederate column did not encounter Union videttes until it had penetrated into the right rear of Crawford's division. This would not have happened if the Federal picket line had been established as far forward as Warren had directed. Meade heard the scattering fire of the skirmish between Warren's videttes and the Southerners as he passed the Aiken house on the way back to his headquarters from a visit to Globe Tavern. Had Mahone swung a little wider to his left, he might have bagged the commander of the *Army of the Potomac*.

While Heth advanced down the Weldon Railroad and

Before the Petersburg campaign, General Robert E. Lee had hoped to avoid fighting Grant near the James River, stating, "If he gets there it will become a siege, and then a mere question of time."

At Globe Tavern

The following selection is taken from the diary of Private Bernard:

Saturday Aug 20 '64

Got orders to move yesterday about 1 o'clock. I saw Capt. Taylor of Hill's staff just before we started who informed me that our destination was down the RR & that 5 brigades were going out to drive away the enemy. The five were Davis's & Walkers of Heth's Division, Clingman's & Colquitt's of Hoke's and ours. The three last moved on the left flank, the two first in the front.

I will not further describe the action than to mention that our brigade was in the warmest place were ever in being subjected to fire from the front, right flank, & rear all at the same time. The flanking brigades drove the enemy into the brigades moving upon the front. The result being the capture of 3000 of them. The brigades in front carried two lines of breastworks but did not attempt the third. The loss in our brigade was 187 Kd, wd & missing out of over 600 muskets carried in, and our reg't lost 6kd, 29wd & 2 missing out of 90 odd officers & arms bearing men carried in. The loss included 2 men in the ambulance corps. The killed were Lts.

Leath Co D, & Beale, Co H, privates Thos. Alley, & Ransome of Co. A, Walker Co. H, David Ridout, Co. F and among the wd were Capt. Jones Commanding Reg't, Serg. Maj. Maclin and privates Frank Robbins & R. A. Machen Co. E, the latter probably mortally. Most of our badly wounded fell into the hands of the enemy when we were withdrawn at sunset.

My brother reached Petersburg in safety yesterday afternoon about 3 o'clock.

Heavy cannonading along the lines on the right last night—too sleepy to get up to see what was "to pay" although the battery not 50 yds from our tent was lumbering away pretty freely. About 3 o'clock this afternoon orders reached us to have cartridge boxes filled & 1 day's rations prepared by 7 o'clock. Conjecture immediately interpreted this as meaning a night march through Dinwiddie to get in the rear of the enemy who still holds the Weldon RR. A few moments ago (6-1/2 PM) we received orders to form at the breastworks with guns & accoutrements at 7 o'clock. What does this mean? Perhaps our guns are to open at the enemy.

attacked the front of the Federal line in the woods north of Globe Tavern, Mahone struck from the right rear. Colquitt's Brigade on the left and Clingman's Brigade on the right rolled up the Union line all the way to the railroad. The left of Colquitt's Brigade emerged into the Globe Tavern clearing, and the commander of the Federal artillery opened fire pursuant to a prearranged plan. But instead of adhering to the scheme and filing out of the line of the artillery's fire, the Northern infantry mostly held its ground. Attacked by Confederates on their front and flank, subjected to friendly artillery fire from the rear, Warren's soldiers cracked and surrendered in droves. Men on both sides were captured and recaptured in this woodland scramble, but when it was over, 2,700 Federal prisoners filed into captivity. West of the railroad, the Northerners held.

Mahone kept Weisiger's Brigade in reserve for the *coup de grace*. But before he could commit it, he found himself attacked in front by Willcox's division and in rear by White's division. Weisiger's Virginians retreated after a sharp struggle and soldiers from Parke's corps reestablished the Federal line in the woods. To the end of his days, Mahone believed that with a few more brigades he could have driven the Northerners from the Weldon Railroad and perhaps have captured them all. But those additional Confederate brigades were on the Peninsula, lured there by Hancock.

At Deep Bottom, Hancock spent the day in a fruitless search for a place to assault the Confederate lines. That night Grant ordered Hancock to send a brigade of cavalry to Petersburg. Potter's division of Parke's corps joined Warren at Globe Tavern.

Lee also withdrew forces from Deep Bottom. Harris', Sanders' and Wright's Brigades of Mahone's Division plodded toward the pontoon bridge at Drewry's Bluff and the trains that would shuttle them to Petersburg. Rooney Lee's cavalrymen started slogging on the muddy roads to the Southside.

No fighting occurred on the Peninsula on 20 August. Grant resolved to withdraw Hancock to Petersburg that night. In the fighting at Deep Bottom, Hancock's men had inflicted about

1,500 casualties on the Southerners at a cost of 2,901 killed, wounded and captured to themselves.

Southside, Beauregard tried to gather sufficient force for another attack on the Federals at Globe Tavern. But Harris', Sanders' and Wright's Brigades arrived after their all night journey in no condition to fight. A.P. Hill rejected a scratch brigade from Johnson's Division while Rooney Lee failed to get farther south than Swift Creek. To make matters worse, Robert E. Lee viewed the situation as another Gettysburg in the making and insisted on a concentrated attack. Beauregard gave up and postponed offensive operations until the following day.

This delay proved fatal to whatever chance the Confederates still had of driving the Federals from the Weldon Railroad. Warren utilized the breathing space to withdraw to a new line of fortifications in the Globe Tavern clearing, where his artillery could be used to greatest effect. Confederate scouts failed to detect this withdrawal.

On the morning of 21 August, the Southerners attacked according to another of Mahone's plans. This plan again called for Heth to assault the front of the Union line with Cooke's and MacRae's Brigades of his own division and Matt Ransom's Brigade of Johnson's Division while Mahone struck the Federal left with four brigades of his own division, plus Scales' Brigade of Cadmus Wilcox's Division and Hagood's Brigade of Johnson's Division.

Mahone and his men emerged from the woods west of the Vaughan Road heading northeast to roll up the line held by Ayres' division for the previous three days. But they found themselves confronted by breastworks to the southeast. Ayres' men had demolished their old line during the night. A.P. Hill ordered Mahone's men to wheel and face the newly discovered Union works. Mahone rode over to Poplar Spring Church Road and guided Hagood's Brigade into position to attack what appeared to be the left of these fortifications.

Hill's wheel was unsuccessful. Only Nathaniel Harris' Brigade on the far left reached the new Federal works, where many of the Mississippians were pinned down by fire and surrendered. The rest of this force retreated in confusion, leaving 24-year-old Brigadier General John Caldwell Calhoun Sanders dead on the field of battle.

Heth's men advanced into the belt of woods north of the Globe Tavern clearing. They drove Union pickets from two lines of razed works. MacRae's Brigade, west of the railroad, debouched from the woods first. The Northern artillery stopped MacRae's soldiers at the woods' edge.

Several minutes later, Ransom's and Cooke's Brigades emerged from the woods east of the railroad. The Northerners considered this attack separate from that of MacRae's Brigade. The Federal artillery blasted Ransom's men as they struggled through the abatis. Potter's division captured several hundred entangled Confederates in a counterattack.

Back west of the railroad, Hagood's Brigade struggled through a swamp and then a wood toward what Mahone had led them to believe was the Federal left. Hagood's men then stormed the entrenched Northern picket line. Thinking they had pierced the main Union line, they headed for the Weldon Railroad and what they thought was the Federal rear. The progress of Hagood's South Carolinians took them to higher ground, where they received a shock. They found themselves facing formidable breastworks—the real Northern main line, which ran along the old bed of the railroad. The South Carolinians were approaching the angle formed by the junction of the refused left of Cutler's division and the right of Charles Griffin's division, which held the breastworks that stretched south for a mile. Enfiladed from the left and under fire from the front, Hagood's men struck the works obliquely. The brigade separated into two sections. A number of the South Carolinians threw down their arms and some of the Federals stopped firing. A Northern officer rode out, seized the colors of one of Hagood's regiments and demanded the surrender of the brigade. When the officer refused to return to his lines, Hagood shot him, took the Federal's horse, and led about a third of his men back to his own lines.

Despite the slaughter, the Confederates did not quit. Barringer's Brigade probed the Union position on the Poplar

Springs Church Road at noon. The North Carolina cavalrymen routed the Federal pickets from their entrenched line but got blasted by Union reinforcements rushed to White's farm on the Weldon Railroad, beyond Griffin's left.

Mahone assured Lee that with two more brigades, he could still drive the Northerners from the railroad. But reinforcements were slow in arriving from the Peninsula, where the Southerners had found Hancock's force gone that morning. Lee ordered the attempt to recapture the railroad abandoned. The Confederates tightened their belts and began using wagon trains to haul provisions, munitions and stores from Stony Creek Depot to Petersburg. The route led along the Flat Foot Road from Stony Creek to Dinwiddie Court House, and thence to Petersburg along the Boydton Plank Road.

Hancock's men staggered into the Globe Tavern clearing that afternoon too exhausted to deliver the counterattack that Grant and Meade urged upon Warren, who wisely declined to engage the Confederates in the wood-fighting at which they excelled. The battle of Globe Tavern had ended. The Northerners had suffered 4,279 killed, wounded and captured. The Confederates lost about 2,300.

Merely cutting the Weldon Railroad did not satisfy Grant. He wanted it wrecked all the way down to Hicksford, 40 miles south of Petersburg. David Gregg's and Kautz's cavalrymen, along with Barlow's infantry division under Miles, began working their way south from Globe Tavern on 22 August.

On the following day, this force arrived at Reams Station, four miles south of Globe Tavern. Matthew Butler's Division, which arrived Southside that morning, crossed Rowanty Creek on Monk's Neck Bridge and began relieving Rooney Lee's horsemen on cavalry picket on the Depot Road west of Reams Station that afternoon. The aggressive Spear chose this moment to pitch into the South Carolinians of Matthew Butler's Old Brigade on the Depot Road. Spear initially routed the South Carolinians, but Matthew Butler soon rallied his Old Brigade. Committing his other two brigades, he drove off Spear.

At Reams Station, David Gregg received word of the

engagement on the Depot Road. Too late to help Spear, he sent a detachment to reconnoiter. The detachment encountered the Confederates, who drove it back towards Reams Station. Gregg fed in his cavalry regiments one by one along with several regiment-sized companies of Miles' *4th New York Heavy Artillery*. The Federals brought the Southerners to a halt within sight of Reams Station. The skirmishing continued late into the night.

When word arrived at Grant's headquarters of the skirmish west of Reams Station, Gibbon's division and four batteries of artillery received orders to reinforce Miles and David Gregg. Hancock was directed to take command of the entire force at Reams Station and with it wreck the Weldon Railroad south to Rowanty Creek. Grant wanted Ord's corps relieved from the trenches so that it could complete the job the rest of the way to Hicksford.

Gibbon's column arrived at Reams Station early on 24 August. Exhausted from their all night march, Gibbon's men slept while Miles' soldiers wrecked the railroad for three miles toward Rowanty Creek. Hancock made no effort to improve the works thrown up by Wright's corps in June.

Hampton also arrived near Reams Station that morning. As usual, he took the initiative and proposed a plan to Lee. It called for Lee to send a force of infantry to strike the Federals at Reams Station. Lee initially rejected the suggestion. Reams Station seemed too far from Petersburg, where the infantry were needed. But before long, Lee reconsidered. Dinwiddie Court House, about 10 miles west of Reams Station, was the key to the Confederate position at Petersburg and Richmond. A Federal force at Dinwiddie Court House would compel the evacuation of Petersburg and Richmond by threatening Lee's line of retreat. Even if the Northerners at Reams Station did not occupy Dinwiddie Court House, their cavalry might undertake another raid on the Richmond & Danville Railroad, Lee's only remaining rail link with the Deep South that had not yet recovered from the Wilson-Kautz Raid. Lee also recognized that inflicting casualties on the Federals would adversely affect the Republicans in the coming presidential election.

After changing his mind, Lee sent four brigades of infantry under Cadmus Wilcox and put A.P. Hill in command of the operation. Later in the day, Lee decided not to attack piecemeal and sent four more brigades of infantry under Heth. Twenty-six guns accompanied the infantrymen, who bivouacked near Holly Church and Armstrong's Mill.

At Bermuda Hundred and Petersburg, the Confederates prepared feints to keep the Federals from reinforcing the force at Reams Station. Hunton's Brigade of Pickett's Division would attack the Northern picket line on Bermuda Hundred while Beauregard sent an easily intercepted message referring to the imminent explosion of a Southern mine at Petersburg.

That night Hill and Hampton planned the following day's battle. Hill would proceed east on the Depot Road. Hampton would leave a reinforced brigade of cavalry to screen Hill's approach and take the rest of the cavalry across Rowanty Creek at Malone's Bridge. He would then advance northward from Malone's Crossing. The two columns would attack simultaneously at 2100.

On 25 August, Hill fell behind schedule. His exhausted men did not move until 0700 and did not cross Monk's Neck Bridge until two hours later. East of Rowanty Creek, the intensity of the skirmishing between the Northern and Southern cavalry prompted Hill to deploy Cadmus Wilcox's command in line of battle. Hill's approach march to Reams Station slowed to a crawl.

Hampton remained on schedule. While the Confederate infantry inched towards Reams Station from the west, the Southern cavalry drove Spear's brigade north from Malone's Crossing. Barringer's Brigade swung to the right to cut the road that ran east from Reams Station to the Jerusalem Plank Road. The delay in Hill's approach allowed Hancock to send Gibbon's division down the railroad to halt Hampton. Back at Reams Station, Miles' men began fortifying.

The feints planned by Lee had no effect on the Federals. What kept reinforcements from Hancock were the repercus-

Lieutenant General A.P. Hill suffered from illness during much of the Petersburg campaign. He was killed in combat on 2 April 1865.

Second Reams Station

The following selection is taken from the diary of Private Bernard:

Entrenchments, Wilcox's Farm Aug 27, '64

Today is my 27th birthday. I must not let it pass without writing something in my diary. I scarcely realize I am so old. And to think of it more than these 4 years wasted, it seems, in this army, necessitating a beginning anew of life should I be spared & to see the end of this war. Thanks to God there are prospects now of its early termination. A great revolution of feeble sentiment is in rapid development in the North, looking to a suspension of hostilities. God grant the movement may result in peace. All eyes are turned to the great Democratic Convention to assemble on Monday next at Chicago.

On Thursday morning last we got in motion a few moments after I finished writing. Passing by an old Mill Dam which I suppose was once the dam of "Armstrong's Mill Pond" & which was only 200 yds from where our brigade camped we moved slowly along, halting frequently & resting, leaning in our route towards the left until we got within a mile of the Railroad just above Ream's Station. Here our brigade & Saunders' some what in the rear of the line of battle to prevent against any attack from the left flank. Without mentioning details, suffice it to say that in our position in the rear we were subjected to a little shelling until the works were carried by the attacking columns when one of Hill's staff officers rode rapidly up to us shouting the "works have been carried & thousands of prisoners captured". In a few moments we were put in line of battle & advanced towards the captured works bearing toward the

sions of Barringer's advance into the *II Corps'* rear. Meade thought that this move was a preliminary to a march around his left flank that would force him to withdraw from the Weldon Railroad.

Because Grant was ill, Meade was in charge. Grant's response to the Confederate threat to Reams Station would probably have been to order an assault on Petersburg, similar to the one that drove the Southerners from the city the following April. Meade characteristically adopted a passive defense. He held the divisions of White and Crawford in

right. When we got within 200 yds. of the works we see in the ditch on our side of the railroad hundreds of Yankees, most of whom however were coming in as prisoners whilst the remainder were moving up the ditch & getting away. These Yankees were, it was said, forming here to sweep around the right flank of the men who had captured the breastworks & no doubt would have done so but for our timely arrival. They did not fire a gun at us as well as I could see as we charged upon them. Saunders' brigade moved down to the extreme left & immediately upon our getting to the works, Hampton's Cavalry bore down upon the enemy's left flank, sweeping everything before them. Upon reaching the works some of our infantry turned the captured guns upon the enemy & did perhaps some of the wildest shooting of the war, causing some of the cavalry as they neared them to reign up their horses and ask "What in

the world was to pay". The first shot fired cut off the top of a pine tree near the gun. The artillery soon came up however & served the pieces. The result of the fight, as far as I have yet learned, was 2000 prisoners, 9 pieces of artillery, & a large number of small arms captured to say nothing of the killed & wounded of the enemy with but slight loss on our part. In our reg't there were but 2 casualties, one killed Joe Bell Co. "C" & Pvt. Marsh Co. I, wounded, which I believe were all the casualties of the brigade. About midnight the infantry were withdrawn from the field & were marched about 5 miles in the direction of Dinwiddie CH. About 9 o'clock next morning we started back to this place & after a long detour in taking a road 2 miles nearer the CH than that by which we marched when going to Reams' Station, we straggled into Petersburg that afternoon, very much broken down by the travel.

---

reserve at Globe Tavern in case the Confederates tried to interpose between Globe Tavern and Reams Station. Orlando Willcox's division, part of Mott's division and the cavalry of the Provost Guard were sent to the junction of the Jerusalem Plank Road and the road to Reams Station to guard the left flank of Grant's command.

Meade's passive defense stretched the Federals so thin that even their engineers went into the line. He sent men to every threatened point except Reams Station, which he expected his most trusted corps commander to hold. Indeed, it appeared that Hancock would hold.

After the derailment of the first Confederate attack plan, Hampton proposed another to Hill. The Southern cavalry would occupy the Federals on the railroad while the Confederate infantry stormed the western face of the Union breastworks.

This plan also failed. Hill moved too slowly. Cadmus Wilcox's command captured the entrenched Federal picket line several hundred yards west of the railroad at 1300. But by this time, Hancock had recalled Gibbon's division to the breastworks except for an outpost at the Lanier house, a few hundred yards south of Reams Station.

An hour later, Cadmus Wilcox sent Scales' Brigade of his own division and George Anderson's Brigade of Field's Division forward against the western face of the Federal works. The assault recoiled from the withering fire. Cadmus Wilcox's Confederates settled down to sharpshooting while they waited for the arrival of their artillery and Heth's infantry.

The Army of Northern Virginia's sharpshooter battalions had not been organized until that spring, though the law authorizing them had been in effect since April 1862. These crack soldiers had stood in the forefront of the campaign of forest warfare that Lee had been waging against the Federals since they crossed the Rapidan in May. At the second battle of Reams Station, Lee's sharpshooters had their best day of the war. They choked off the ammunition supply of the Federal artillery by making a dead zone of the railroad embankment between the caissons and limbers to the east and the cannon to the west. By massacring the battery horses, they made it impossible for the Union artillery to escape in case of defeat. Finally, they kept down the heads of the Northern infantry.

Heth's first two brigades arrived at 1500. Hill meanwhile had fallen ill, as was his characteristic at critical moments. He wanted to abandon the operation, but Heth dissuaded him. Hill sent orders to Hampton to advance when he heard the sound of the infantry's assault. Heth deployed the arriving

Confederate artillery and allowed the infantry assault to remain in Cadmus Wilcox's hands.

The Northerners knew it was coming. Miles received a brigade of Gibbon's division as a reinforcement and deployed one of its regiments to enfilade any Confederate attack on the northwest angle of the breastworks. The Federals stood three ranks deep at this point, which Miles further reinforced with a cannon from the battery in the northern return of the works. East of the railroad, the remainder of Gibbon's command hurriedly constructed a southern return to the works. Hancock ordered the Union detachment at the junction of the road from Reams Station and the Jerusalem Plank Road to arrest stragglers. Orlando Willcox's division was summoned to Reams Station.

Hampton's initiative seemed wasted. Hill had failed to catch the Federals off guard. The Confederates were now staking everything on a frontal assault against fully manned breastworks, which ordinarily was suicidal. To make matters worse, Cadmus Wilcox was preparing another piecemeal assault. Though he had four brigades of infantry at his disposal, only two of them would make the attack. The other pair would wait in support.

The preliminary artillery barrage began at 1630. The Southern cannon fired over the heads of the Federals manning the western face of the fortifications but into the backs of Gibbon's men, forcing them to jump to the outward side of the breastworks. One of the Federal cannon west of the railroad was knocked out.

Cadmus Wilcox sent the Southern infantry forward at 1700. The center of the Confederate front line advanced under the cover of woods and became locked in hand-to-hand combat with the Federals. The left stampeded the regiment posted by Miles in ambush and then had to wheel to face the northern side of the works while under fire. The right, which only had to cross an open field, stayed put under the orders of Brigadier General John R. Cooke. He did not want the right to be repulsed before the rest of the line reached the Union breastworks.

Forest Warfare

Early in 1864, Robert E. Lee quietly ordered a change in the organization of his forces that would exert a profound influence on the coming campaign. He directed the creation of a sharpshooter battalion in several of the infantry brigades in the Army of Northern Virginia, an arrangement that the Confederate Congress had authorized previously.

A sharpshooter battalion consisted of a company from each of the regiments in its brigade. The companies included two commissioned officers, two sergeants, two corporals, 30 privates and two men for ambulance corps duty. Officers and men were all veterans. The men were selected on the basis of marksmanship. The sharpshooters were armed with long-range, small-bore Enfield rifle-muskets. They used only long English-made cartridges, never ammunition of Confederate manufacture. At their disposal were also two globe-sighted rifles, for sniping.

The primary duty of the sharpshooters was to establish and occupy the skirmish line while Confederate infantry was in contact with the enemy. The sharpshooters would serve as pickets all day. At night one of the regiments of their brigade would relieve them. During the Virginia campaigns of 1864 and 1865, the sharpshooters were on the front line almost every day.

The organization of sharpshooter battalions was part of Lee's adoption of the tactics of forest warfare. He hoped to fall upon Grant's command while it

---

As the sound of fighting grew in the center, the commander of the supporting brigade behind Cooke saved the day with another display of Southern initiative. Brigadier General William MacRae ordered his brigade across the open ground along the Depot Road. The left of his brigade jostled into motion the immobile right of Cooke's Brigade. Cooke's men were blasted by the Federal artillery, but MacRae's battle line approached the Union earthworks unscathed. The Northern guns had run out of ammunition shooting at Cooke's Brigade and the Federal infantry, cowed by the Confederate sharp-

was entangled in the Wilderness and rout it as the French and Indians had Major General Edward Braddock's numerically superior British and Colonial force at the battle of the Monongahela in 1755. The Wilderness would confine the Federals to the roads and each tree would furnish a Southern fortification to impede their progress. The Confederates would use their knowledge of paths and byways to ambush and annihilate the Northerners.

Lee failed to destroy Grant's army in the Wilderness, but the Southerners continued to wage forest warfare all the way down to and across the James River. The terrain around Petersburg and Richmond was even more favorable than the Wilderness to Lee's tactics. Several Federals thought the landscape along Hatcher's Run made the Wilder-

ness seem hospitable. Some of the war's most successful Confederate ambushes took place around Petersburg on 22 June, 23 June, 18 August, 19 August, 30 September and 27 October.

Coupled with Grant's aggressiveness, the forest warfare that Lee waged until the fall of Petersburg had the unintended effect of creating a war of attrition that worked in his favor. Grant's command always outnumbered Lee's in bodies, but until the very last stage of the Petersburg campaign, Lee's command exceeded Grant's in the number of men willing to fight. Lee's advantage in this unplanned war of attrition reached its peak in August 1864, when Federal prisoners significantly outnumbered Federal killed and wounded. Natural selection in Grant's command had produced a soldier unlikely to fight.

---

shooters, fired high. MacRae's soldiers poured into the works and the Northerners began grounding their arms.

The Federals also started surrendering at the northwest angle as the left of Lane's Brigade swung around into the railroad cut. Miles' command, divided at least six ways by its leader, collapsed. The Confederates captured the cannon at the northwest angle and, sweeping along the northern return, the other three guns of its battery.

The Southerners also drove south along the railroad embankment, fighting hand-to-hand. When the Northerners in the southwest angle of the works turned to face MacRae's men, part of McGowan's Brigade advanced, took the Federals from behind and made them prisoners. Eight Union cannon fell into Confederate hands in the southwest angle, and the Southerners quickly turned them on the Federals.

What was left of Miles' command fell back to the woods 200 yards east of the railroad. Hancock ordered Gibbon's men to retake the lost breastworks and while Gibbon responded immediately, his men moved in the wrong direction. They attacked toward the northern return instead of wheeling to attack the western face of the works. Most of Gibbon's division disintegrated under the fire of the captured cannon and the Confederate riflemen along the railroad embankment. A few regiments on Gibbon's far right helped a fragment of Miles' command recapture the three cannon in the northern return. This motley group of Federals worked their way across the railroad still farther to the north and enfiladed the Southerners, whose main line now ran along the embankment.

Two brigades from Mahone's Division arrived as the final attack took place. Cadmus Wilcox initially ordered both of them to the left, but Weisiger's Brigade was diverted to the right and took position with McGowan's men at the embankment. Sanders' Brigade joined Scales' Brigade in driving off the Federals who enfiladed the Southern line from the north.

Meanwhile, Hampton swept up from Malone's Crossing. His men overwhelmed the Federal outpost at Lanier's farm and arrived opposite the southern return just as Gibbon's men recoiled from their misdirected assault. Fire from the embankment and from the Confederate cavalrymen had Gibbon's soldiers hopping from one side of the works to the other. Finally, both the Southern infantry and cavalry attacked simultaneously. The Confederates pocketed many of the Federals, while others escaped into the woods.

Orlando Willcox's division of Parke's corps arrived in time to help cover Hancock's retreat. Willcox's interception of and obedience to the orders that were meant for the detachment of Mott's men had eliminated whatever chance there was of his troops arriving at Reams Station on time to be of assistance to

Hancock. The Federals had lost more than 2,700 men, nine cannon, numerous flags and 3,000 stands of arms. Confederate losses totaled 720.

A downpour followed the battle. The infantry of both sides staggered back into the Petersburg lines the next day. Union and Confederate cavalrymen confronted each other at Reams Station while the Southerners buried the dead.

Grant's Fourth Offensive had ended. The Northerners had lost almost 10,000 men. More than half were prisoners, an indication that the Federals were losing the will to fight. But Lee, whose casualties numbered about 4,500, was no more inclined to counterattack than he had been on 18 June. His remaining soldiers were exhausted.

William Mahone

During the siege of Petersburg, many Federals considered Major General William Mahone the most formidable of Lee's subordinates. Officers on Meade's staff held the opinion that Mahone had occasioned more trouble to the Union forces around Petersburg than all of Lee's other generals combined.

Mahone was born in 1826 in Southampton County, Virginia, the site of Nat Turner's Rebellion five years later. The son of a tavern keeper, Mahone entered Virginia Military Institute in 1844—reputedly with money that he won in a poker game from a man who had won it in the same game from Mahone's father.

Graduating from VMI as adjutant of the Corps of Cadets, Mahone worked as a civil engineer and a teacher at Rappahannock Academy in Caroline County. In 1849, the Orange & Alexandria Railroad employed him as a surveyor. During the following year, he served as chief engineer of the Fredericksburg Plank Road. He subsequently went to work as chief engineer of the Norfolk & Petersburg Railroad. In 1858, he became the Norfolk & Petersburg's president and general superintendent as well.

Mahone began the war as a brigadier general of Virginia Militia. In April of 1861, he assisted in forcing the Federals from Portsmouth's Gosport Navy Yard by means of a ruse. The cheering of his men, as empty trains pulled in and out of the station across the Elizabeth River in Norfolk, created the impression that large Southern reinforcements were arriving. The Northern commandant of the navy yard was intimidated into withdrawing.

In Confederate service, Mahone first became colonel of the 6th Regiment Virginia Infantry and then, in November of 1861, brigadier general of Mahone's Brigade, part of the Norfolk garrison. From the start, he developed a reputation as a disciplinarian. His men had brigade drill every morning for two hours, battalion drill for two hours every afternoon and dress parade every evening. He also developed a reputation as an eccentric. A scrawny little man with a squeaky falsetto voice and a flowing triangular beard, he wore a decidedly unmilitary uniform—a long trailing coat and a wide brimmed hat. Because his dyspepsia forced him to subsist on milk and eggs, he always kept a cow and chickens near his tent.

He did not initially distinguish himself in combat. His brigade broke under enemy fire at the battle of Seven Pines. At the battle of Malvern Hill, he and his men redeemed themselves. Mahone was superficially wounded in the abdomen at Second Manassas. He was of such slight build that when his wife was told that it was a flesh wound, she declared such a thing impossible.

After his recovery, he led his brigade capably during the Chancellorsville campaign on ground that he had surveyed in 1850. At the battle of Gettysburg, his brigade saw practically no battle action, which gave rise to an unpleasant controversy in the Confederate newspapers after the retreat to Virginia.

At the battle of the Wilderness, on 6 May 1864, he was in command of the flank attack that Longstreet launched to drive back the Federal left. After the battle, command of Richard Anderson's Division devolved upon Mahone as its senior brigadier when Lee chose Richard Anderson to command Longstreet's corps after its commander suffered a debilitating wound.

In command of a division on the familiar ground around Petersburg, Mahone became the terror of Grant's command. On 22 June, near the Wilcox farm, he took three of the five brigades of his division and routed the Union *II Corps*, capturing more than 1,600 prisoners, nine flags and four cannon. On the following day, near the Gurley house, he employed three of his brigades to capture almost 500 prisoners from the Federal *VI Corps*. At the first battle of Reams Station on 30 June, Mahone and two of his brigades participated in a rout of retreating Northern cavalry resulting in the capture of 1,000 prisoners and 15 cannon. At the battle of the Crater on 30 July, he used three of his brigades to restore the Confederate line, capture 1,100 prisoners and 16 flags of the Union *IX Corps* and recapture four cannon. At the battle of Globe Tavern on 19 August, three brigades led by Mahone captured 2,700 prisoners and nine flags. At Burgess Mill on 27 October, the three brigades he commanded captured 400 prisoners and three flags and fatally disrupted Grant's last attempt of 1864 to drive the Confederates from Petersburg and Richmond. Three days later, the pickets of Mahone's Division carried off 230 of their Federal counterparts in the most successful trench raid of the siege.

From his assumption of the command of Richard Anderson's Division on 6 May 1864, until the re-election of President Abraham Lincoln on 8 November, Mahone engineered the capture of 6,700 prisoners, 42 colors and 15 cannon.

After the war, Mahone returned to engineering and the presidency of the Norfolk & Petersburg Railroad. He arranged the combination of that railroad, the South Side Railroad and the Virginia & Tennessee Railroad into the Atlantic, Mississippi & Ohio Railroad, the forerunner of the Norfolk & Western Railroad, which is now part of the Norfolk Southern Corporation.

Mahone was a Readjuster in Virginia's postwar Funder Readjuster controversy. The Funders favored paying Virginia's prewar debt in full. The Readjusters advocated deducting from it a substantial portion allocable to the state of West Virginia. In 1877, he ran for Governor of Virginia but withdrew. Two years later, he engineered the election of a Readjuster governor and legislature. To accomplish this, the hero of the Crater aligned himself with former slaves and Republicans. The Legislature named him United States senator in 1881.

By the end of his term, the tide had turned in favor of the Democrats—both nationally and in Virginia—and the state legislature did not reelect him to the Senate. In 1889, he lost the race for Governor by a wide margin. He died in 1895, vilified by Virginia's conservatives. While they adopted the battle of the Crater as the symbol of their victory over Reconstruction, they suppressed the memory of the military and political deeds of the Crater's hero.

Mahone's mausoleum, in Petersburg's Blandford Cemetery, overlooks the graves of many of his men. It is said that the mausoleum is marked only with the letter "M" instead of his full surname because he did not want to distract attention from them.

CHAPTER VII

Fort Harrison and Peebles Farm

While Grant's Fourth Offensive ground to a halt, Sherman's army group got under way in Georgia for a maneuver aimed at cutting the last railroad into Atlanta. At Petersburg, Lee began scraping the bottom of the Confederate manpower barrel.

Lee knew that Grant had cut the Weldon Railroad because of the way he employed his superior numbers. To remedy the situation, Lee attempted to increase the number of men in his own command. Lee bombarded the War Department with suggestions aimed at achieving this end. He wanted most detailed men recalled to their units, 5,000 African-Americans to work on fortifications, more blacks to replace white soldiers in rear echelon positions such as teamsters and militia, and reserves to hold the trenches in order that his veterans might strike the Federals a blow.

While Lee scrounged for men and Grant's soldiers sweated away fortifying the recent extension of the Federal line to the Weldon Railroad, Sherman's soldiers outflanked General John B. Hood and forced the Confederates to evacuate Atlanta on 1 September 1864. Sherman occupied the city on the following day. The capture of Atlanta vindicated the Lincoln administration's hard war policy and Grant's generalship. It also justified the terrible casualties of the spring and fall and shifted to the Confederates the burden of persuasion in the coming election.

At Petersburg, Lee continued to prepare to take the offensive. Scouts had informed Lee of the vulnerability of City Point. On 3 September, he directed Hampton to reconnoiter the area with the idea of inflicting damage there.

A shotted salute from all of Grant's batteries of 4 September confirmed the reports of Atlanta's fall. Meanwhile, Beauregard quietly departed Petersburg for an inspection of Wilmington's defenses. During his absence, President Davis appointed him to oversee military affairs in the West. Beauregard had left Petersburg for the duration and the Cockade City had lost a brilliant defender.

By 5 September, the partisan scouts who roamed the woods in Federal occupied territory had reported on Northern dispositions around City Point. While City Point itself seemed secure, a Federal cattle herd at Coggins Point was lightly guarded. The scouts also brought news that the Federals were extending their military railroad to the Weldon Railroad.

Hampton proposed a deep strike into the Union rear to capture the cattle herd at Coggins Point. The plan's goal was unusually modest for Hampton. All his previous schemes had called for direct blows to Federal combat units. Lee, who rarely interfered with the plan of a subordinate, approved of Hampton's proposal.

Meanwhile Lee's strategy of threatening Washington had produced an uneasy equilibrium in the Shenandoah Valley. It was similar to the equilibrium reached at the end of Jackson's Valley campaign of 1862, when it had preceded a withdrawal of Confederate forces from the Valley to smite another Federal command besieging Richmond. But there were significant differences that made such a Southern move difficult now. Jackson had ended his 1862 campaign at the Valley's upper end, at Port Republic, less than a week's march from Richmond. Early was near the Valley's lower end, at least two weeks away from the Confederate capital.

Federal cavalry raids had not impaired Lee's supply lines in 1862. But Early's men had to defend the undevastated portion of the Valley above Fisher's Hill while the Confederates at Richmond and Petersburg replenished food reserves exhausted during the interruptions of rail traffic in June, July and August. Early's soldiers hastened to bring in the harvest while Sheridan familiarized himself with his new command.

Lee wanted Early to take aggressive action. When Early did not move, Lee suggested the return of Kershaw's Division and of Richard Anderson, with whom Early did not get along. It was Lee's intention, if Early complied with this suggestion, to combine Kershaw's Division with the reserves at Petersburg—Hoke's Division and three brigades of Field's Division—and use this force to strike Grant's left. Early was given the option of waiting for Rosser's Brigade to arrive before returning Kershaw's Division. Sheridan's cautiousness had lulled Early into overconfidence, and he started Richard Anderson and Kershaw's Division on their way to Lee on 15 September.

But by the second week in September, Sheridan had gotten used to his new command and wanted to attack Early. Secretary of War Edwin M. Stanton and Halleck would not issue orders for such an offensive, and Grant did not trust them to forego intercepting such orders issued by himself. Lincoln suggested that Sheridan be reinforced to break the deadlock. The situation required Grant's personal presence.

On 13 September, Grant left Petersburg to meet with Sheridan. The conference took place at Charles Town three days later. Sheridan was confident that he could defeat Early—in part because Sheridan knew of the departure of Kershaw's Division on the previous day. Grant personally ordered Sheridan to attack.

While Grant conferred with Sheridan, Hampton moved into position to execute the attack on Coggins Point. On the following day, on which Grant departed for Petersburg, Hampton successfully executed the attack. The Confederate cavalry returned to Petersburg on 18 September with more than 2,400 head of cattle. But the Federals could easily replace such losses so long as the James River remained open to their shipping. Lee had damaged nothing more than their pride, though he had learned a great deal about the vulnerability of their left rear.

On 19 September, Sheridan routed Early at the battle of Opequon Creek. Early lost the battle for want of a reserve, which Kershaw's Division might have provided. News of the victory quickly reached Grant, who braced in case Early returned to Petersburg to reinforce Lee.

But Early remained in the Shenandoah Valley. On 22 September, Sheridan's numerically superior forces routed Early again at Fisher's Hill, near Strasburg. Early retreated up the Valley as far as Brown's Gap. Lee received word of the defeat at Fisher's Hill on 23 September and immediately ordered Kershaw's Division, which had reached Gordonsville, to return to Early. Richard Anderson was allowed to go back to the Army of Northern Virginia.

By the time Kershaw's Division rejoined Early, the Federal infantry had halted at Harrisonburg. Twenty-seven miles to the south, Union horse soldiers were taking possession of Staunton. The Northern cavalrymen then proceeded eastward along the Virginia Central Railroad, ripping it up as they went. On 28 September, at Waynesborough, Early's reinforced command began sweeping the Federal cavalry off the vital tracks. Rosser's Brigade of Southern horse soldiers left Petersburg for the Shenandoah Valley that same day.

Meanwhile, Grant put aside plans for a contemplated operation against Fort Fisher on 5 October and ordered an offensive around Petersburg on 29 September. The offensive would follow the familiar pattern of a thrust at Richmond from the Peninsula to draw the Southerners away from Petersburg, then an attack Southside on the Confederate supply lines. As in August, Grant hoped to take Richmond, but he would be satisfied with cutting the South Side Railroad or at least preventing Lee from reinforcing Early.

There were differences between Grant's plans of August and September. Butler, not Hancock, would command on the Peninsula. The force there would consist entirely of Butler's men—the X Corps under David Birney, the XVIII Corps under Ord and the Cavalry Division of the Army of the James under Kautz. Southside, the force at Meade's disposal would include Charles Griffin's and Ayres' divisions of Warren's corps and Potter's and Orlando Willcox's divisions of Parke's corps, along with David Gregg's cavalry division. Hancock's corps would get a rest.

Butler delivered his best performance of the war. He produced a plan that shifted the axis of his drive on Richmond upriver from previous offensives launched from Deep Bottom. There would be no attempt to turn the Confederate left, but surprise attacks on the Southern right and center. Ord's men would cross the James to Aiken's Landing on a pontoon bridge to be erected that evening. David Birney's men would cross on the upper Deep Bottom pontoon bridge, followed by Kautz's cavalry. Ord would attack north on the Varina Road, Birney would storm New Market Heights to the east and Kautz's cavalry would exploit David Birney's success by driving for Richmond.

Despite Butler's precautions, the Confederates detected the crossing. At 0630 on 29 September, Lee ordered the three brigades of Field's Division at Petersburg back to the Peninsula. But Lee's reaction was too late. Butler's men were already reaping the benefits of a divided Confederate command on the Peninsula. Ewell, on the Southern right, led a force that consisted primarily of reservists, though it included the veterans of Fulton's Tennessee Brigade. John Gregg, on the Confederate left, commanded his own Texas Brigade and DuBose's Georgia Brigade. Ewell chose to defend Signal Hill, on his own right near the James. John Gregg chose to defend New Market Heights, on his command's left and inland. The African-American division of Birney's corps dashed itself valiantly but vainly against John Gregg's men. But Stannard's division of Ord's corps drove up the Varina Road, overran the picket line that constituted Ewell's left and stormed Fort Harrison which was part of the entrenched camp at Chaffin's Bluff and the keystone of the Southern position on the Peninsula.

Fortunately for the Confederates, the Federals failed to exploit their success. Stannard's division had suffered heavily in casualties and lost cohesion. Heckman's division, ordered to support Stannard, meandered off into a swamp on the right

Federals engage Confederates near Richmond during Grant's 29 September offensive. Initially, the attack went off well with the Union troops carrying Fort Harrison, but this success was not exploited.

and extricated itself only one brigade at a time. Meanwhile, Ord was wounded as he led a small band of Stannard's men toward the vital pontoon bridges over the James. Command devolved upon the incompetent Heckman, exchanged after his capture at Drewry's Bluff in May. First he failed to prevent John Gregg, who had abandoned New Market Heights to Birney's soldiers, from joining Ewell. Then Heckman frittered away his own division in piecemeal attacks on the Southern fortifications.

Birney's men arrived in the afternoon and accomplished little more. Foster's division attacked Fort Gilmer from the north at 1330, but John Gregg's veterans manned the fort, not reserves as had occupied Fort Harrison that morning. A few Federals made it to the row of sharpened stakes projecting from the fort's ramparts, but no farther. Birney allowed a brigade of Paine's black division to stand by without helping, except for the *5th United States Colored Troops*.

David Birney's next attack was delivered at 1430 by his

incompetent brother, William Birney, who threw his brigade preceded by a single battalion of the *7th United States Colored Troops* against Fort Gilmer from the east. The Confederates inflicted frightful casualties on the battalion, while the two black regiments to the right and left were also punished.

At 1300, a provisional brigade from Pickett's Division arrived and took position near Forts Hoke and Maury, on the south face of the Chaffin's Bluff perimeter. By 1430, Law's Brigade of Field's Division arrived and moved to support Forts Johnson and Gilmer to the east. George Anderson's and Bratton's Brigades of Field's Division arrived before dark, but the Confederates failed to mount a counterattack against the decimated, disorganized and hungry Northerners. Lee overruled a proposal from Field that the Southerners attack with what they had, because, as on 20 August on the Weldon Railroad, he wanted to deliver a concentrated blow. The Federals began turning the captured works to face the Confederates.

David Birney's capture of New Market Heights opened the way for Kautz. By 1300, Kautz had arrived at the Intermediate Line of Southern fortifications by way of the New Market and Darbytown Roads. Alternatively resting and riding, his troopers made their way northwest cross country, encountering resistance at this line of fortifications on each road they tried. His final thrust toward Richmond came at midnight on the Creighton Road, northwest of the Nine Mile Road and almost at the Mechanicsville Turnpike. The Federals opened on one another first, then took fire from the militia manning the works at this point. Kautz headed his exhausted soldiers home.

Meade spent the day feinting in a vain attempt to hold the Confederates at Petersburg. David Gregg's cavalrymen probed all the way to the vicinity of Armstrong's Mill. Hampton's horsemen drove Gregg's men back to Wyatt's farm on the Lower Church Road, east of Arthur's Swamp.

That night a race began on the Peninsula with the Federals hastening to fortify the open rear of Fort Harrison and the Confederates striving to bring up enough reinforcements to

Troops of the V Corps *advance against Confederate earthworks at Peebles farm on 30 September. The fortifications were carried and one gun captured. It was a success on an otherwise dismal day for Grant.*

drive the Federals out of the fort. Confederate reinforcements consisted primarily of the reserves Lee had accumulated at Petersburg for his now thwarted offensive against Meade's left. On the morning of 30 September, the Federals were in the lead. No attack took place that morning because of Lee's determination to mount a concentrated assault.

Southside, Meade's strike force got under arms before daybreak. But his soldiers did not get under way until 0900. Charles Griffin's division led the infantry column of four divisions west on the Poplar Springs Church Road. David Gregg's cavalrymen advanced on the Vaughan Road, on the left of the footsoldiers.

At 1100, Warren's men began arriving at the junction of the Poplar Springs Church Road and the Squirrel Level Road. Dearing's Brigade of cavalry, supported by a battery in a redoubt on its left, held the Confederate works at Peebles farm just west of the intersection. James Archer's and Mac-Rae's Brigades of Heth's Division had left these works on the preceding day to take position near Battery 45 in the main line around Petersburg while Lee scraped that front for forces with which to counterattack at Fort Harrison.

By 1300, Warren had deployed Charles Griffin's division in front of the Confederate works facing the intersection. Warren moved Ayres' division north to guard his right and to allow the two divisions of Parke's corps to advance behind Griffin whose division drove Dearing's Brigade from the earthworks, capturing one of the cannon in the redoubt. It was U.S. government issue, captured at Second Reams Station.

The Federal column had orders to proceed west and then north, first to the Boydton Plank Road and then the South Side Railroad. The way was open, but the Federals moved slowly. Warren's men marched up the Church Road and drove Dearing's men from a lunette on the Pegram farm, then stopped. Parke brought up Potter's division and placed it on Warren's left. Orlando Willcox took position to support Potter.

Delay followed delay. The Confederates used the time to bring up reinforcements. Hampton left Matthew Butler's Division to prevent David Gregg's horsemen from advancing on the Vaughan Road and ordered Rooney Lee's cavalrymen to the unfinished fortifications guarding the Boydton Plank Road northwest of the Federal infantry. At 1400, while awaiting transportation at Dunlop's north of Petersburg, Lane's and McGowan's Brigades of Cadmus Wilcox's Division received orders to return to the Southside. They began retracing their steps through Petersburg. At the same time, A.P. Hill ordered Cooke's and Davis' Brigades of Heth's Division from Petersburg to the Boydton Plank Road.

While Lane's and McGowan's Brigades abandoned their journey to Chaffin's Bluff, the Confederates there finally attacked Fort Harrison. The assault proved a repetition of the 24 June fiasco, but with the roles of Field and Hoke reversed. This time Field, on the left and with more ground to cross, was to advance part way and then await the onslaught of Hoke's Division on the right. The first problem came from George Anderson's Brigade. Nearly without field officers because of its losses in August, this unit lacked the discipline to stop its

Fort Harrison and Peebles Farm

The following selection is taken from the diary of Private Bernard:

Sunday afternoon Oct. 2 '64

Went in to Petersburg yesterday & there heard the sad news of my Brother Dick's death. He was killed while on picket near Mt. Jackson in the Valley on Friday Sept. 23. The fatal bullet struck him upon the neck, producing instant death. Poor fellow, he had passed through many hard fought battles and at last has filled a soldier's grave. I can scarcely realize that he is now among the dead. His comrades performed the last sad offices to his remains, giving them a hasty burial before the enemy got possession of the field. His memory will ever be fondly cherished by relatives & friends, beloved by all who knew him.

During the past 48 hours there has been fighting on our right upon the farms of Messrs. Peebles, R.H. Jones & Pegram. One result certainly was the capture of about 1400 prisoners up to yesterday midday. The rumors are rather conflicting, but in the main they are favorable. I hear nothing reliable from the extreme left, except that attempts to dislodge the enemy from the captured salient (Fort Harrison) have failed, but on the other hand, attempts of the enemy to carry other points have also been equally repulsed.

Our reg't furnished the 100 men for picket last night, our company contributing a part of the 100. The rifle pits were, most of them, filled with water, which with the rain & the constant sharpshooting of the enemy made the tour of duty a most disagreeable one. Banging away at the enemy served very well to keep our eyes open. All night long, notwithstanding the constant firing, our men & the enemy were exchanging words. At day light we had a short truce to relieve the pickets. There has been but little picket firing today, both parties being disposed to keep up the truce.

charge. The Federals mowed down the impetuous Georgians. On the far left, Law's Brigade became entangled in picket fighting. Bratton's Brigade advanced alone a few minutes after Anderson's Brigade. The Northerners blasted Bratton's South Carolinians. At 1400, after the Federals had repulsed the disjointed attacks of Field's soldiers, the left of Hoke's

Division struck. The Northerners in Fort Harrison decimated Clingman's and Colquitt's Brigades while Hoke's other three brigades failed to advance.

About the time that this fiasco played itself out, Meade visited the Federal strike force at Peebles' Farm. But he neglected to take command and coordinate the efforts of Parke and Warren. At 1600, Parke ordered Potter to advance without reference to the units on his left and right. Parke shifted all of Orlando Willcox's division to Potter's left, expecting Griffin's division to advance on Potter's right, but Griffin did not advance.

By this time, the brigades of Lane and McGowan had arrived in the fortifications on Jones farm, in Potter's front just short of the Boydton Plank Road. MacRae's and James Archer's Brigade of Heth's Division were on the way. Lane took position on the right, McGowan on the left. When Heth and his men arrived, MacRae's Brigade moved into position behind Lane's right, Archer's Brigade behind McGowan's left. Cadmus Wilcox took command of the four Southern infantry brigades. Heth, the ranking officer on the scene, took command of the Confederate right.

The sharpshooter battalions of Lane's and McGowan's Brigades drove the skirmishers of Potter's lead brigade back from the Jones house. Simon Griffin, the commander of this brigade, led the first of his two lines of battle forward to recapture the house. At 1700, Simon Griffin's soldiers drove the Confederate sharpshooters from the Jones house. All that intervened between the Federals and the Boydton Plank Road now was a ravine and a strip of woods. But out of the ravine burst Wilcox's battle line. His men crumpled up the flanks of Simon Griffin's first line of battle and put it to flight. Such of the first line as escaped envelopment communicated the panic to the second line, which fled back to Pegram's farm. The second line of Curtin's Brigade, on the left of Simon Griffin's brigade, retreated to its left, toward Hartranft's brigade. Rooney Lee's cavalrymen, MacRae's Brigade and part of Lane's Brigade enveloped and captured most of Curtin's first line. These Confederates drove Hartranft back toward Pegram's farm along the course of Arthur Swamp. McGowan's and Archer's Brigades and the left portion of Lane's Brigade swept on to the same destination along the Church Road. This force arrived ahead of the Southerners working their way through the tangled watercourse and met Griffin's and Orlando Willcox's divisions supported by two batteries. As on 18 August, the superior Northern numbers, bolstered by overwhelming artillery support, brought the Confederates to a halt.

Once again the Federals spent the night fortifying while the Confederates brought up reinforcements for a counterattack. On the morning of 1 October, as Early finished clearing Northern horse soldiers from the Virginia Central Railroad and prepared to encamp near Staunton, Hill attempted to repeat Mahone's maneuver of 19 August. While Cadmus Wilcox demonstrated with McGowan's and Lane's Brigades on the Church Road at Pegram's farm, Heth attacked down the Squirrel Level Road intending to roll up an unanchored Federal right.

This time Warren was in charge of the Northern right and he had learned his lesson on 19 August. Cadmus Wilcox's men advanced in the rain and gobbled up almost 200 of Parke's pickets, but Heth's men probed in vain from dawn until mid-morning. They found Warren's soldiers dug in and supported by artillery and lost 400 men in their efforts to find a way into the Federal rear.

That afternoon, Meade used the newly constructed military railroad to speed Mott's division on its way to reinforce the Union left. Hampton tried unsuccessfully to envelop the Federal cavalry at Wilkinson's farm on the Vaughan Road. The Northern horsemen retreated to McDowell's farm, and Hampton failed to drive them from that position.

On the Peninsula, Lee's artillery opened fire on Fort Harrison at 0830, but Lee declined to send his infantry forward. Butler dispatched Alfred Terry and Kautz up the Darbytown Road to probe the Richmond defenses. They approached the Confederate Intermediate line at 1400 and skirmished with the forces of the Department of Richmond until dark. Then

During the action near the Darbytown Road, Federal guns boom away against their enemy counterparts. Lee's 7 October offensive on the Darbytown Road was broken up by cannons and infantry armed with repeating rifles.

they withdrew, having come closer to Richmond than any other Federals would until the city's fall, on 3 April 1865.

A reconnaissance in force by Mott's division on the morning of the following day convinced Grant to call a halt to his offensive. He had not forced Lee to withdraw men from the Shenandoah Valley or prevented Lee from reinforcing Early though he had captured the important Confederate work at Fort Harrison. More importantly, he had also taken the New Market Heights position which had withstood his Peninsula offensives of July and August and forced Lee to transfer to the Peninsula reserves accumulated for an offensive against the *Army of the Potomac*'s left rear. Had Lee beaten Grant to the punch in September and launched that offensive, Hampton's cattle raid would have borne the same relationship to it as Stuart's ride around McClellan did to the Seven Days Battles. Finally, Grant had pierced the Squirrel Level Road line Southside and was now dangerously close to the Boydton Plank Road and the South Side Railroad. On the Peninsula, the Northerners had lost 3,327 men, the Southerners about 1,700. The Federals lost 2,889 men Southside to inflict about 1,300 casualties on the Confederates there.

The capture of Fort Harrison and New Market Heights

made it worthwhile for Grant to have his men hold their gains on the Peninsula. This compounded Lee's manpower problems by requiring him to defend a much longer line in front of Richmond and Petersburg. To occupy that extended line made a Southern offensive Southside practically impossible. Lee had to keep so many men on the Peninsula that he decided to make a virtue of necessity and take the offensive there.

The attack took place on the morning of 7 October, two days after Rosser's Brigade joined Early in the Shenandoah Valley. Its goal was to roll up the Federal right and drive Butler's men back into the James. Lee gave the lead role in the attack to the infantry divisions of Field and Hoke, originally earmarked for the canceled Southside offensive.

Before dawn, while Hoke's Division waited on the New Market Road, Field's Division trudged into position opposite Kautz's cavalrymen on the Darbytown Road. Gary's Confederate horsemen opened the ball by driving in the Federal pickets on the Charles City Road, then turning toward the Darbytown Road. Field's Division attacked Kautz at 0900. Bratton's Brigade was on the left of the Darbytown Road, facing Spear's brigade. George Anderson's Brigade, on the right of the road, confronted West's brigade. Spear's men gave way first. Some of Bratton's men wheeled to their right to drive off West's troopers. Kautz's division was soon in retreat, which turned into a rout when Gary's cavalrymen appeared in their rear. The Confederates captured nine pieces of artillery.

Hours passed while the Southern infantry made its way through the underbrush and across Four Mile Creek toward the right of the X Corps, a line of trenches extending several hundred yards north of the New Market Road. Pond's brigade of Terry's division held these works. At first, the brigade's right was in the air. But the delayed advance of the Southerners gave Terry sufficient time to bring up Hawley's and Plaisted's brigades and place them at right angles to the right of Pond's brigade. Several batteries unlimbered in support of the Northern infantrymen, some of whom carried Spencer repeating rifles.

The Federal artillery broke up Hoke's Division before it could deliver its attack against the Northern line south of the Darbytown Road. The terrain made Field's attack against the refused Federal right north of the road disjointed. On Field's right, Union fire killed the commander of the Texas Brigade, John Gregg. Anderson's Brigade failed to close with the Northerners. Repeating rifles inflicted heavy casualties on Bratton's Brigade. Law's Brigade, on Field's left, recoiled almost instantly from the fire it encountered. In the afternoon, the Confederates withdrew. The Federals reoccupied Kautz's works on the Darbytown Road and dug in along the return which had withstood Field's men. Butler's soldiers had inflicted about 700 casualties on the Confederates at a cost of 437 to themselves.

On the following day, Parke's and Warren's corps demonstrated southwest of Petersburg to prevent Lee from taking more men from the Southside to use in a Peninsula offensive. The demonstration proved unnecessary. Lee had already abandoned the offensive for the time being. Southside and on the Peninsula, both sides concentrated on constructing new lines of trenches.

As the fighting died down around Petersburg, Grant urged Sheridan to drive all the way down the Shenandoah Valley to the Virginia Central Railroad and follow it across the Blue Ridge, then to Charlottesville, and finally to Richmond, wrecking it as he marched. But Sheridan was oblivious to the strategic importance of such a movement and the Lincoln administration did not want to hazard its inherent risks. Sheridan began withdrawing down the Shenandoah Valley, making sure that he left the countryside wasted behind him.

The last repercussion of Grant's Fifth Offensive began on 12 October. On that day, Butler received intelligence that the Confederates were building a fort on the Darbytown Road near the Federal picket line. Grant ordered Butler to undertake a reconnaissance in force on the next day and destroy the fort if possible.

Butler sent two divisions of Alfred Terry's X *Corps* out to examine the Confederate positions on the Darbytown and

Charles City Roads. William Birney's African-American division advanced south of the Darbytown Road, Ames' division north of the road. Kautz's cavalry covered the ground from Ames' right to the Charles City Road. Gary's Southern horse soldiers skirmished with the Federals during their two-mile advance. The Northern infantrymen found the Confederate fortifications confronting them too formidable to attack, but Kautz reported the works in front of him slight. Terry ordered Ames to move to the right and look for weak spots in the Southern line. Ames thought he found a spot with no works about half a mile south of the Charles City Road.

Pond's brigade drew the assignment of charging through the gap. At 1400, 570 of its men began their advance through thick underbrush. At first only the Hampton Legion of Gary's command resisted them. Pond's men flanked the Hampton Legion, but before they could exploit this advantage, the Texas Brigade and Law's Brigade of Field's Division arrived. The Federals found themselves under fire from three sides. To make matters worse, instead of there being no works at this point, there were works that formed a cul-de-sac into which the Northerners had thrust themselves. Some of Pond's men reached the Confederate breastworks. Fewer than half of them made it back across the 800 yards they had advanced. By nightfall, the Federals had returned to their own lines. They had lost 437 men and inflicted only about 50 casualties on the Secessionists.

Grant's Railroad

Nicknamed "Grant's Railroad" by newspapermen, the City Point & Army Line had its origin in mid-June 1864. Grant wanted a rail connection between his City Point supply depot and his troops, and he summoned construction teams of the United States Military Railroads of Virginia.

Construction began on 18 June, when the crews arrived at City Point. They began by rebuilding most of the City Point Branch of the South Side Railroad. The workers busied themselves reconstructing broken bridges, replacing rotten ties, substituting Northern T-rails for Southern U-rails and narrowing the gauge from five feet to four feet eight inches to accommodate Federal locomotives and cars.

The railroaders also built stations for loading, unloading, storing and issuing supplies. Wood Pile, the station closest to City Point, served as the fuel stop. Four miles from City Point, at the junction of the railroad and the Cedar Level Road, stood Cedar Level Station. A short distance further along the line was Clark Station. Five and a half miles from City Point, the crews built Pitkin Station.

By 5 July, the gandy dancers had the railroad in running order for seven miles out of City Point. Regular trains began operating on 7 July, when a convoy of 90 steamers, tugs and barges delivered 24 locomotives and 275 cars. The *1st Connecticut Heavy Artillery* and its flatcar-mounted seacoast mortar Dictator shared the mile and a half of railroad beyond Pitkin Station with trains carrying supplies for Forts McGilvery and Stedman.

On 29 August, after cutting the Weldon Railroad, Grant issued orders to extend the City Point & Army Line to the Weldon Railroad in rear of the Union fortifications. By 1 September, the *Construction Corps* had begun work on a new section that branched off to the southwest from Pitkin Station. In 10 days, the corps laid nine miles of track to the Weldon Railroad. This section of the line included five new stations: Birney, Meade, Hancock, Parke and Warren. Fourteen and a half miles separated City Point from Warren Station at the end of the section.

The corps took special pains to protect the line from Confederate fire. In some places, crews erected earthworks. In others, the men sank the track up to five feet. The noise and smoke of locomotives attracted Southern fire, but the Secessionist shells inflicted no serious injuries.

As Grant extended his left toward the South Side Railroad, the *Construction Corps* extended the City Point & Army Line. In November, the crews added the Patrick Branch. It ran two and a quarter miles from Warren Station to Patrick Station at Peebles Farm, which the Federals had taken at the end of September. In December, the crews added the Gregg Branch. This branch, east of the Weldon Railroad, ran from Hancock Station to Fort Blaisdell on the Jerusalem Plank Road, a distance of two and a quarter miles. In February 1865, the *Construction Corps* built the last branch of the railroad. This branch ran south from Warren Station down the old line of the Weldon Railroad for two miles, then turned west for three miles before terminating at Humphreys' Station near the junction of the Vaughan and Squirrel Level Roads.

The City Point & Army Line made it possible for Federal troops to live in relative comfort and plenty that winter while the opposing Confederates shivered and starved. Bread baked at City Point could be distributed still warm all along the Union fortifications.

Grant's Railroad had become so extensive that a story made the rounds about some Union soldiers who reached a railway near Petersburg one day. These men assumed the railroad was Confederate and began tearing up the tracks. Hearing a whistle in the distance, they prepared to capture the approaching train. But when the locomotive appeared, they realized that they had been tearing up the City Point & Army Line.

The railroad had other humorous aspects besides its size. For example, hasty construction caused many steep grades. A member of Grant's staff wrote of the railroad that "its undulations were so marked that a train moving along it looked like a fly crawling on a corrugated washboard."

Despite the grades, the City Point & Army Line's engines hauled an average of 15 loaded cars per train. In many cases, they hauled as many as 23 loaded cars. During the railroad's existence, it carried 785,981 passengers (all other Union military railroads in Virginia carried only 421,493), some 362,506 tons of food; 76,540 tons of weapons, ammunition and explosives; 9,665 tons of medical supplies and 193,652 tons of quartermaster stores. The tonnage carried exceeded the total tonnage of all other Union lines in Virginia for the same period.

On the morning of 3 April 1865, within hours after the Cockade City fell, the *Construction Corps* resumed activating the track of the City Point Branch into Petersburg. By this time, the corps consisted of about 2,000 men. When President Lincoln went to view the captured city that day, he entered Petersburg on a special train consisting of a locomotive and a coach. "Has this railroad got a lawyer?" the former corporate counsel for the Illinois Central Railroad said with a smile before boarding.

CHAPTER VIII

Fair Oaks and Burgess Mill

By the second week in October, 1864, Abraham Lincoln seemed likely to be returned to office in the coming November election. On 15 October, the probability of Lincoln's reelection increased when Hood abandoned his attempt to maneuver Sherman out of Atlanta. Since part of Lee's reserves were with Early in the Shenandoah Valley and the rest had been used up defending against Grant's Fifth Offensive and in the first battle of the Darbytown Road on 7 October, Early was left with the burden of persuading the Northern electorate to change administrations.

On 19 October, Early sprang a surprise attack on Sheridan's army at Cedar Creek, near Winchester. The attack was initially successful, and the Confederates took many prisoners and captured numerous cannon. But Sheridan, who was absent at the battle's inception, returned and led his army in sweeping the Confederates from the field. Grant's batteries at Petersburg delivered another hundred gun salute on the following day.

As in September, Grant began considering an offensive to follow up Sheridan's success in the Shenandoah Valley, either to prevent Lee from sending reinforcements there, or to take advantage of the absence of those reinforcements. If the Federals were fortunate, they might force the evacuation of Petersburg and Richmond—an outcome that would be an October surprise in the Lincoln administration's favor.

Grant's orders were issued on 24 October. They called for a demonstration by Butler's command on the Peninsula while

Incapacitated by a wound on 6 May 1864 Longstreet, Lee's "Old-Warhorse," finally returned to command in October of that year.

Meade's *Army of the Potomac* struck for the South Side Railroad west of Petersburg. Grant did not take any half measures this time. Butler's command was to carry three days' rations, an amount appropriate for a force that was going forth to battle instead of mounting a diversion. The *Army of the Potomac* was to take six days' rations, twice the amount ordinarily carried by a strike force, plus a herd of cattle—an indication of the sense of insecurity created by Hampton's cattle raid. All detailed men were to be given muskets and put in the ranks.

Meade planned to advance Parke's and Warren's corps on the east side of Hatcher's Run while a force led by Hancock crossed to the far side. This force would consist of two infantry divisions of the *II Corps* and David Gregg's cavalry division. Meade expected that Parke's and Warren's corps would encounter unfinished earthworks. But if they came up against fully manned fortifications, they were not to attack. Instead, Warren's corps would cross Hatcher's Run at Armstrong's Mill and attempt to recross above Burgess Mill. Hancock would bypass Burgess Mill, recross Hatcher's Run on the Claiborne Road, and use Butterworth's Road for the last leg of his thrust to the South Side Railroad.

The politically ambitious Butler ordered more than a mere demonstration. He intended to end the war by capturing Richmond. Weitzel's *XVIII Corps* was to cross White Oak Swamp and attempt to turn the Confederate left on the Williamsburg and Nine Mile Roads. Alfred Terry's *X Corps* would meanwhile demonstrate on the Darbytown and Charles City Roads.

Unfortunately for the Federals, Grant's plan found the Southerners at the top of their form. Longstreet had returned from the long convalescence following his wounding in the Wilderness to take command on the Peninsula on 19 October. This master of defensive strategy divined Butler's intentions from his preliminary movements on the evening of 26 October. Longstreet set his men in motion to counter Butler's maneuver.

Southside, the actual leadership of the Confederate right wing had devolved upon Hampton, the junior major general there except for the only other Southern major general to approach him in competence—Mahone. As usual, Hampton rose to the occasion. First, he placed his dismounted cavalrymen—perhaps 20 percent of his force—in the far right of the recently completed breastworks between Petersburg and Hatcher's Run. Second, he formulated the Confederate response to a Federal advance south and west of Hatcher's Run. His cavalry would contain the Northerners while the infantry counterattacked into their rear across dams that Hampton had recently erected between the Boydton Plank Road and Armstrong's Mill.

Meade's Federals hit the road before daybreak on 27 October. Thomas Smyth's brigade of Egan's division led Hancock's force across Hatcher's Run on the Vaughan Road as the sun rose. By 0900, Parke's corps had found the Southern entrenchments in its front unassailable. Soon afterward, a reconnaissance by Gregory's brigade of Warren's corps showed that the Confederates had fortified all the way to Hatcher's Run.

David Gregg's mounted division advanced on Hancock's left. Attempting to envelop the Northern cavalry, Hampton ordered Rooney Lee's Division up from the south while Matthew Butler's Division blocked off the roads north and west to the Federal horsemen. Dearing's Brigade was ordered to screen the Boydton Plank Road from the advance of the Union infantry.

The plan might have succeeded in annihilating David Gregg's division if A.P. Hill had not ordered Dearing's Brigade to remain at Burgess Mill. The envelopment of Gregg's horse soldiers was proceeding apace when Hampton discovered the Federal infantry in his rear as a result of Hill's orders to Dearing. Hampton ordered his troopers to retreat. Matthew Butler retired cross-country to the White Oak Road. Rooney Lee proceeded along the south bank of Gravelly Run to the Boydton Plank Road. Hancock's infantry took position at Burgess Mill, far short of the Claiborne Road crossing of Hatcher's Run.

Humphreys, Meade's chief of staff, ordered Warren to reinforce Hancock. Warren started Crawford's division to Hancock's support. Crawford did not cross Hatcher's Run at Armstrong's Mill until noon. He then received orders to advance along the right bank of Hatcher's Run, no easy task in light of terrain that made the Wilderness seem hospitable. Ayres' division remained east of the run.

Hancock was instructed to halt at noon. He waited at Burgess Mill while Crawford's division advanced on his right. It became clear to Meade and Grant that they had underestimated the distances between their starting points and their goals. When they arrived at Burgess Mill in the early afternoon, Grant and Meade gave Hancock the option of either crossing Hatcher's Run and turning the Confederate works to the east, or withdrawing. At that point, the three

Action on the Boydton Plank Road

The following selection is taken from the diary of Private Bernard:

On picket near the W. W. Davis's house on Squirrel Level Road Monday Oct 31

After a rest of more than two weeks, which we spent in the pine grove near Mr. Branch's place last Thursday morning we were put in motion and before sunset our brigade found itself charging the enemy near the Burgess Farm on the Boydton Plank Road. Our brigade lost in this action 410 kd, wd & missing, most of the latter whom are no doubt prisoners—our regiment 43kd, wd & missing—2 kd Jno E. Burwell Co "E" & King Co "G", 12 wd and 30 missing. Our company lost kd as mentioned above, 1 wd Corp. Jno Turner and 4 missing privates Wm. S. Clopton, Craig Riddle, Henry Ellington &

Jas. Keen. More stands of colors were captured by our brigade, 2 of which were captured by members of our reg't, six pieces of artillery were also captured but could not be brought off. The enemy's line was completely cut in two but we had not force enough to follow up our advantage. The enemy must have suffered heavily, as they withdrew their troops from the Plank Road Thursday night. The heavy loss of prisoners on our part was due to the men losing their way in the dense woods. However many instances of men being captured two or three times & finally getting away. The recruits distinguished themselves by the valor with which they fought.

Next morning we returned to our old camp in the pine grove, but at dark marched off to the breastworks near battery No. 45.

generals began to downplay the operation by referring to it as a reconnaissance.

While the Confederate cavalry contained Hancock's command, Hill called up reinforcements and sent them to Heth, the ranking Confederate on the far right. The brigades of Harris, MacRae, Sanders and Weisiger reached Heth in the early afternoon. Retaining Harris' Brigade to bolster Dearing's Brigade at the Boydton Plank Road crossing of Hatcher's Run, Heth deployed the other three brigades under Mahone in accordance with Hampton's defensive plan.

On the Peninsula, Alfred Terry's men demonstrated from the New Market Road to the Charles City Road while Weitzel's men advanced toward the Confederate left. By 1300, after skirmishing with Gary's Southern cavalrymen, Weitzel's soldiers had reached the Williamsburg Road near the 1862 battlefield of Seven Pines. From there they could see a line of fortifications a mile and a half to the west. The fortifications were held by three cannon and a few troopers.

Major General Godfrey Weitzel deployed his men to attack. He put Marston's division north of the road. Cullen's brigade was in line of battle supported by the division's other two brigades. Heckman's division took position south of the road, with Fairchild's brigade supported by the rest of the division. Holman's brigade of the black division received orders to cross the York River Railroad at Fair Oaks Station still farther to the right and turn the Confederate left. The African-American division's other brigade remained in reserve.

The advance of Weitzel's corps began at 1530. By that time, the situation had changed. The Federals no longer confronted works nearly empty of defenders. Instead, they encountered works manned by the Texas Brigade, with George Anderson's and Benning's Brigades in support. Longstreet had guessed from the length of Terry's demonstration that another force would try to turn the Southern left. Field was ordered to shift in that direction. His veterans blasted the Northerners with deadly musketry. The fire pinned down many of the Federals behind a little crest. Confederate skirmishers advanced and gathered up 600 prisoners and 6 battleflags.

Holman's black troops marched northwest on the Nine Mile Road. The African-Americans attacked where the road entered the Confederate fortifications. Gary's pickets repulsed Holman's left, but his right entered the works and captured two cannon. The blacks did not hold the guns for long, though. The rest of Gary's Brigade arrived on the right of Holman's troops and drove them from the works. As the African-Americans reformed, orders recalling them arrived from Weitzel.

Butler, who had accompanied Weitzel, realized that Long-

Major General Godfrey Weitzel.

street must have weakened his line elsewhere in order to have massed so many men on the Williamsburg Road. Orders went to Terry to press his demonstration against the recently constructed Confederate line that extended from a mile north of Fort Gilmer to within a half mile of the Charles City Road.

Terry had his *2nd Division* astride the Darbytown Road, with his *1st Division* on its right and his *3rd Division* on its left. He ordered forward the *1st* and *2nd Divisions* to seize the Confederate rifle pits and, if possible, the Southern main line. The *1st Division*—its ranks filled with recruits and veterans with expiring enlistments—was easily repulsed by Field's remaining soldiers. Hoke's men yielded some rifle pits to the *2nd Division*, but the Federals failed to pierce the main Confederate line.

As Butler issued orders for the withdrawal of his men to their fortifications, Crawford neared a point opposite the Southern works resting on Hatcher's Run. Hancock was preparing to force a crossing of the run with McAllister's brigade of Mott's division. But the increasing skirmisher fire

Petersburg and the Shenandoah Valley

When Jubal Early sneezed, Robert E. Lee caught cold. Early's drive down the Shenandoah Valley in late June and the beginning of July in 1864 constituted Lee's principal strategic response to Grant's arrival at the gates of Richmond. Stonewall Jackson's threat to the Federal capital had seriously interfered with the Union advance on Richmond in 1862. Lee hoped to repeat the formula.

Events in the Shenandoah critically influenced the Petersburg campaign. Early's march on Washington diverted the *VI* and *XIX Corps* from Grant's command at Petersburg at the beginning of July. The burning of Chambersburg, Pennsylvania, by Early's cavalry at July's end drew two Northern cavalry divisions away from Petersburg and threatened to force the return to Washington of Grant's entire command. At the beginning of August, Lee responded to the reinforcements sent to the Shenandoah by Grant by sending a cavalry division and an infantry division to Early, then a few days later dispatching another cavalry division and putting another infantry division and perhaps still other forces under marching orders. Grant launched his Third Offensive in late July, his Fourth Offensive in mid-August, his Fifth Offensive

on his right alarmed Hancock and he deployed Pierce's brigade of Mott's division in the woods on that flank.

Mahone was deploying his attack force in the woods between Crawford and Hancock. As usual, Mahone led three brigades, which he deployed two up and one in support. In the first line, MacRae's Brigade was on the right and Weisiger's Brigade—Mahone's Old Brigade—was on the left. Sanders' Brigade was in reserve.

At 1630, as Crawford's advance brushed against the extreme left of Weisiger's Brigade, Mahone ordered his men forward. The North Carolinians and Virginians overwhelmed the right of Pierce's brigade. The Confederates captured three flags and 400 prisoners. Sweeping on, the Southerners took two cannon in the middle of Pierce's line. The Confederates then put to flight Pierce's left and drove across the open field

in late September and his Sixth Offensive in the fourth week of October to prevent Lee from reinforcing Early or compel the return to Petersburg of forces already sent to the Shenandoah.

Lee's ploy did not succeed in breaking Grant's grip on Petersburg, but it still benefitted the Southern cause. From the start, Early faced a Northern army in the Shenandoah that outnumbered his own. He succeeded in drawing from Petersburg another Union force at least twice his command's size. Despite his epic defeats at Sheridan's hands, Early eased Lee's task of holding Petersburg and Richmond.

By the end of October, Early no longer posed a serious threat to Washington. But Sheridan had too much respect for Early to march on the Virginia Central Railroad, as Grant wished. Stalemate prevailed in the Shenandoah Valley through the winter. Both sides withdrew substantial forces from the Shenandoah in December and January, but events in the Valley continued to influence the opposing commands at Petersburg. The beginning of the end for Lee's command came in early March of 1865 when Sheridan turned east, eventually to join Grant's army group at Petersburg, instead of following orders, which called for him to proceed all the way down the Valley and then head for Sherman's command in North Carolina.

to the Boydton Plank Road. With MacRae's Brigade on the right and Weisiger's Brigade on the left, they faced south and advanced to sweep the Federals from the field.

Mahone's men did not know it yet, but they had advanced into a trap. A belt of trees screened from view four brigades of Federal infantry behind them—McAllister's brigade of Mott's division and the three brigades of Egan's division. Egan ordered McAllister to forego crossing Hatcher's Run. His brigade must about face and attack. The onslaught of McAllister's brigade precipitated a hand-to-hand struggle for the two guns captured by Mahone's men from Pierce's brigade. On the Boydton Plank Road flank of Mahone's force, Hancock's aide-de-camp took part of Rugg's brigade and reopened the plank road to the Northerners.

The Federals south of Mahone's soldiers swung into action.

Part of De Trobriand's brigade wheeled about and drove for the still contested two-gun battery. The remnant of Pierce's brigade rallied and joined this attack. The Federals pocketed about half of MacRae's Brigade, capturing two flags and inflicting almost 600 casualties, mostly prisoners. Weisiger's Brigade was driven back in confusion into the woods to the east. Sanders' Brigade halted the Federal advance at the woods' edge.

That any of Mahone's two lead brigades escaped was due to the attacks that the Confederate cavalry and Nathaniel Harris' Brigade launched at the sound of Mahone's firing. Harris' and Dearing's Brigades advanced across Hatcher's Run to pin down Thomas Smyth's brigade and part of Willett's brigade of Egan's division. Dismounted Southern horsemen of Matthew Butler's Division drove down the White Oak Road where they occupied Kerwin's brigade of cavalry, parts of Willett's and Rugg's brigades of Egan's division and several regiments of De Trobriand's brigade of Mott's division. One of Hampton's sons was killed and another seriously wounded in this attack. Rooney Lee's Division, striking up the Boydton Plank Road from Gravelly Run, engaged the remaining two brigades of Federal cavalry.

Darkness brought the fighting to an end. Meade offered to reinforce Hancock with Ayres' division of Warren's corps during the night, but Hancock elected to withdraw. His men and guns had nearly exhausted their ammunition, and the single road available to him could not accommodate ordnance wagons in addition to Ayres' division Hancock needed both to hold his ground.

The retreat along this wagon track took place in the same miserable downpour that made Butler's withdrawal so unpleasant. But Meade's soldiers were also harassed by wandering bands of Weisiger's men, 400 of whom wandered into Crawford's division and Hancock's column. Hancock left almost 300 wounded on the battlefield because his ambulances could not accommodate them. In the confusion, some of his pickets also remained on the field.

The decision to retreat was wise. The Confederates had

gathered their forces to destroy Hancock. In the morning, the Southerners had to content themselves with taking prisoner his wounded and stragglers instead of his whole command.

Instead of producing victories as at Fort Harrison and Peebles' farm, this attempt to capitalize on Sheridan's successes in the Shenandoah Valley had resulted in a pair of fiascoes. Instead of receiving an October surprise, the Lincoln administration had to engage in a coverup. Grant and Meade continued to downplay the ambitious goals of the offensive—Grant's Sixth—by referring to it as a reconnaissance. The secretary of war, who as a matter of custom reduced all Federal casualty figures by half before disclosing them to the press, also tried to keep a lid on the truth. But as the election neared, word of the disasters leaked out and the price of gold on the New York Stock Exchange rose.

Winfield Scott Hancock

Generals Grant and McClellan concurred in more than just their assessments of the importance of James River as an avenue of approach to Richmond. They also agreed in the esteem in which they held the military qualities of Major General Winfield Scott Hancock, whom McClellan termed "the Superb." During the Petersburg campaign, Hancock frequently functioned as a de facto army commander, exercising independent command several times.

A Pennsylvanian named after Dinwiddie County's Lieutenant General Winfield Scott, Hancock attended West Point and began the Civil War as a quartermaster in California. After journeying east, he received command of one of McClellan's brigades during the Peninsula campaign. By the battle of Fredericksburg, Hancock had risen to lead a division. After the Chancellorsville campaign, he received command of a corps.

At the battle of Gettysburg, Meade put Hancock in charge of a wing of the *Army of the Potomac*. On the late afternoon of 1 July, Hancock made the key decision regarding whether to fight the battle there while Meade remained in the rear and expedited the arrival of reinforcements. Wounded at Gettysburg in the hour of victory, Hancock did not return to the command of his corps until the following spring.

In the battle of the Wilderness, almost half of Grant's forces eventually came under Hancock's orders. In the Petersburg campaign, his authority often extended beyond his own corps. He was given command of all the Union forces before Petersburg for several hours on the morning of 16 June, until Meade arrived. Hancock led the three divisions of his own corps, a brigade from each of two other corps, and three cavalry divisions at the first battle of Deep Bottom in July. At the second battle of Deep Bottom in August, he led the three divisions of his own corps, two divisions of David Birney's corps and David Gregg's cavalry division. Later in August, Hancock commanded two divisions of his own corps, one division of Parke's corps and David Gregg's cavalry division at the second battle of Reams Station. During the battle of Burgess Mill in October, Hancock led two divisions of his own corps, one division of Warren's corps and David Gregg's cavalry division.

Caution and lack of initiative characterized Hancock's performance at Petersburg. His caution sometimes worked to his advantage. At the battle of Burgess Mill on 27 October, the care he took to properly picket his right helped his command avoid the kind of disaster that had befallen Warren's corps on 19 August. On the other hand, Hancock's reluctance to take big chances ruled out decisive results. Though the bold Grant wanted Hancock to cut loose from the Deep Bottom bridgehead and drive for Richmond and the Virginia Central Railroad in his July and August expeditions to the Peninsula, Hancock on both occasions insisted on forming a continuous line behind Bailey's Creek and each time got little closer than that to the capital or the railway.

On the one occasion when he relaxed his guard, catastrophe ensued. Despite the attack of Hampton's cavalry on 23 August, Hancock allowed 24 August to pass without having Gibbon's tired soldiers properly complete the earthworks at Reams Station begun by the *VI Corps* in June. On 25 August, it became apparent that the position had needed another 30 yards of slashing more than Gibbon's men needed rest.

Hancock's only display of in-itiative during the entire campaign came during the night of 15 June, when he ordered the divisions of Gibbon and David Birney to advance against the points of opposition in their fronts. Though the orders were not executed until the following morning, Hancock failed to exploit the opening his men made in the Confederate line.

Despite his shortcomings, Hancock remained one of the most trusted of Grant's corps commanders. Unlike Warren, who also occasionally exercised independent command, Hancock never gave anyone the impression that he was looking for an excuse to depart from the orders of his superiors. And except for his lapse at Second Reams Station, he always executed those orders with exemplary technical competence.

A Democrat, Hancock had political ambitions that his captures of guns and colors at first and second battles of Deep Bottom advanced. But his disastrous defeat at the second battle of Reams Station wrecked whatever prospects he had as a dark horse candidate for the Democratic vice presidential nomination.

After Burgess Mill, Hancock left the *Army of the Potomac* to take a recruiting command in Harrisburg, Pennsylvania. He finished the war in charge of the Shenandoah Valley, which had become a quiet sector, and he remained in the postwar army.

In 1880, Hancock finally ran for president as the nominee of the Democratic Party. Despite the votes of many former Confederates, he lost narrowly to his Republican opponent, James A. Garfield.

Hancock died in 1886. His body still bore the scars of Gettysburg, but it was said that if his heart could have been examined, written on it would have been "Reams Station."

CHAPTER IX

The Apple Jack Raid

The decisive political event of the Civil War took place on 8 November 1864. Lincoln won reelection by the modest margin of 55 percent to 45 percent. The Southerners tried to steel themselves for four more years of hard war.

Ten days after the election and two days after Sherman departed Atlanta on his march to the sea, Lee received intelligence that Grant's men were preparing to move out with 12 days' rations. This signified another effort to turn the Confederate right, but of proportions greater than any previous attempt. Burke's Station, deep in Lee's right rear, seemed a possible Federal objective.

Lee consulted with Longstreet and Hampton about counterattacking such a Northern movement. Longstreet suggested cutting in between the Federals and their base of supplies at City Point. Lee accordingly planned to strike the Union left, but the intelligence of a move by Grant's force proved false.

By the end of November, Kershaw's Division had returned to Lee from the Shenandoah Valley. Grant responded by withdrawing some of the Union forces from the Valley. The first division of Horatio Wright's corps to leave the Shenandoah reached Petersburg on 6 December.

Grant finally launched another offensive on the following day. Command of the operation fell to Warren. His corps, reinforced by Mott's *II Corps* division and David Gregg's cavalry division, broke camp and headed south on the Jerusalem Plank Road. Warren's mission was to complete the

Soldiers participate in the election of 1864. The presidential election pitted Abraham Lincoln against the former commander of the Army of the Potomac, George Brinton McClellan. Though McClellan was still popular with the troops, the majority of them voted to return Lincoln to office.

destruction of the Weldon Railroad down to the bridges over the Meherrin River, a task which Grant's August offensive had failed to accomplish. The vanguard of the expedition camped near the Nottoway River that evening.

On the morning of 8 December, Warren's men marched through Sussex Court House with David Gregg's cavalry division in the lead. The Northerners reached the Weldon Railroad near Parham's Store, on the Halifax Road just south of where it and the Weldon Railroad, which ran parallel to it, crossed the Nottoway. The Federals brushed aside a few bands of Confederate cavalry and began tearing up the rails.

Early the next day, the Northerners passed through Jarratt's Station. David Gregg's cavalrymen remained in the lead. At 1000 that morning, at a creek just north of the Meherrin River, the Federals encountered significant resistance for the first time. The resistance came from the Confederate garrison at

Hicksford. David Gregg's troopers managed to cross the creek, but the enemy stiffened as the Federals neared the Meherrin River. Soldiers of the Army of Northern Virginia's Cavalry Corps barred the way.

Hampton had rushed Waring's Brigade of Matthew Butler's Division and Barringer's Brigade of Rooney Lee's Division into the path of the Northerners, whom Lee thought were bound for Weldon. Hampton's troops and the garrison of Hicksford halted the Federals at Belfield, just north of the vital bridges over the Meherrin River. Late in the afternoon, Warren received intelligence that Confederate infantry was bearing down on him. This news, along with deteriorating weather and dwindling rations, prompted Warren to issue orders for a retreat.

While Hampton's troopers and the Hicksford garrison battled Warren to a standstill, A.P. Hill's corps marched to their assistance. Hill's men had taken the Boydton Plank Road to Burgess Mill on 7 December. On the following day, they marched to Dinwiddie Court House and turned south on the Court House Road. Spending that night four miles south of Dinwiddie Court House, the foot soldiers crossed the Nottoway River into Greensville County on the Double Bridges, near Wyatt's Mill, on the afternoon of 9 December.

Meanwhile, the divisions of the Northern *VI Corps* and the Southern Second Corps continued to arrive at Petersburg from the Shenandoah Valley, and intelligence that Hill's corps was in pursuit of Warren had reached City Point. Grant ordered Miles' division of the *II Corps* to cross Rowanty Creek and see if Confederate weakness there could be exploited. Launched as Hill neared the Nottoway, Miles' probe met with such stiff resistance that Grant attempted no attack on Lee's right.

After crossing the Nottoway, Hill came to Fields Crossroads. One way led due east to Jarratt's Station. The other led southeast to Belfield. Mahone, who had grown up in adjacent Southampton County, urged Hill to let Mahone's Division take the road to Jarratt's Station and attempt to cut off the Federals while the rest of Hill's Corps went on to Belfield. The

Wade Hampton

Widely reputed to be the richest man in the South, Wade Hampton of South Carolina lacked military training and opposed secession. But once war broke out, he raised his own legion—a unit consisting of artillery, cavalry and infantry—and led it to Virginia. At the first battle of Manassas, he fought as an infantryman and distinguished himself as a combat leader. After he recovered from the wound suffered at that battle and had participated in the battle of Seven Pines, he was assigned to the cavalry and excelled as a brigadier and as a division commander.

The death of Jeb Stuart on 11 May 1864 left Hampton first in line for command of the Army of Northern Virginia's Cavalry Corps. But because Hampton lacked the formal military training provided by West Point, Lee hesitated to fill the vacancy. Hampton quickly removed any excuse for denying him the position. During the month of June, he gave a dazzling display of the initiative that made him among the most valuable of Lee's subordinates during the last year of the Civil War. The re-

sults were Confederate victories in the battle of Trevilian Station, the battle of Samaria Church and the first battle of Reams Station. In these battles and the movements leading up to them, Hampton demonstrated that he was not only capable of corps command, but of independent command. His tactics were as outstanding as his strategy and his infantry experience showed. Like Lieutenant General Nathan Bedford Forrest, but unlike Stuart, Hampton fought his men more as mounted infantry than as cavalry, dismounting them to go into battle.

On 11 August 1864, Lee officially appointed Hampton to Stuart's vacant position. Lee dispatched Hampton to Culpeper Court House with his Old Division and orders to take charge of the rest of the Confederate cavalry in Northern Virginia.

Grant's August offensive forced Hampton's recall while he was still on the way to Culpeper Court House. At the second battle of Deep Bottom on 18 August, Hampton again displayed his initiative. His plan to envelop and destroy the Federal right did not succeed, but the initiative he displayed on 24 and 25 August resulted in a major Confederate victory at the second battle of Reams Station.

In mid-September, Hampton planned and led the successful Beefsteak Raid. Later in the month, he helped fend off Grant's first thrust toward the South Side Railroad. In late October, Hampton provided the plan of battle that thwarted Grant's last attempt of 1864 to cut the South Side Railroad at Burgess Mill. Personal tragedy struck during that action when one of his sons was killed and another was seriously wounded. Hampton vowed that he would never have a son under his command again.

On 9 December, during the Apple Jack Raid, Hampton helped save the important bridge of the Weldon Railroad over the Meherrin River at Hicksford. That evening he prevailed upon A.P. Hill to adopt Mahone's plan to cut off the Federals, but Hill's failure to approve it when initially proposed by Mahone earlier that day gave the Northerners time to escape.

In late January of 1865, Lee reluctantly yielded to another of Hampton's initiatives. Hampton departed for South Carolina with two brigades of horseless cavalry as well as orders to recruit new mounts and oppose Sherman's advance. Lee expressed the desire that Hampton should return to Petersburg with the two brigades remounted in the spring, but developments in the Carolinas kept Hampton and his force engaged there until the war's end.

Command of the Cavalry Corps of the Army of Northern Virginia eventually passed to Lee's nephew, Fitzhugh Lee. With Hampton's departure, the type of disaster that befell the Confederates at the battle of Five Forks became possible. It is unthinkable that Hampton would have conducted himself like the Virginians Pickett and Fitzhugh Lee, who slipped away from their men in the face of the enemy, leaving none of their subordinates in charge—for that peculiar institution of the Old Dominion—a shadbake.

After the end of hostilities, Hampton's efforts to preserve his lands met with success. Before his death in 1902, he served two terms as governor of South Carolina and another two as United States senator.

One of the reasons for the demise of the Confederacy, Yankee rein-forcements. Troops such as these, who joined the Army of the Poto-mac outside Petersburg, swelled Federal ranks while the Confederates scrounged for manpower.

Southerners would then destroy Warren's isolated force. But Hill elected to take the least imaginative course and proceed to Belfield with both divisions.

The Confederate infantry halted that night at another crossroads about six miles from Belfield and six miles from Jarratt's Station. While their tired men tried to rest in the intensifying cold, Hill and Hampton conferred. The result of the conference was the reversal of Hill's decision of that afternoon and the belated adoption of a modified version of Mahone's suggestion. Hampton would follow Warren north while Hill attempted to cut the Northerners off by marching on Jarratt's Station.

That night the cold turned first to rain and then sleet. The sleeping soldiers of both sides awoke to find themselves buried in snow and ice. Hill's advance on Jarratt's Station came too late. Instead of starting from the town's outskirts, as they would have done if Mahone's counsel had prevailed on the previous afternoon, the Southern footsoldiers started from six miles away. They found only a rear guard at Jarratt's

Station. The main body of Federals had gotten a big head start.

Warren's retreat turned ugly. As they pillaged the countryside, the Northerners broke into reserves of Apple Jack that gave the raid its name. They became drunk and destructive. Confederate partisans lurking in the woods retaliated by murdering and mutilating Union stragglers. The Federals escalated the war of reprisal that begat reprisal by setting fire to every building they sighted, even the slave quarters.

Lee had wanted to respond to the Apple Jack Raid in accordance with the plan of the previous month for dealing with the falsely rumored raid on Burke's Station—by counterattacking the Federal left and thereby isolating the raiders. But he could not find a spot where the Northern left was vulnerable. As Warren retreated, Lee ordered Longstreet to reconnoiter on the Peninsula preparatory to an attack there. Longstreet advanced on the Peninsula, but he too failed to locate a site where he could strike with any likelihood of success.

Hill's Corps failed to overtake Warren, who recrossed the Nottoway on 11 December and met two divisions of Parke's *IX Corps* sent to rescue the raiders. The Weldon Railroad would resume running from Hicksford to Stony Creek by the following March, but another opportunity for the Confederates to cut off and capture a substantial Union force had slipped away.

As Hill's Corps returned to Petersburg and the Apple Jack Raid came to an end, Butler prepared an expedition to capture Fort Fisher and cut off Wilmington, the Confederacy's last major port. The expedition sailed from Virginia on 20 December. The Southern response was to take Hoke's Division from Lee and send it to Wilmington by rail. On 25 December, before many of Hoke's men had arrived, Butler's scheme of destroying Fort Fisher by exploding a bomb ship moored nearby had failed and the Federal expedition soon returned. No longer politically invulnerable because of an imminent election, Butler was relieved of his command by Grant.

Trench Raids and Picket Affairs

Complex trench networks developed during the Petersburg campaign, particularly just east of the city, where the combatants were separated by only a matter of yards. Each side typically had in advance of its main line rifle pits or an entrenched picket line. Videttes manning the advanced position provided the soldiers in the main line with warning of an enemy attack. Behind the rifle pits or entrenched picket line was the main line, a series of batteries and forts linked by an infantry parapet or trench. Wooden entanglements—abatis, fraises and chevaux-de-frises—stood in front of the main trenches and forts, which incorporated traverses to shield the defenders from enfilading fire and bomb-proofs to protect them from shell fragments. A maze of covered ways and communication trenches extended from the main line to secondary lines and the rear.

Frequent skirmishes took place on the picket lines, where the opposing sides were in closest contact with one another. Most were not part of any larger operation, but occurred between companies, battalions or regiments. Sometimes, though, these fights involved whole brigades and once in a while they even drew in entire divisions. They did not appreciably modify the lines, but they accounted for a substantial portion of the campaign's casualties. The biggest of these affairs took place in late 1864.

On 10 September, Mott's division of Hancock's corps seized part of the entrenched Confederate picket line in front of Fort Mahone, a Southern work known as "Fort Damnation," opposite Fort Sedgwick, called "Fort Hell," on the Jerusalem Plank Road. The Northerners took 83 prisoners and suffered 54 themselves.

Early in the month of October, Mahone learned from some Union deserters the procedure and schedule followed when one group of Federal pickets relieved another. At 2100 on 30 October, he put this knowledge to work to get a measure of revenge for the punishment his men had absorbed at the hands of Hancock's corps during the battle of Burgess Mill, three days earlier. Dressing the sharp-shooters of his division in blue, Mahone employed them to gobble up 230 pickets of Miles' division near Fort Sedgwick without the firing of a shot or the loss of a Confederate soldier. It was the most successful trench raid of the war.

In the early morning hours of 5 November, Wallace's Brigade of Johnson's Division rushed Gibbon's picket line near Fort Morton, which stood just north of the Baxter Road. The Confederates captured about 100 stunned Federals and began reversing the entrenched Northern picket line. But McAllister's brigade of Mott's division flanked the Southerners on the right and drove them back to their own lines. The Southerners in turn also lost about 100 men.

Another vicious trench fight took place on the night of 18 November. Pickett's Virginians seized part of the entrenched picket line on the Bermuda Hundred front from some green and unreliable Pennsylvanian units. By morning, Union counterattacks had recaptured the line. But the Northerners had lost about 100 men, the Confederates only a handful.

CHAPTER X

The Battle of Hatcher's Run

Christmas time in 1864 at Petersburg was for the Confederates a season of starvation balls, where guests pooled their viands in the hope of recapturing the variety and plenty of a pre-war repast. Shortly after the New Year, Sherman's movements began to have a direct influence on matters at the Cockade City. In response to a clamor for protection by South Carolina, Kershaw's Old Brigade of Kershaw's Division was dispatched there from Lee's command.

While this development took place, Grant launched another expedition against Fort Fisher. This time he sent Alfred Terry in command of the same portion of the *Army of the James* that Benjamin Butler had led against the fort in December. On 15 January 1865, assisted by the navy, Terry's men took Fort Fisher by storm. This closed the Confederacy's last major port and cut off Lee's command from supplies carried in by blockade runners.

About a week later, Fitzhugh Lee's Division of cavalry arrived on the Peninsula from the Shenandoah Valley. But on 27 January, Lee lost his figurative right arm. The destruction of the Weldon Railroad and the shortage of forage had such a terrible effect on Confederate horseflesh that almost half of the Southern cavalry now lacked mounts. To make a virtue of necessity, Lee yielded to a Hampton plan for Matthew Butler's Division to turn its horses over to Rooney Lee's Division and proceed to South Carolina, where new mounts were available and Sherman's forces were about to resume their advance. With the horseless cavalrymen went Hampton, who

Confederate works at Hatcher's Run.

had displayed more initiative during the Petersburg campaign than any of Lee's other subordinates. It was hoped that Butler's Division and Hampton would return to Lee's command in the spring.

At the very end of the month, a Confederate peace delegation conferred with Lincoln at Old Point Comfort. The Southerner envoys flattered themselves that they could reach a compromise with Lincoln. Very early in February, negotiations collapsed. Lincoln made it clear that he would accept nothing less than unconditional surrender.

During the peace negotiations, the Confederate Congress finally forced Davis to name a supreme commander. Davis named Lee, whose problems subsisting the Confederacy's largest army delayed his coming to grips with the deteriorating situation in the Carolinas.

On 5 February, Grant launched another offensive at Petersburg. Besides seeking to exploit any fall in Southern morale resulting from the collapse of peace talks, he also wanted to cut off wagon traffic on the Boydton Plank Road. The Federal *II Corps*, now under Humphreys, advanced the Northern line to Armstrong's Mill on the near bank of Hatcher's Run. On

Major General Andrew A. Humphreys led a division until he accepted the position of Meade's chief of staff shortly after the battle of Gettysburg. When W. S. Hancock gave up command of the II Corps because of his failing health, Humphreys replaced him.

Humphreys' left, Warren's corps advanced across the run and halfway to Dinwiddie Court House. The redoubtable David Gregg had resigned command of his cavalry division on the eve of the battle for personal reasons. Under lrvin Gregg, the division occupied Dinwiddie Court House but captured few wagons.

The Confederate reaction was anticipated by Humphreys. Calling up McAllister's brigade from Mott's division and Ramsey's brigade from Miles' division, Humphreys posted them on the right of Thomas Smyth's division. This would prevent the Confederates from cutting in between Smyth's division and the rest of the Federal forces—a repeat of their successful maneuver of 19 August, when Mahone nearly destroyed Warren's corps.

Humphreys guessed correctly. Receiving news of the Federal advance while at communion in St. Paul's Church in Petersburg that morning, Lee immediately ordered a counterattack. Late in the afternoon, Heth struck with Cooke's, MacRae's and McComb's Brigades. The attack fell at the right angle where Smyth's division joined McAllister's brigade,

Hatcher's Run

The following selection is taken from the diary of Private Bernard:

Thursday Feb 9 '65

Back at camp again after a very severe five days campaign beginning Sunday afternoon, ending yesterday afternoon. Monday evening our division led by Gen. Finnegan charged the enemy & drove them beautifully for more than a mile. The engagement took place in a body of woods on the right of Hatcher's Run & about 3-1/2 miles below Burgess Mill. The enemy had first attacked Pegram's division, turning it back, and had been in turn driven by Evans' division, which they then drove back & were driven just as we were put in line

of battle. We lost in our reg't 23 kd & wd. The kd were Billy Willson of our company, a good fellow & fine soldier, Geo. Spence of Co. H, a good soldier, Pattaway of Co K and Baughn of Co G. Among the wd were "Billy" Scott & Hamilton Martin of our company, both excellent soldiers, Lt. Ben Grasswit & Doncey Dunlop of Co C, Bob Eckles & Jackson Bishop of Co A. I myself received a slight scratch on the cheek, the position of my head only saving me from a dreadful wound or perhaps death. In company E several others were struck—David Meade, Thad Branch, Ben Peebles & Ello Daniel.

I hope to return to my friends as safe guard today.

*A line of **V Corps** Federals battles Rebel cavalry during the opening of Grant's first offensive of 1865 which began on 5 February.*

which had arrived in the nick of time. Three times the Confederates came howling out of the woods. Though some of Smyth's men wavered, McAllister's brigade fought off the Southerners. Evans' Division of Gordon's Corps arrived on Heth's left too late to participate in the attack.

Despite the departure of Butler's Division, lack of forage had forced the Confederates to disperse their cavalry. Stationed at Stony Creek, Rooney Lee's cavalrymen plodded north in response to the Federal advance. Rooney Lee's movement made Meade worry about his left rear. Meade ordered Warren and Irvin Gregg to withdraw to the Vaughan Road crossing of Hatcher's Run. The withdrawal took place during the early morning hours of 6 February.

Later that morning, Meade ordered Humphreys and Warren to advance westward and bring to battle any Confederates outside the Southern works. Humphreys complied with this order but encountered no Southerners in the open. Warren misinterpreted Meade's order and did nothing until noon, when Meade arrived in person and made his intent unmistakably clear. In response to Meade's instructions, Irvin Gregg's cavalrymen rode out on the Vaughan Road. Crawford's division, followed by two brigades of Ayres' division, took the Dabney Mill Road through the tangled underbrush toward Burgess Mill. Winthrop's brigade of Ayres' division, supporting the cavalry on the Vaughan Road, prepared to follow Crawford and the rest of Ayres' division. Charles Griffin's division remained in reserve near the crossing.

In front of the Federals stood John Pegram's Division of Gordon's Corps. This division extended all the way from the Dabney Mill Road to the Vaughan Road. Pegram's right, on the Vaughan Road, had no difficulty halting the advance of the Federal cavalry. The Southerners there kept up the pressure so well that Winthrop's brigade could not withdraw to join the rest of Ayres' division.

But on the Confederate left, the tide of battle surged back and forth. At first, Crawford's men forced the Southerners back from Dabney's Mill and its fort-like sawdust pile toward their works at the Crow house. Then Evans' Division arrived

City Point

Interdiction of Federal shipping on the James River could have been disastrous for the Northerners of the *Army of the James* and the *Army of the Potomac*. All of their supplies came up the river. City Point, Petersburg's deepwater port, became not only Grant's headquarters but his command's supply base and one of the world's busiest seaports.

Eight wharves handled up to 75 sailing ships, 40 steamboats and 100 barges a day. Thousands of soldiers and civilians unloaded the men, munitions and stores on those vessels. Mountains of crates and barrels rose and a small city developed that included a prison, a bakery with a capacity of 123,000 loaves a day and sutlers' shacks and huts where soldiers with the wherewithal could supplement their rations.

The Confederates were not oblivious to the effect that denying the James to Northern shipping would have on Union plans. Luckily for the Federals, the results of Southern designs and efforts were so negligible that they have scarcely left a mark on history. In late May of 1864, Beauregard wanted to storm Fort Powhatan and set up batteries there that would iso-

late Butler in Bermuda Hundred. But Davis withdrew the troops necessary for Beauregard to carry out the plan. During late June and early July, Lee prodded Ewell to take steps to deny the James to Federal vessels. July saw the height of Southern plans and efforts to this end.

On 11 July, Ewell finally got moving on a project to interdict Grant's supply line by placing torpedoes in the river. The operation immediately hit a snag because no boats were available. While the Southerners gathered boats, Ewell dispatched Cutshaw's Battalion of artillery to conduct a series of attacks on Northern supply vessels. On 14 July, the Confederate artillerists unlimbered at Wilcox's Landing and drove downriver two ascending Union merchantmen. On the following day, the Southern gunners put to flight the Federal gunboats near Deep Bottom. They repeated this achievement 24 hours later. By 17 July, the Confederates had finally gathered sufficient boats to deploy torpedoes in the James. But the project came to an abrupt end that day when a Federal gunboat captured the boats and their cargo.

Two days later, Major General Bushrod Johnson proposed detailing 1,000 men to chop down trees and float them down the James to interrupt Grant's supplies. Nothing ever came of this wild idea, which Johnson's superiors greeted with silence. They had something more conventional in mind. Lee and Ewell were contemplating the positioning and fortification of a heavy battery on the north bank of the river. Wilcox's Landing, which had high banks and dominated the deep channel, seemed the best location for the projected battery. But the first battle of Deep Bottom discouraged the Confederates from building fortifications below Bailey's Creek. On 11 August, a Confederate agent planted a time bomb in a lighter that blew up at City Point, showering Grant's headquarters with debris.

Just before the beginning of December's Apple Jack Raid, a force of Confederate sailors left Drewry's Bluff in another attempt to interfere with Federal shipping in the James. These Southerners carted torpedo boats around the Union left by way of Franklin in Southampton County. The Federals received intelligence of the approach of this force before it reached its put-in point at Smithfield, far downriver from City Point.

Grant and Rear Admiral David B. Porter prepared an ambush on 8 December, but the Confederate sailors got wind of it and hauled their boats back to Drewry's Bluff.

Later that month and for much of January, most of the Union fleet was absent from the James to support the expeditions of Butler and Alfred Terry against Fort Fisher. On the night of 23 January, the Confederate Navy tried to take advantage of this situation by having three Southern ironclads and their escorts attempt to descend the river. The Secessionist plan was to negotiate the obstructions, sink any opposing Union vessels and destroy the Federal supply dump at City Point by bombardment. But two of the ironclads and several escorts went aground. When a Federal land battery and a Union monitor shelled the Southern vessels, one of the escorts blew up, but the tide floated the other Confederate ships and they returned to Drewry's Bluff in the morning. The Southern vessels attempted to descend the river again on the following night, but they made even less progress toward their goal and returned to the base even more ignominiously.

on Pegram's left. The Confederates drove the Northerners back to the mill. There Warren deployed Ayres' two brigades and Pearson's brigade of Griffin's division on Crawford's left. The Federals forced the Confederates back again, killing Brigadier General John Pegram in the process.

Now came the final reversal of fortune. As Gordon's men retreated through the frigid wilderness, a gap developed between Pegram's and Evans' Divisions. Into the gap plunged another Confederate reinforcement, Mahone's Division, the crack outfit of Lee's command during the Petersburg campaign. With Mahone on leave, Brigadier General Joseph Finegan was in command. Finegan led Mahone's Division in a charge that routed the units of Warren's corps at Dabney's Mill and drove them back in the gathering darkness upon Wheaton's division of Horatio Wright's corps, near the Vaughan Road crossing of Hatcher's Run. The next day, Warren advanced with Crawford's division in a storm and drove the Confederate skirmishers back into their main works near the Crow house. But no general engagement developed in the execrable weather. The battle came to an end.

The Federals had extended their lines to Hatcher's Run, a good starting point for future operations against the Southern right. 1,539 Northerners were killed, wounded or missing as opposed to about 1,000 Confederates.

The Southerners also made progress as a result of the battle, though not of a strategic sort. The hardships endured by Lee's soldiers because of the miserable Confederate supply system prompted an outcry that resulted in the ouster of one of President Davis' favorites, Commissary General Lucius Northrop. Within a matter of weeks, the supply situation improved insofar as rations were concerned.

While this development took place, legislation was pending in the Southern Congress to accept slaves and free blacks into the ranks of the Confederate Army. Around 15 February, in the midst of these deliberations and a wave of desertions, the soldiers of the Army of Northern Virginia voted overwhelmingly, regiment by regiment, to adopt resolutions in support of the legislation.

As the end of the month approached, Lee began to take steps to oppose Sherman's advance more effectively. The Southern general-in-chief relieved the ailing Beauregard of command of Confederate forces in North and South Carolina. To take Beauregard's place, Lee recalled Johnston to duty.

CHAPTER XI

The Battle of Fort Stedman

*T*he beginning of the end for the Confederates at Petersburg began with another of Grant's swipes at their supply lines. On 27 February 1865, Sheridan rode out from Winchester with two cavalry divisions. He had orders from Grant to break the Virginia Central Railroad at Staunton, continue down the Shenandoah Valley, cross the Blue Ridge and capture Lynchburg. There Sheridan would break up the South Side Railroad. Afterward, he would continue on down into North Carolina, where he would rendezvous with Sherman.

Sheridan's force reached Staunton on 28 February. Finding that Early and a small Confederate force occupied Waynesborough, 14 miles east on the Virginia Central, Sheridan made a fateful decision. He would depart from Grant's orders, complete Early's destruction and accomplish the wrecking of the Virginia Central that he and "Black Dave" Hunter had failed to effect the previous June. Then Sheridan would join Grant's forces on the Peninsula.

On 2 March, Sheridan's troopers smashed Early's command at Waynesborough. The Federals then began systematically destroying the Virginia Central. When they got to Charlottesville, they began ripping up the Orange & Alexandria Railroad in the direction of Lynchburg while continuing to wreck the Virginia Central toward Gordonsville. For good measure, they also destroyed the James River Canal from New Market to Goochland Court House. When Sheridan had finished wreaking havoc on Richmond's supply lines to the west, he bypassed the city at a respectful distance and headed

Desperation and Desertion

The following selection is taken from the diary of Private Bernard:

Monday Night, March 20 '65

On picket yesterday & last night; had quite a dull time; all intercourse with the enemy prohibited. Heard during night shots fired at deserters—the first early in the night & the last between 1 & 3 o'clock. This firing at deserters, a thing of nightly occurrence. A few minutes ago I heard as many as eight or ten shots fired, apparently on our brigade picket line. Night before last, it is said, one deserting "Gopher" (Floridan) was killed & another captured by an officer who stationed himself outside of the picket lines & laid in wait for them. This is the first instance of killing or capturing deserters going from the picket line of which I have heard for several months.

Heard musketry & a little artillery on the lines across the James this morning about 10-1/2 o'clock. Heard much artillery firing for about 2 hours this afternoon apparently at Petersburg. Rumor says Johnson has whipped Sherman near Raleigh N.C.

I expect a fifteen day furlough tomorrow.

Private Bernard's furlough came two days later. Before it ended, the Confederates had abandoned Petersburg and Richmond. Despite his best efforts, Private Bernard was unable to make it from his father's home in Orange County back to the Army of Northern Virginia before it surrendered. He contemplated joining Johnston's army in North Carolina, but sought a parole after that army surrendered. In a few weeks, he resumed the practice of law in Petersburg. Eventually he was elected Petersburg's Commonwealth Attorney.

After the War's end, Petersburg's former Confederate soldiers established the A. P. Hill Camp, United Confederate Veterans. Bernard became a member. The Southern Historical Society published several of his addresses and some by other members of the camp. In 1892, A. P. Hill Camp authorized Bernard to compile and edit some of these addresses as a book entitled *War Talks Of Confederate Veterans.*

Bernard continued to write and publish about the War. At the time of his death in 1911, he was at work on an edition of his war reminiscences that he intended to call *Musket & Cartridge Box.*

The flamboyant Confederate John Gordon had seen action in some of the greatest battles of the war including Antietam, Gettysburg and the Wilderness. When he surrendered at Appomattox, he was a major general and corps commander.

for White House Landing with the Confederate cavalrymen of Rosser's Division dogging his tracks.

On 13 March, while Sheridan's troopers rode toward White House Landing, the Virginia Legislature passed a law to admit free blacks and slaves into the army. Recruitment began at once.

Two days later, Sherman drove off a small Confederate force at Averasboro, North Carolina. On 19 March, the same day as Sheridan's cavalrymen reached White House Landing, half of Sherman's command withstood the ravaged might of Johnston's entire army at the battle of Bentonville. Sherman moved on from Bentonville and encamped at Goldsboro on 21 March. There he united with Major General John M. Schofield's *Army of the Ohio*, which had advanced inland from Wilmington and New Berne.

Davis and Lee realized that the Confederates must abandon Petersburg and Richmond and retreat into the hinterland before Grant and Sherman united and surrounded or overwhelmed Lee's command. Lee had known since childhood that Tidewater Virginia was ultimately indefensible against an enemy who had command of the sea. This had been impressed on him by his father, a Revolutionary War hero. Only a shift in the command of the sea brought about by European intervention had made possible the successful siege of Yorktown in 1781. But as of early 1865, no European power had intervened on behalf of the South. And the Confederacy's attempts to interfere with Federal shipping on the James River had been ineffective.

Lee's command would have to abandon Petersburg and Richmond when Sherman crossed the Roanoke (Staunton) River. That day was not far off, because Johnston's dwindling army could not even be relied upon to slow Sherman down anymore. But Lee did not want to abandon Petersburg and Richmond before the roads dried. His ravaged horseflesh would need every advantage in order for his army to escape Grant's clutches and unite with Johnston in North Carolina. Lee therefore considered a number of schemes for buying time.

The plan he adopted originated with Gordon, who proposed an assault on Fort Stedman, about a mile south of the Appomattox River. As the operation evolved, the attackers came to include Pickett's Division, two brigades of Johnson's Division, two brigades of Cadmus Wilcox's Division, all of Gordon's Corps except for a skirmish line left to hold its works southwest of Petersburg, and Rooney Lee's Division of cavalry. The operation would begin shortly after midnight on 25 March. Confederate infantry would storm Fort Stedman, then roll up the Union line to the right and left. Three specially selected combat teams would penetrate into the Federal rear and seize Battery No. 4, Fort Friend and the Dunn House Battery in the second Federal line, which consisted of turned Confederate works. Rooney Lee's cavalrymen would pound through this breach toward City Point. At the very least, the Confederates hoped to force Grant to withdraw his left. This would facilitate their retreat to North Carolina. If all went according to plan, they might cut the *Army of the Potomac*

Sites of the battle for Fort Stedman in a sketch made in 1886.
Above is Fort Haskell from Gracie's Salient. In the bottom picture,
Fort Stedman was located in front of the clump of trees. When Gor-
don launched his attack, his troops moved over the ground on the
left.

off from the James River, destroy the huge depot at City Point and capture Grant.

While the Southerners prepared to attack Fort Stedman, Grant came to the conclusion that he must attempt to destroy Lee's forces without waiting for Sherman to arrive in Virginia. Everyday Grant feared that he would wake up the following morning to find Lee and his command gone from the siege lines and hastening toward Johnston in North Carolina.

On 24 March, as Sheridan's troopers entered Federal lines on the Peninsula, Grant issued instructions for the offensive that the imminent Confederate assault on Fort Stedman was intended to delay. He ordered a movement against Lee's right to begin five days later.

That night, as a preliminary to the operation, Ord pulled three Union divisions out of the Bermuda Hundred and Peninsula lines. The Federals in these units withdrew so quietly that their absence went unnoticed by the Southerners opposite them. Grant planned to employ this force Southside.

Confederates of Gordon's Corps tear through abatis in their charge against Fort Stedman. The attack was a desperate gamble to force Grant to retract his left and allow the Army of Northern Virginia to join Joseph E. Johnston's army in North Carolina.

Meanwhile, problems with the arrival of supporting and exploiting troops delayed the Confederate attack on Fort Stedman. It was after 0400 on 25 March when Gordon finally gave the order to advance. The initial onslaught was successful. Gordon's and Johnson's infantry pierced the Union line on both sides of Fort Stedman and took the fort from behind. Within minutes, the Southerners had possession of the Northern trenches from Battery X to Battery XII. They even captured a Federal brigadier during an unsuccessful counterattack.

Then luck ran out for Gordon. Battery No. IX on the breach's northern shoulder held. So did Fort Haskell on the southern shoulder. Many Confederates fell out to plunder captured bombproofs and camps. Darkness, rolling terrain and the presence of the reserves of Parke's *IX Corps* hindered penetration by Gordon's special combat teams. The only special guides to approach their goal were blasted by the Union artillery in Fort Friend. By daybreak, the attack had stalled. Lee and Gordon knew they must withdraw. They

Union troops bring Confederate prisoners into camp. Thousands of Confederates were captured during the final battles of the war.

refrained from committing the two brigades of Cadmus Wilcox's Division

Brigadier General John Hartranft, whose division was in reserve near the southern shoulder of the penetration, took charge of the Federal counterattack. Artillery from the reserve of Parke's corps unlimbered on the high ground between the breach and Meade's Station on the Military Railroad. These cannon and those in Fort McGilvery, Battery IX, Battery No. 4, Fort Friend and Fort Haskell laid down a devastating fire. The Confederates had interposed between Meade and his *Army of the Potomac*, which left Parke in command as senior corps commander. Parke ordered up reinforcements from Warren's and Horatio Wright's corps, but Hartranft had mopped up the last pockets of Confederate resistance by 0830, before the reinforcements arrived. The parade of Confederate prisoners elated President Lincoln, who had arrived at City Point from Washington the previous evening.

To make matters worse for Lee, the Federals responded by attacking the far Confederate right on the supposition that Lee had weakened it to provide forces for the attack on Fort

Stedman. Humphreys and Wright seized much of the entrenched Confederate picket line southwest of Petersburg, but found the main line still well manned. Humphreys' corps abandoned its gains, but Southern counterattacks failed to budge Wright's corps.

Pickett's Division had such difficulty with rail transportation that only three of its four brigades departed the Peninsula, and they did not arrive until midday. Rooney Lee's cavalrymen also arrived too late to take part in Gordon's attack.

The battle of Fort Stedman was a disaster for Lee's command. Lee had lost irreplaceable men and, on the right, irreplaceable ground. Confederate casualties numbered about 4,000. The Federals lost 2,087 killed, wounded and missing. The Northerners, who captured many flags, noted the refusal to fight of many Southern enlisted men.

Confederate Desertion

Every year, during the winter, Southern soldiers deserted from the Army of Northern Virginia in droves. With bitter cold in Virginia and Sherman moving north through the Carolinas, the winter of 1864-1865 saw a heavier run of deserters than usual.

The floodgates opened after the battle of Hatcher's Run. On many nights between mid-February and the end of March, Grant's command received more than 100 Southern deserters. According to Confederate records, 2,934 Southern soldiers deserted from 15 February 1865 to 18 March 1865. Northern records show that 1,767 of these Confederates deserted to the enemy. Subtracting that 1,767 from the grand total of deserters gives the number of Southern deserters who presumably just went home.

Complete Union records survive of the number of Confederate deserters to the enemy from 9 February 1865 to 28 March 1865: 2,213 Southerners deserted to the enemy during this period. No record exists of the total number of Southern deserters from 9 February 1865 to 28 March 1865. Assuming the same proportion of Confederate deserters went home during this period as during the shorter period from 15 February 1865 to 18 March 1865 yields 1,455 as the number of Southern deserters who just went home. Lee's command probably lost about 3,600 soldiers to desertion from 9 February 1865 to 28 March 1865.

But that year's great wave of desertion began during the night of 9-10 January. It ended on 28 March the day before the spring campaign began. Assuming that Southerners deserted to the enemy or to their homes in the same proportions as during the period from 15 February 1865 to 18 March 1865, gives 92 as the average number who deserted each day. Multiplied by the days from 10 January to 28 March yields 7,259 as the number of Confederates in that period. Based on the figures from 9 February 1865 to 28 March 1865, the average number of those who deserted each day is 76. This yields 5,928 as the number of Southern deserters between 10 January and 28 March.

Lee's army thus lost at least a division and a half to desertion between 10 January 1865 and the opening of the spring campaign. On top of this, a brigade of infantry and two brigades of cavalry were sent to South Carolina during the month of January. The Confederates at

Petersburg also lost about a brigade in combat in February's battle of Hatcher's Run, a division in combat on 25 March and another division in combat on 31 March and 1 April.

The Southerners were scarcely able to man their lines on 2 April, when they lost at least another division and a half.

No wonder the Federals made such short work of Lee's command on the retreat to Appomattox. Lee's command had lost at least 40 percent of its strength— about six divisions, or 25,000 men—to desertion, combat, and transfer between 10 January 1865 and 2 April 1865.

Confederate Desertion to the Enemy													
9 February-28 March 1865													
9-28 February	AL	AR	FL	GA	LA	MD	MS	NC	SC	TN	TX	VA	?	Total
AOJ	17			54			3	22	6		1	210	18	331
AOP	67		52	44	18	3	38	334	167	17		74	3	807
Total	84		52	98	18	3	41	356	173	17	1	284	21	1,148
1-28 March	AL	AR	FL	GA	LA	MD	MS	NC	SC	TN	TX	VA	?	Total
AOJ	21		51	66	1		23	32	61			83	15	353
AOP	34		21	41	16		29	413	48	12		63	35	712
Total	55		72	107	17		52	445	109	12		146	50	1,065
Grand Total	AL	AR	FL	GA	LA	MD	MS	NC	SC	TN	TX	VA	?	Total
	139	0	124	205	35	3	93	801	282	29	1	430	71	2,213
AOJ = Army of the James							AOP = Army of the Potomac							

CHAPTER XII

Five Forks and the Fall of Petersburg

On 27 March 1865, as Sheridan's cavalry finished crossing from the Peninsula to the Southside, Sherman arrived at City Point by steamer and conferred with Grant and Lincoln. The Northern president and his two leading generals discussed the final campaign against Lee's command. Apprised of the offensive that Grant intended to launch on 29 March, Sherman declared that he would be ready to move out from Goldsboro by 10 April.

The conference convinced Grant that he must attempt to take Petersburg and Richmond with his own command immediately. The date when Sherman would be ready to march against Lee, 10 April, would not be soon enough. Nor was Grant willing any longer to wait until 29 March to launch the drive on the Confederate right that he hoped would pry the Southerners from their capital. He moved up the starting time for his Ninth Offensive of the Petersburg campaign to the very evening of his conference with Lincoln and Sherman.

Like Grant's First Offensive of the campaign, this one began with a crossing of the James River. The three divisions that Ord had pulled out of line on the Peninsula a few days earlier now set out on a night march to the Southside. Longstreet remained unaware that they were gone.

Meanwhile, Sheridan's crossing of the James River on the previous day had not gone unnoticed by the Confederates. Lee believed that Sheridan's destination was the South Side

Railroad. To defend this railroad, Lee on 28 March issued orders for his cavalry to concentrate at Five Forks. Fitzhugh Lee's Division rode out that day for Five Forks from its position on the Nine Mile Road, east of Richmond. This left Longstreet with only Gary's Brigade to reconnoiter on the Peninsula and made it even more difficult for the Southerners to detect the absence of the three divisions with Ord.

That evening, Ord and his three divisions arrived behind Humphreys' corps on the Southside. This gave Grant a concentration of force that he had not achieved in any of his previous offensives. That same evening, the *Army of the James'* *Cavalry Division*—now under Brigadier General Ranald MacKenzie, who had replaced Kautz when that officer took command of one of Weitzel's infantry divisions—also departed the Peninsula for the Southside. MacKenzie's cavalry division arrived at daybreak on 29 March. Shortly afterward, Ord's force relieved Humphreys' corps in the trenches. The next step of Grant's plan then got under way.

At this point, the plan called for Grant's left to make a grand right wheel in the Southside. Parke's corps held the Northern right, to the lower Appomattox. Then came Wright's corps and Ord's force, which extended all the way to Hatcher's Run. These units would form the pivot for Grant's left. Humphreys' corps would be the innermost performing the right wheel. It would cross Hatcher's Run on the Vaughan Road and close up with the Confederate works at Burgess Mill. To the left of Humphreys, Warren's corps would cross Rowanty Creek at Monk's Neck Bridge and guard Humphreys' left by taking position at the junction of the Vaughan and Quaker Roads. At the extreme left of the Federal line, Sheridan and three cavalry divisions—the two that he had brought from the Shenandoah Valley plus David Gregg's old division, now under Major General George Crook—would cross Rowanty Creek at Malone's Bridge and proceed to Dinwiddie Court House, where the horse soldiers would menace Lee's communications.

Grant's plan was flexible. It gave him two main options. First, he could cut loose for Burke's Station, the crossover of

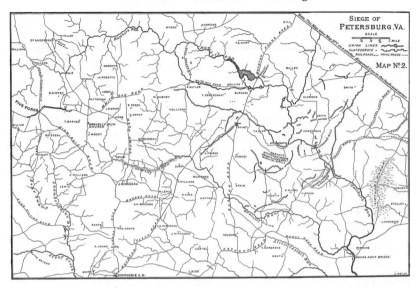

the Richmond & Danville Railroad and the South Side Railroad. The notion of such a movement had circulated since first put forth by Warren the previous June. This would involve taking everyone to the left of Parke, leaving Parke to hold the Union army's entrenched camp Southside and Weitzel to hold Bermuda Hundred and the Peninsula trenches. Alternatively, Grant could refrain from cutting loose for Burke's Station and just work his way around the Confederate right. Sheridan could lead the way or he could cut loose with the cavalry, raid Lee's railroad communications and join up with Sherman in North Carolina.

The first day's advance went relatively smoothly. Humphreys encountered no major difficulty. Farther to the west, Griffin's division of Warren's corps drove back Johnson's Division in a skirmish on the Lewis farm near the junction of the Quaker and Boydton Plank Roads. Out on the end of the Northern line, Sheridan's cavalrymen were unopposed by anything stronger than Southern cavalry videttes. Sheridan reached Dinwiddie Court House at 1700. But he had to leave Custer's division seven miles behind to protect the wagons, mired in the muddy roads west of Monk's Neck Bridge. This was a precaution against an attack by Rooney Lee's Division, which Sheridan had detected on his left. Rooney Lee was en route from his post at Stony Creek to Five Forks pursuant to General Lee's orders of the previous day. Rosser's Division, which had taken position on the Nottoway River, accompanied Rooney Lee.

As Sheridan neared Dinwiddie Court House, Fitzhugh Lee's Division passed through Petersburg. General Lee ordered Fitzhugh Lee to take charge of the Army of Northern Virginia's Cavalry Corps. His division reached Sutherland Station near sunset. Rooney Lee's and Rosser's Divisions did not arrive there that day because of the length of their detour west of Dinwiddie Court House.

The crossing of Rowanty Creek by the Federals moved Lee to shift McGowan's Brigade to the far side of Hatcher's Run and concentrate at the South Side Railroad Station the three brigades of Pickett's Division at Petersburg. From there, the decrepit cars of the railroad carried Pickett's men to Sutherland Station, 10 miles west of the Cockade City. The last cars did not arrive until late at night.

To provide a new reserve, Lee shifted Hunton's Brigade of Pickett's Division to Manchester from the Williamsburg Road on the Peninsula. Lee considered shifting more men Southside, but Longstreet remained unaware of Ord's departure. By the end of the day, Hunton's orders were to proceed to Petersburg by way of Richmond. Lee shifted William Pegram's Battalion of artillery to Burgess Mill.

The events of 29 March convinced Grant to forego a raid on the railroads. He directed Sheridan to advance into the right rear of the Confederates. Sheridan ordered Devin's division to Five Forks. Meade instructed Humphreys and Warren to extend their lines westward for a linkup with Sheridan.

On the rainy morning of 30 March, Lee resumed shifting his forces to his right. Fitzhugh Lee's Division proceeded to Five Forks, where it fended off Devin's advance. General Lee reinforced Pickett with Wallace's and Ransom's Brigades of Johnson's Division, both mauled at Fort Stedman, and dispatched Pickett's force to Five Forks with orders to retake Dinwiddie Court House. To make up for the departure of

Johnson's brigades, Cadmus Wilcox's Division and Gordon's Corps extended to their right.

Pickett's five brigades of infantry rendezvoused with Fitz-hugh Lee's Division at Five Forks late in the afternoon. Sheridan soon detected the presence of Southern infantry. Rooney Lee's and Rosser's Divisions arrived at Five Forks that evening. While the Confederates deployed, the Federals stumbled sluggishly in the mud. Humphreys advanced to the Confederate main line, but Warren failed to extend to his left and link up with Sheridan, who failed to take Five Forks.

Giving up on the Burgess Mill area, Grant fidgeted. First he ordered an assault on the Petersburg defenses for the following morning. At the same time, he offered to send Sheridan Warren's corps to turn Lee's right. Later, Grant canceled the orders for the assault and resolved to pursue the turning operation.

That night, Sheridan sent Grant word of the presence of Pickett's infantry at Five Forks. This meant that Sheridan would be unable to link up with Warren's left. Grant asked Meade to inform Warren of this, but Meade omitted to do so. Early on the morning of 31 March, Sheridan received Grant's offer of Warren's corps. Sheridan replied that he would prefer to have the assistance of Horatio Wright's corps, which had fought under him in the Shenandoah Valley.

Pickett entrenched at Five Forks while also preparing to turn Sheridan's left. Early that morning, with Rosser's and Rooney Lee's Divisions preceding the infantry, Pickett marched south along the Scott Road with Chamberlain's Bed to the east. Fitzhugh Lee's Division, under Colonel Thomas Munford, remained in front of Five Forks with orders to make a frontal attack when Pickett's guns were heard on the Federal left. At Little Five Forks, Pickett's column turned south on to the Ford Station Road. The infantry would cross Chamberlain's Bed at Danse's Ford. The cavalry would cross at Fitzgerald's Ford, downstream. Pickett's command would envelop and rout Sheridan and recapture Dinwiddie Court House.

Unfortunately for the Confederates, Southerners captured

by Sheridan's patrols betrayed Pickett's plan. To guard the Federal left, Sheridan committed the division of George Crook: Davies' brigade took position behind Danse's ford, Charles Smith's brigade held a post behind Fitzgerald's ford a mile south, and Irvin Gregg's brigade remained in reserve at the junction of the Adams and Brooks Roads. To the north, Fitzhugh's brigade of Devin's division held its position in front of Five Forks. Farther east, Stagg's brigade occupied the Crump Road. Gibbs' brigade stood at the fork of the two roads.

The Federal cavalry awaited Pickett's onslaught. At 1000, the ball opened. Rooney Lee's Division, at the head of Fitzhugh Lee's force of Southern cavalry, drove in the pickets of Smith's brigade guarding Fitzgerald's ford. Smith reinforced his picket line, but the Confederates hurled the Northerners back across Chamberlain's Bed. The dismounted North Carolinians of Barringer's Brigade and a mounted squadron of Virginians from Chambliss' Brigade then attacked across the swollen creek. Smith's reserves struck the Southerners and pushed them back in turn with heavy losses. The fighting here died down to desultory skirmishing, as it did in front of Five Forks, where Munford's division had attacked Fitzhugh's brigade at the sound of Rooney Lee's guns.

Farther east, Humphreys' corps had shifted to its left and relieved Griffin's division of Warren's corps. The roads were so bad that Meade feared that neither of these corps could be supplied with rations. It seemed there would be no movement of troops that day. All Northern efforts were going into resupply.

Ayres' division of Warren's corps had advanced to a position where it threatened to cut the White Oak Road beyond the return west of the Claiborne Road. Lee determined to prevent this by attacking the exposed Federal left, unguarded by Sheridan's forces because of the Confederate infantry threatening him. Johnson would undertake to attack with three brigades from three different divisions. He formed line of battle with Stansel's Brigade of his own division on the right and Hunton's Brigade of Pickett's Division on the left.

McGowan's Brigade of Cadmus Wilcox's Division moved out of the works and shifted toward the right of Stansel's Brigade.

Warren precipitated a battle by sending Ayres forward at 1030, while Sheridan repelled Rooney Lee's attack. At 1100, as Winthrop's brigade of Ayres' division reached the White Oak Road, Hunton's and Stansel's Brigades struck. McGowan's Brigade, not yet in position, joined in the assault.

The Southerners crumpled up Winthrop's brigade as quickly as Davis' and Walker's Brigades had crumpled up Hayes' brigade on 18 August. Winthrop's men briefly rallied on Gwyn's brigade, to their right, only to give way again. Hunton's Virginians hit Gwyn's now exposed left and forced him back. McGowan's Brigade was momentarily checked by the *Maryland Brigade* on Winthrop's left but soon drove the Marylanders back through Coulter's brigade of Crawford's division as it went to the support of the *Maryland Brigade*. Outflanked on the left by McGowan's Brigade, Coulter's brigade also collapsed.

The two remaining brigades of Crawford's division were thrown into confusion by Ayres' fugitives. These brigades—Baxter's and Kellogg's—deployed with a gap between them. Stansel's Alabamians turned Baxter's left and McGowan's South Carolinians turned Kellogg's right. Crawford's line collapsed. Three Southern brigades were driving twice their numbers of Northern brigades back across a branch of Gravelly Run toward the Boydton Plank Road. The routed Federals rallied behind and to the right of Charles Griffin's division, which had formed line behind the run when heavy musketry became audible. Griffin's men and the corps artillery drove back Confederate skirmishers.

Warren asked Humphreys, to his right, to make a diversion to take pressure off the *V Corps*. Humphreys ordered Miles' division to advance with two of its brigades about 1230. Ramsey's and Madill's brigades crossed Gravelly Run. Several hundred yards beyond, near the crest of a ridge, the Federals engaged Wise's Virginia Brigade. Lee had ordered this unit to advance and protect Hunton's left. Ramsey's brigade, in the lead, initially suffered a repulse. So did part of

Scott's brigade which clumsily probed a section of rifle pits west of the Boydton Plank Road that Miles thought empty. Miles tried again. Sending Ramsey's brigade back across the run to pin down Wise's Virginians, Miles used Madill's brigade to turn Wise's left. The maneuver worked. Wise's brigade collapsed. Some 100 prisoners and a flag were taken. Nugent's brigade mopped up.

The collapse of Wise's Brigade forced Stansel's and Hunton's Brigades to shift to their left. Johnson and, his immediate superior, Richard Anderson quickly realized that the line behind Gravelly Run was untenable for their exhausted soldiers. They authorized a withdrawal to a line of works that Ayres' men had erected south of White Oak Road the previous evening. The absence of fresh troops influenced Johnson and Anderson in this decision. Ord's crossing of the James paid its first dividend.

Warren prepared to advance with Charles Griffin's division and recover the ground lost by his corps. The advance was set for 1345, but at that time Warren failed to move. Not until 1430, with Miles' division advancing on its right and the rest of Humphreys' corps reconnoitering still farther to the east, did Charles Griffin's division of Warren's corps advance. By 1530, it had driven the Confederates from the captured works and back into the fortifications at the junction of the Claiborne and White Oak Roads. The Federals had severed Lee's direct line of communications with Pickett.

At 1430, unaware that the Northern infantry was beginning its final push to the White Oak Road but elated by the repulse of the Confederate cavalry that morning, Sheridan prepared to order Devin's division to advance on Five Forks, thinking that it was still occupied by Pickett's infantry. The Northern cavalry leader was soon unpleasantly surprised when that infantry appeared on his left flank.

The firing at Fitzgerald's ford that morning had drawn toward it most of Davies' brigade, which had been guarding apparently unthreatened Danse's ford. This force was heading back to its original position as Sheridan prepared to advance on Five Forks. But before the balance of Davies' brigade arrived and before a Northern advance on Five Forks began, Corse's Brigade of Pickett's Division drove in the pickets of the lone Federal battalion left to guard Danse's ford. The battalion's main body, strongly posted, repulsed the first Confederate advance. But Corse's Virginians quickly outflanked the battalion and put it to flight. Only then did the rest of Davies' brigade arrive. It was too late. Corse's men smashed the head of the column and the rallying battalion from the ford. Davies' brigade fell back to the Adams Road and the rest of Pickett's infantry forded Chamberlain's Bed.

As Pickett's soldiers surged east, Federal reinforcements came to the assistance of Davies' brigade. Devin sent first a regiment from Stagg's brigade, which now occupied the J. Boisseau farm except for a small detachment still on the Crump Road. Personally accompanying the regiment, Devin found a precarious situation. He ordered Fitzhugh's brigade to leave a single regiment to hold the Dinwiddie Road and assist Davies' brigade on the Danse's Ford Road. Fitzhugh's brigade formed line near the Williams' house. Davies' brigade passed through Fitzhugh's men on its way to the J. Boisseau farm to reform, as did the regiment from Stagg's brigade. Fitzhugh's soldiers repulsed an attack by Corse's Brigade at 1430. Back on the Dinwiddie Road, though, Morgan's Brigade of Munford's command overwhelmed the weakened force from Fitzhugh's brigade remaining there. Munford's men headed into the right rear of the balance of Fitzhugh's brigade.

Pickett committed William Terry's Brigade on Corse's right. Overlapped on both flanks, Devin ordered Fitzhugh's brigade to retreat and called up the main body of Stagg's brigade. Fitzhugh's troopers withdrew a short distance to the east. Stagg's brigade took position on Fitzhugh's left, but Pickett's infantry put Stagg's brigade to flight and Munford's cavalry drove off Fitzhugh's men. Stagg's and Fitzhugh's brigades then joined Davies' men on the J. Boisseau farm. Pickett had cut these Federals off from the direct route to the Northerners at Dinwiddie Court House, but Devin led the three brigades toward that destination by way of the Boydton Plank Road.

Munford's Confederate cavalry pursued. All of these units, except for Corse's and William Terry's Confederate Infantry Brigades were effectively out of the battle.

Sheridan deployed his remaining forces to defend Dinwiddie Court House if Pickett turned south or to strike Pickett's right if his infantry pursued the isolated brigades under Devin to the Boydton Plank Road. Gibbs' brigade took position at the junction of the Adams and Brooks Roads. Irvin Gregg's brigade, which like Davies' brigade had initially marched to the sound of the guns at Fitzgerald's ford, received orders to set up on Gibbs' left and strike the Confederates in their right rear if they proceeded toward the Boydton Plank Road. Custer was directed to bring up two of his brigades and leave the third to guard Sheridan's wagon trains.

At the junction of the Crump and Dinwiddie Roads, Pickett's soldiers ceased their pursuit of Devin's and Davies' fugitives. Turning southward, the Virginians collided with Gibbs' and Irvin Gregg's brigades. These two brigades held off Pickett's soldiers for two hours. Then the Southerners dislodged Gibbs' brigade, which made Irvin Gregg's position untenable. The Federals fell back from the Brooks Road line. Their retreat in turn rendered untenable the position of Charles Smith's brigade at Fitzgerald's ford. This outfit had held Fitzhugh Lee's two cavalry divisions at bay for more than three hours. At 1730, Smith's brigade joined the retreat toward Dinwiddie Court House. Fitzhugh Lee's forces pursued.

By this time, Custer had put his two brigades into line half a mile north of Dinwiddie Court House, supported by artillery. Pennington's brigade held the ground east of the Dinwiddie Road, and Capehart's brigade deployed west of the road. Irvin Gregg's and Gibbs' brigades passed through Custer's troopers while Smith's brigade took position on Capehart's left. Gregg's brigade then deployed on Pennington's right and Gibbs' brigade continued on its way to the rear.

Pickett's infantry arrived hot on the heels of the retreating

While Five Forks was a military victory for the Union, it also resulted in the destruction of Major General Gouverneur Warren's reputation. His name was cleared many years later by a court of inquiry after Warren had died.

Federals. The Confederate footsoldiers struck Pennington's brigade and forced it back to a crest, where Pennington's horse soldiers held. On the far left, Smith's brigade also gave way, but darkness put an end to the fighting. Both sides slept on their arms.

During the day's fighting, Grant's command had lost about 2,250 men, Lee's Confederates some 1,650. But the Northerners had clearly gained an advantage over the Southerners. They had cut the White Oak Road, Pickett's direct link with Lee. Even worse for the Confederates, Pickett had failed to recapture the key to their position—Dinwiddie Court House.

But a change for the better seemed imminent for the Confederates. As night fell, it appeared that Dinwiddie Court House would fall into Pickett's hands early the next day. Sheridan knew that his men could not hold it by themselves. He asked Grant for reinforcements, and Grant readily supplied them. At 2000, Warren's corps received instructions to withdraw from the White Oak Road to the Boydton Plank Road and send Charles Griffin's division to Sheridan. This would reopen Pickett's direct line of communication with

Burgess Mill, but Grant plainly considered it a lesser evil than the loss of Dinwiddie Court House.

Warren had already sent reinforcements to Sheridan pursuant to a suggestion from Meade. Hearing the sound of battle to the southwest receding, and inferring that the Confederates were forcing Sheridan back, Warren dispatched Bartlett's brigade of Griffin's division cross-country in the afternoon with orders to hit the Southerners in flank and rear. Bartlett's brigade reached Dr. Boisseau's farm as night ended the fighting. At 2200, Munford's scouts detected the presence of Bartlett's brigade at Dr. Boisseau's farm. Pickett decided to retreat in the face of this threat to his left.

Half an hour later, Grant ordered Warren's entire corps to Sheridan's assistance and notified Sheridan to expect Warren's force at midnight. But the destruction of the Boydton Plank Road's bridge over Gravelly Run delayed Warren's progress. So did haggling with Grant and Meade over the order of march and the route to be taken. Not until 0200 did the tired soldiers of Warren's corps begin crossing Gravelly Run, with Ayres' division in the lead.

The retreat of Pickett's force began soon afterward. His infantrymen slogged directly to Five Forks, with Munford's horsemen covering their rear. The rest of the cavalry recrossed Chamberlain's Bed and proceeded to Five Forks by way of Little Five Forks. Custer's division trailed Pickett's infantry column.

Pickett called for reinforcements and protection on his left. He wanted to retreat past Five Forks and beyond Hatcher's Run. But Lee ordered Pickett to hold Five Forks at all hazards. Its loss would allow the Northerners to cut all of Lee's remaining supply lines and his easiest line of retreat from Petersburg, due west on the Cox Road.

The presence of the Federals at Dinwiddie Court House threatened all the lines of retreat for Lee's command from the Petersburg-Richmond position. Lee knew he must prepare to withdraw from that position and he notified President Davis accordingly. The Union occupation of Dinwiddie Court

House also cut off the Southern cavalry from forage at Stony Creek Depot.

In obedience to Lee's orders, Pickett halted at Five Forks. He assumed that Lee would make a diversion in his favor and send him reinforcements. Pickett's infantry was posted behind the White Oak Road, with the three brigades of his own division on the right and the two brigades from Johnson's Division on the left. Ransom's Brigade of Johnson's Division held the extreme left, almost a half a mile west of the White Oak Road's junction with the Gravelly Run Church Road. The brigade took position with its left refused.

The infantry strengthened the earthworks commenced on 30 March. The artillery sought such fields of fire as existed in the flat pinelands. Rooney Lee's cavalrymen took up a position on the infantry's right. Munford's horsemen guarded the infantry's left. Roberts' Brigade picketed the now open White Oak Road from Munford's left to the right of the main Confederate position near the Claiborne Road. Rosser's Division went into reserve north of Hatcher's Run.

At Petersburg, a desperate Lee prepared to strike Grant if the opportunity arose. Lee ordered up reserve artillery to strengthen the thin lines that he contemplated thinning further. Early on the morning of 1 April, as these movements took place, Lee received intelligence for the first time of the presence of Ord's force in front of A.P. Hill, between Petersburg and Hatcher's Run. Lee immediately ordered Longstreet to attack to draw Federals back to the Peninsula. Longstreet also was given the option of sending reinforcements to Petersburg. Lee then proceeded to Anderson's headquarters near Burgess Mill. Longstreet did not think an attack would be effective in the presence of Northern gunboats. Instead, he sent out scouts to verify the intelligence of Ord's absence from the Peninsula. Lee ordered Longstreet to hasten troops to Petersburg if the scouts confirmed Ord's absence.

By 0900, Warren's corps had reached Sheridan. Ayres' division halted at J. Brooks' farm. Charles Griffin's and Crawford's divisions stopped farther north on the Crump Road, one-half mile south of J. Boisseau's farm. Ordered by

Meade to report in person to Sheridan, Warren had sent an aide instead and had remained with his corps to expedite its movement.

To reinforce the pursuit of Pickett's command, Sheridan called up the third brigade of Custer's division from its position guarding the supply train at the junction of the Vaughan and Monk's Neck Roads. Merritt was put in overall command of the pursuit and was assigned Devin's division as well. Capehart's and Pennington's brigades of Custer's division soon reached the Confederate position at Five Forks. The Southerners repelled Custer's initial probes. Devin's division advanced up the Dinwiddie Road and took position on Custer's right, but also found the Confederate works too strong to carry. The Federal cavalrymen erected their own breastworks in the woods to the south of the White Oak Road.

Wells' brigade of Custer's division reached Dinwiddie Court House with Sheridan's wagon train at 1100. Crook's division assumed the task of guarding the wagons except for Irvin Gregg's brigade, which took possession of Little Five Forks to prevent a repetition of the previous day's Confederate flank attack. Mackenzie's division also reached Dinwiddie Court House that morning. In the saddle since 0330, Mackenzie's men required rest.

By noon, Sheridan had formed his battle plan. He had to attack because a resumption of the recent rains could hinder the forwarding of supplies so much that he might have to withdraw eastward across Rowanty Creek. Custer would feint toward the Confederate right, Warren would assail the left and Devin would then make a frontal assault. This would cut the Southerners at Five Forks off from the rest of Lee's command and drive them west.

At 1300, Sheridan dispatched Wells' brigade to join the rest of Custer's division. Warren received orders to advance up the Gravelly Run Church Road to the White Oak Road, form his entire corps and strike Pickett's left. Sheridan had learned of the withdrawal of Humphreys' corps from the White Oak Road to the Boydton Plank Road. Afraid that a Confederate advance on the White Oak Road would take Warren in flank and rear, Sheridan ordered Mackenzie to cut this route.

Toward 1400, Mackenzie's division struck the Southern picket line at the junction of the Crump and White Oak Roads. His troopers broke the line and scattered the pickets of Roberts' Brigade, reestablishing Pickett's isolation. Some of Roberts' horsemen retreated to Burgess Mill. Others fled toward Five Forks. From those of Roberts' troopers who reached Five Forks, Munford learned of the loss of the White Oak Road. Munford reported this matter to Fitzhugh Lee. But Fitzhugh Lee was impatient to get to a shad bake to which Rosser had also invited Pickett. Fitzhugh Lee instructed Munford to investigate the matter and rode off across Hatcher's Run with Pickett. In an incredible dereliction of duty, Pickett neglected to inform anyone of his whereabouts or place Rooney Lee, the ranking officer remaining, in command.

While Pickett and Fitzhugh Lee feasted on shad that Rosser had seined in the Nottoway River, the usually balky Warren moved heaven and earth to get his men in position to attack. Despite muddy roads clogged with led cavalry horses, despite soldiers exhausted from the previous day's fighting and the previous night's march, Warren completed his dispositions by 1600.

During the interval, Sheridan fretted that Custer's and Devin's divisions would use up all their ammunition. This might have wrecked Sheridan's plan, because the cavalrymen would then have had to replenish their ammunition from the wagon train at Dinwiddie Court House—making it impossible for them to participate in any attack at Five Forks. But even though Grant had authorized Sheridan to relieve Warren of command if that was necessary to get the V Corps moving and fighting properly, Sheridan declined to take this drastic action.

Warren's corps formed in view of Munford's cavalrymen. The leaderless Confederate force at Five Forks was paralyzed though unit commanders could make individual adjustments. Munford led Fitzhugh Lee's Division into position as an extension of Matt Ransom's return. But in the absence of an overall commander, coordination was impossible. Ransom refused to allow Munford to position MacGregor's Battery of horse artillery advantageously.

At 1615, Warren's corps advanced. But instead of encountering Southerners, it encountered Mackenzie's troopers. Sheridan had wrongly supposed that Pickett's left extended to the Gravelly Run Church Road. In fact, it was more than 700 yards to the west. Sheridan ordered Mackenzie's men to advance to Hatcher's Run and then follow the run westward to the Ford Church Road. Warren had formed his battle plan based on Sheridan's misinformation. Ayres adjusted by himself and wheeled to move due westward. But Crawford's and Charles Griffin's divisions kept heading northwestward. Warren and Sheridan were riding with Ayres. As Ayres' men engaged the Confederate infantry in Ransom's return, Warren departed from Sheridan and rode off to the right in search of Crawford and Griffin.

The Northern cavalry began its holding attacks. The Southerners repulsed the Union horsemen. The fire from Ransom's return caused some of Ayres' soldiers to waver. Having lost contact with Ayres' right, Crawford's and Griffin's divisions struggled northwestward through bogs and thickets for several hundred yards before wheeling to the left. As Ayres' division neared the angle where Ransom's return met Pickett's main line, Warren found Griffin 800 yards to the north, at the "Chimneys." Griffin's division had meandered into position between Crawford and Ayres from its station behind them. Warren had Griffin's division wheel to the left and Griffin's men began driving back Munford's right.

As Griffin led his men forward, Sheridan, Ayres and Ayres' officers rallied the waverers in Ayres' division and swept into the angle where Ransom's return met Pickett's main line. With the situation on Ayres' right unclear, Sheridan ordered Ayres to halt and reform. Sheridan was also concerned that Ayres' men might advance into a firefight with attacking Union cavalrymen.

About 1,000 yards to the north, Warren rode on in search of

Sheridan encourages his men during the battle of Five Forks. On 1 April 1865, this Federal victory was followed by an attack on the Petersburg fortifications. The Confederate defenses finally collapsed.

Crawford's division. The first of Crawford's brigades that Warren found was Kellogg's brigade on the divisions' left. Warren ordered Kellogg's brigade to halt so that the rest of Crawford's division could form up on its right. But when Warren went on in search of the rest of the division, orders came from Sheridan directing Kellogg's brigade to advance. The brigade quickly drove back Munford's left center. In the woods still farther to the north, Warren's couriers finally found Crawford. After trying to form on Kellogg's brigade but failing to find that unit, Crawford ordered his men westward. They drove back Munford's extreme left.

The three Confederate infantry brigades on the left of the White Oak Road line swung back to form a line along the Ford's Church Road. This line was at a right angle to the White Oak Road line. Crawford's division had its right on Hatcher's Run and overlapped the left of the Confederates in the Ford's Church Road line. Because of atmospheric conditions that stifled the sound of the conflict, the appearance of Crawford's soldiers 100 yards from the road's crossing of Hatcher's Run was Pickett's first sign that a battle was raging practically under his nose.

Pickett managed to dash across Hatcher's Run and down the Ford's Church Road before Crawford's men barred the way. When Fitzhugh Lee failed to get across the run, he hurled Rosser's Division toward Five Forks. Rosser's troopers were repulsed but bought Pickett precious time by causing Crawford's soldiers to pause. Fitzhugh Lee then formed Rosser's Division astride the Ford's Church Road to guard the South Side Railroad.

Arriving at Five Forks, Pickett pulled part of Mayo's Brigade out of the White Oak Road line. Knowing that Crawford outflanked the Confederate Ford's Church Road line, Pickett deployed Mayo's Brigade to form a return from the left of that line. MacGregor's Battery, which had limbered up and retreated from its position behind Matt Ransom's return, unlimbered in support of Mayo's Brigade.

After repulsing Rosser's desperate charge, Crawford's division turned down the Ford's Church Road. Mackenzie's troopers sealed off the Hatcher's Run crossing of the Ford's Church Road to Rosser and Fitzhugh Lee and continued to drive Munford's horsemen westward. Crashing into Mayo's Brigade, Crawford's soldiers routed it and captured three of MacGregor's four cannon. Several hundred yards to Crawford's left, in a hand-to-hand struggle, Charles Griffin's division overwhelmed the Southerners at the base of the Ford's Church Road line and took flags and prisoners. At the "Angle," Sheridan ordered Ayres' men to resume their advance along the White Oak Road line. Fitzhugh's and Pennington's cavalry brigades stormed the Southern breastworks at Five Forks just before the arrival of first Griffin's division from the north and then Ayres' division from the east.

Confusion prevailed in the Union ranks at Five Forks for a short time after its capture. Sheridan sought to form a battle line facing westward. He put Devin's division on the left,

Griffin's division on the right and Ayres' division behind Griffin.

Near the western end of the Confederate White Oak Road line, the Southerners prepared their last stand. Brigadier General Montgomery D. Corse on his own initiative directed his brigade, the last intact brigade of Pickett's infantry, to take position facing east on the western edge of the Gilliam field. On Corse's right and rear, Rooney Lee's Confederate cavalrymen held off Custer's frantic assaults.

The momentum of Crawford's division carried it into a position facing Corse's Brigade. Riding at the head of Crawford's division, Warren ordered this tired and disordered formation to attack. At first the men refused to advance. Then Warren picked up the corps battle flag and led his soldiers in person. Southern resistance was fierce and Warren had a horse shot out from under him but Crawford's division overwhelmed Corse's Virginians. The Union victory was complete.

As darkness fell, Rooney Lee's Division covered the Confederate retreat. Pickett led the remnants of his command toward Exeter Mills to cross the Appomattox River and link up again with the rest of Lee's forces. The Southerners had lost about 500 killed and wounded and approximately 2,000 prisoners. Sheridan's forces suffered fewer than 1,000 casualties. The Northerners also captured 13 colors and six cannon.

Now came one of the war's cruelest injustices. After the V Corps had won the battle with Warren at its head, Sheridan relieved Warren of command. The reasons were ostensibly Warren's slowness, though Sheridan failed to act at the time of the allegedly offensive conduct, and Warren's failure to participate in the fight, though he was in its forefront. There may have been bad blood between the two because of Warren's failure to arrive on time to support Sheridan on 8 May 1864 at Spotsylvania Court House, but the ambitious Sheridan had also shown himself capable of cheating his old friend George Crook of the credit for the decisive maneuver at the battle of Opequon Creek on 19 September 1864. In any

Gouverneur K. Warren

Like Hancock, Major General Gouverneur Kemble Warren sometimes held independent command during the Petersburg campaign. Also like Hancock, Warren was a hero of Gettysburg. After that battle, he received command of Hancock's corps while Hancock recuperated from his Gettysburg wound.

An engineer, Warren often displayed the caution and deliberation that marred the careers of so many of his colleagues during the Civil War. Warren's failure to attack on 2 December 1863 during the Mine Run campaign was the beginning of the end of his relationship with Meade. In the spring of 1864, upon Hancock's recovery, Warren received command of the *V Corps*. Warren's failure to beat the Confederate infantry to Spotsylvania Court House on 8 May 1864 strained still further his relationship with Meade and may

have sowed the seeds of Warren's ultimate undoing with Sheridan.

Meade wanted to relieve Warren of command for his balkiness in the initial assaults on Petersburg. Warren's late June suggestion that the army cut loose for Burke's Station fell on deaf ears, although Grant seriously considered this option in March of 1865. Warren's failure to attack in support of Burnside's corps at the Crater further displeased Meade, but Warren still received command of the mid-August advance to the Weldon Railroad. The force he commanded eventually consisted of his own four divisions, three divisions of Parke's *IX Corps* and two cavalry brigades.

Nagged by Grant and Meade into advancing into a wilderness that exposed his men to vicious Southern ambushes on 18 and 19 August, Warren beat a masterful tactical retreat on 20 Au-

event, a Court of Inquiry held many years later found Sheridan's relief of Warren unjustified.

News of the disaster at Five Forks reached Lee about 1730. Shortly afterward, he ordered Richard Anderson to take Wise's, Hunton's and Stansel's Brigades to the Ford's Church Road crossing of the South Side Railroad. Anderson was to gather up Pickett's survivors and retreat to Sutherland Station.

gust. This retreat bears comparison with the brilliant tactical withdrawal executed by Beauregard on 18 June. Fighting on his own terms on 21 August, Warren delivered a bloody repulse to the Confederates. But he could not please Grant and Meade. They were disgusted by Warren's failure to counterattack back into the thickets where so many of his men had fallen prey to the Southerners. Despite this and his failure to support Parke adequately at Jones Farm on 30 September, Warren received another independent command in early December. He led three divisions of his own corps, one division of Humphreys' *II Corps* and David Gregg's cavalry division on the Apple Jack Raid. Warren's hasty withdrawal when Confederate infantry approached did nothing to increase his esteem in the eyes of Grant and Meade.

By March, Warren's superiors could not endure him anymore. Grant and Meade wanted subordinates who would do as they were told without any backtalk. When Warren's superiors ordered him to report to Sheridan on the eve of Five Forks, they authorized Sheridan to relieve Warren of command if Sheridan thought the *V Corps* would march and fight better under another leader.

Warren gave one of his best performances of the war at the battle of Five Forks. It was Warren, not Sheridan, who led the charge that drove the Confederates from the field. At best, Sheridan's sack of Warren was unjustified—as the court martial that finally vindicated Warren concluded. At worst, it was the act of a man so ambitious that he would cheat even a friend— and Warren and Sheridan were not friends—of credit for winning a battle. Warren's vindication came many years later. Unfortunately for him, it came posthumously. He had died in 1882.

At the same time, Grant received word that Mackenzie's men had cut the White Oak Road and that Sheridan was ready to attack at Five Forks. Grant ordered Humphreys to swing his left around to the position held by Griffin's division on the previous day and block the White Oak Road near the Claiborne Road return. This would protect Mackenzie.

By 1830, Anderson's force had moved out of the Burgess Mill entrenchments. Cadmus Wilcox and Heth shifted to the left to compensate for the absence of Anderson's force. Lee ordered Longstreet to send Field's Division from the Peninsula to Petersburg.

News of the Northern victory at Five Forks reached Grant at his headquarters at Dabney's Mill at 2100. This time Lee's audacity in detaching Anderson's force did not meet with a passive response of the sort that Meade had orchestrated on 25 August. Fearing that Lee would detach still more troops for another attempt to smash Sheridan, Grant ordered an assault all along his lines. The instructions to Humphreys, on the left of Grant's command, included the proviso that if the *II Corps* could not carry the Confederate works immediately, Humphreys must send Miles down White Oak Road to Sheridan.

By midnight, Humphreys' reconnaissances in force had ascertained that the Southern position at Burgess Mill could not be stormed. Miles' division moved out on White Oak Road shortly afterward. About the same time, Mahone at Bermuda Hundred received orders from Lee to dispatch Nathaniel Harris' Mississippi Brigade to Petersburg because Longstreet's march there from the Peninsula would take considerable time.

The other Union corps commanders got their men under arms, but their assaults were postponed until dawn. During the interval, Grant narrowed the number of assaults to two. This was the number of corps whose commanders thought an assault feasible. Parke of the *IX Corps* believed he could storm Fort Mahone on the Jerusalem Plank Road. Horatio Wright of the *VI Corps* was confident that his soldiers could break the thin Confederate line between the Cockade City and Hatcher's Run. The Federals bombarded the Southern lines all night long as Field's Division and Nathaniel Harris' Brigade hastened toward Petersburg.

The Federals struck before either Field or Harris arrived. Preceded by a diversion mounted by Orlando Willcox's division east of Petersburg, the other two divisions of Parke's corps attacked astride the Jerusalem Plank Road at 0430, Hartranft's division was on the right, Potter's on the left. Parke's soldiers captured the first line of Confederate works

John Grubb Parke was Burnside's successor as commander of the IX *Corps.*

from Grimes' Division of Gordon's Corps, along with 12 cannon, 800 prisoners and several colors. On the right, Hartranft's division took Miller's Salient as well. On the left, Potter's division bogged down among the numerous traverses. The main Southern line remained intact, and Gordon soon began counterattacking the Federal lodgement, which extended for 400 yards on either side of the Jerusalem Plank Road.

Wright's corps advanced at 0440. His staff had reconnoitered the point of attack, opposite Forts Fisher and Welch, two nights earlier. Here the Federals held the Confederate entrenched picket line captured on 25 March. But for that, Wright would have considered the Southern lines facing him impregnable. Two lines of abatis separated by a row of pointed stakes stood in front of deep ditches, high parapets and artillery batteries every few hundred yards.

Leaving only a holding force in the Union works, Wright's corps formed with its *1st Division* on the right, its *2nd* in the center and its *3rd* on the left. Under heavy fire, the men of this formation cut away the abatis and swarmed over the Confederate fortifications at the junction of Lane's and McComb's Brigades. Momentum carried some of Wright's soldiers to the

A young Confederate lies in the Petersburg trenches where he fell. Beside him are his musket and ram rod along with torn paper cartridges. He was one of the defenders of Fort Mahone during the fighting on 2 April.

Boydton Plank Road and beyond to the South Side Railroad. One of these men killed A.P. Hill as the unlucky Southern corps commander reconnoitered west of the Boydton Plank Road. Detaching a brigade to expand the lodgement to his right, toward Petersburg, Wright reformed the rest of his corps and drove southwestward down the line of Confederate works. McComb's Brigade fought desperately, but the overwhelmingly superior Federal numbers dictated that there could be only one outcome to this struggle. One by one, several batteries fell into Northern hands as McComb's men were forced back.

Davis' Brigade held the Southern line between McComb's right and Hatcher's Run. As Wright's Northerners neared the run, Davis' Mississippians hurried to abandon the works. But it was too late. Wright's soldiers annihilated McComb's and Davis' Brigades by pinning them against ponds formed by the dams in Hatcher's Run. Thomas Harris' brigade of Turner's division in Ord's force occupied the works abandoned by Davis' Brigade before 0700. Those of Wright's men who had reached Hatcher's Run did an about face and started slogging back toward Petersburg. Wilcox was counterattacking and driving back the Union brigade detached to guard the right of Wright's breakthrough.

Beyond Hatcher's Run, Heth's four Confederate brigades in the fortifications that stretched from Burgess Mill westward to the Claiborne Road return began to abandon them. By 0830, the two divisions of the *II Corps* that remained with Humphreys had occupied the Southern trenches from Burgess Mill all the way out to the Claiborne Road.

Sheridan had not required the assistance of Miles, who was returning to Humphreys on the White Oak Road. When Miles' division was two miles west of the junction of the Claiborne and White Oak Roads, Humphreys ordered Miles' division and the rest of the *II Corps* to pursue Heth's men by the Claiborne Road toward Sutherland Station. Meade overruled Humphreys and ordered Miles to march to Petersburg by the first road after the crossing of Hatcher's Run. The rest of the corps was ordered to move on Petersburg by the Boydton Plank Road.

After crossing Hatcher's Run, Miles' division caught up with Heth's force before reaching the first road to Petersburg. Heth's men occupied a ridge parallel to the South Side Railroad, south of Sutherland Station. By this time, Heth had been called to Petersburg to take command of the other remnants of Hill's Corps. Command of the four Southern brigades at Sutherland Station passed to Cooke, the senior brigadier there. At 1000, from behind hastily erected fence rail breastworks, Cooke's men repulsed an attack on their left by Nugent's and Madill's brigades of Miles' division.

Several miles westward, Sheridan's men pursued Richard Anderson's force, which after Wright's breakthrough had been ordered to retreat on the Namozine Road toward Amelia Court House. Lee notified President Davis that the Confederate retreat from Richmond and Petersburg would have to begin that night—if the Federals could be held that long.

The men of Wright's corps were exhausted. They had been under arms for 18 hours. Gibbon, whose corps was part of Ord's force and had been unmasked by Wright's rolling up of the Southern line down to Hatcher's Run, received permission to pass his men through Wright's soldiers. With parts of Wright's corps on his right and left, Gibbon pushed up the Confederate line of works toward Petersburg where his men recaptured the ground lost to Wilcox's counterattacks. By noon, Gibbon's corps encountered Nathaniel Harris' Brigade of Mahone's Division just outside Forts Whitworth and Gregg. The Federals paused.

To the west, Miles launched another assault against Cooke at 1230. The Confederates at Sutherland Station repulsed this second attack on their left by Madill's brigade.

Eastward, Gordon's counterattacks took their toll on Parke's corps. Some of Parke's men broke and ran. Grant and Meade ordered substantial reserves to Parke's assistance, including the garrison of City Point and even part of Wright's corps. Parke's corps was in the same trouble it had run into at The Crater, the same difficulty that Gordon's force had run into at Fort Stedman—Parke's soldiers held part of the enemy line, but enemy fire swept the ground between the captured enemy trenches and their own. Reinforcements had to charge across a fire-swept no man's land. Those who ran to the rear and survived the hail of Southern lead did not rally and return. Gordon's woefully outnumbered Confederates prepared for a final onslaught to drive out Parke's corps.

Confronted by Gibbon's corps, Nathaniel Harris' Mississippians withdrew into Forts Whitworth and Gregg as the vanguard of Field's Division filed into the old Dimmock Line. Foster's division of Gibbon's corps attacked Fort Gregg but met with repulse at the hands of the motley garrison, which included many of Wilcox's men. Gibbon ordered Foster to renew the assault. This time two brigades of Turner's division supported Foster while Turner's other brigade—Thomas Harris' brigade—attacked Fort Whitworth. Because Longstreet's soldiers had finally arrived, the Confederates in Fort Whitworth were ordered to withdraw. Most of them escaped, but the order came so late that Thomas Harris' brigade of Turner's division captured a number of soldiers from Nathaniel Harris' Mississippi Brigade. The rear of Fort Gregg was now protected only by a palisade. At 1430, Gibbon's men captured

Fort Gregg at bayonet point after one of the most desperate struggles of the war.

Grant did not exploit the fall of Fort Gregg by attacking the old Dimmock Line. He had used up almost all of his reserves. Of Ord's force, only William Birney's African-American division was fresh, but Grant and Meade regarded *United States Colored Troops* as nothing but glorified ditch diggers despite their admirable combat record. The two divisions of the *II Corps* with Humphreys were ordered to the support of Miles. Any chance of storming Petersburg on 2 April were allowed to slip away.

At 1500, before the arrival of Humphreys, Miles mounted another attack on Cooke. This time, he feinted toward Cooke's right with Nugent's brigade deployed in a strong skirmish line. Then Ramsey's brigade struck Cooke's left. Sweeping down inside the Confederate breastworks, Ramsey's soldiers took 600 prisoners, one battleflag and two cannon. Miles had revenged himself for the rout of his command at Second Reams Station on 25 August 1864. The four Confederate brigades at Sutherland Station—Cooke's, MacRae's, McGowan's and Scales'—had all participated in that Southern victory. Now the proud soldiers of those commands were scattered fugitives. Some crossed the Appomattox at Exeter Mills while others moved upriver to Amelia Court House. Humphreys and reinforcements for Miles arrived on the Cox Road after fighting had died down.

As Miles launched his successful attack against Cooke, Lee issued orders for the abandonment of Petersburg and Richmond. Gordon, who was about to administer what he hoped would be the coup de grace to the Federals on the Jerusalem Plank Road, called off his counterattack. His men and Parke's remained locked in combat over Fort Mahone, with each side holding part of that fortification. Near Fort Gregg, the Confederates of Field's Division and the Federals of Wright's corps and Ord's force glowered at one another. Humphreys' corps remained at Sutherland Station mopping up Cooke's fugitives. As dusk fell, Sheridan's men had a brisk skirmish

Grant Versus Lee

During the Petersburg campaign, Grant outmaneuvered Lee from start to finish. Grant accomplished this by no means easy feat by exploiting Lee's preoccupation with the safety of Richmond.

In June 1864, Grant exploited Lee's fears for Richmond to enable Union forces to cross the James without interference. As a result, Lee almost lost Richmond by losing Petersburg and failed to deliver the devastating Southside counterattack that the Federals feared. The first Deep Bottom operation in July drew an inordinate number of Confederates from Petersburg to the Peninsula, which significantly increased the chances of success for the explosion of the mine—chances which Grant's and Meade's meddling with Burnside's battle plan decreased.

In August, Lee reacted predictably to the second Deep Bottom operation. Again he stripped the Petersburg lines to defend Richmond. As a result,

Grant gained a stranglehold on the Weldon Railroad. Grant succeeded with the same maneuver in September. The capture of Fort Harrison was a greater threat to Richmond than Lee had faced in any of the previous months. It drew from Petersburg the reserves that Lee was hoarding for a Southside offensive against the Federal left. Why Grant abandoned this successful one-two punch in late October is a mystery. Maybe he thought that Lee must eventually devise a devastating response. But the late October offensive was one of Grant's least successful—an almost unmitigated disaster.

The final instance of Grant outmaneuvering Lee occurred in March and April of 1865, when Grant managed to hide the crossing of Ord's detachment from the Peninsula to the Southside. The extra force provided by this transfer of manpower gave Grant the numbers Southside to make the single thrust opera-

with Anderson's rear guard at the Namozine Road crossing of Namozine Creek.

In the fighting that day, Battle Sunday, the Federals lost 3,361 killed, wounded and missing. Southern casualties totaled about 6,500, most of them prisoners.

The Confederate retreat from Petersburg began at 2000. The

tional strategy that he employed even more successful than the one-two punches of 1864.

Lee recognized that Grant's victories stemmed from skillful employment of his superior numbers. To Lee's credit, he used every expedient at his disposal to increase the size of his own forces. But he was unable to increase them to the point that he could protect Richmond and take the offensive elsewhere. Lee also knew that command of the sea was essential to the Federals. But the resources of the South never permitted him to mount an effective challenge to Northern control of the James.

But if Grant so consistently outmaneuvered Lee, why did it take so long for the Union to capture Richmond? The Southerners had three tremendous advantages that largely offset Grant's skill. First, the rifled musket had dramatically increased the effectiveness of the defense since the Mexican War, in which Grant, Lee and many of the other officers of the Civil War had first experienced combat. Secondly, the defense was also favored by the terrain around Petersburg. The Northerners thought that in places this landscape made the Wilderness seem hospitable. To compound this second advantage, the Southerners knew the ground while the Federals had to rely on maps that varied widely in their degrees of accuracy. Finally, there was also a significant difference between the instrument wielded by Grant and that employed by Lee. Grant may have had more bodies in his command, but until the very last stages of the campaign, the Confederates had more men willing to fight. Compounding this advantage was the absence of a leader like Hampton or Mahone in the Northern ranks until Sheridan returned from the Shenandoah Valley in late March of 1865 at the top of his form.

---

artillery and wagon trains led the way across the Appomattox River and headed westward. Longstreet and remnants of Hill's command were next in line. Gordon covered the rear and fired the bridges. Mahone's men abandoned the Howlett Line and trudged toward Chesterfield Court House. The Southern forces on the Peninsula, under Ewell, crossed the

Confederates captured during the final days of the campaign. The dejected soldiers are lined up for their first decent rations in some time.

James River to Chesterfield County at and below Richmond and proceeded to the Genito Road. The assembly point for all of Lee's remaining forces was Amelia Court House. As the Southerners pulled out of Richmond and Petersburg, they set fire to the military stores in the railroad yards and warehouses. Looters and rioters ran wild in the two cities that night.

Grant issued orders for an assault on the Petersburg and Richmond lines early on the morning of 3 April. But before 0300, Orlando Willcox's men discovered that Lee had abandoned Petersburg. They entered the Cockade City and quickly put an end to the chaos that prevailed there. Weitzel's command brought peace to Richmond at daybreak.

Six days later—on Palm Sunday, 9 April—Grant would accept the surrender of the remnant of the Confederate command that his soldiers had mortally wounded at Petersburg. Lee's capitulation at Appomattox Court House set in motion a chain reaction that during the next 11 weeks resulted in the surrender of all Confederate armed forces in the field, from the North Carolina piedmont to the Indian Territory.

After months of siege and battle, Federal soldiers enter Petersburg on 3 April. Richmond, the Confederate capital, fell the same day.

The Petersburg Court-house after the fall of the town on 3 April. Six days later, Lee gave in to Grant at Appomattox. The surrender of Confederate forces throughout the South took place over the next 11 weeks.

Besieged! Great Sieges in Civil War			
Siege	Besiegers/ Besieged	Dates	Length
Yorktown	U.S.*/C.S.	5 April-3 May 1862	29 days
Corinth	U.S.*/C.S.	30 April-30 May 1862	31 days
Suffolk	C.S./U.S.*	12 April-12 May 1863	31 days
Vicksburg	U.S.*/C.S.	25 May-4 July 1863	41 days
Port Hudson	U.S.*/C.S.	21 May-9 July 1863	50 days
Knoxville	C.S./U.S.*	17 Nov.-4 Dec. 1863	18 days
Petersburg	U.S.*/C.S.	15 June 1864-3 April 1865	292 days
Atlanta	U.S.*/C.S.	20 July-2 Sept. 1864	45 days
Savannah	U.S.*/C.S.	12-21 Dec. 1864	10 days
Mobile	U.S.*/C.S.	26 March-12 April 1865	18 days
* denotes victorious side.			

Guide for the Interested Reader

In writing this book, I relied upon the following works and sources among those listed in their bibliographies.

William Glenn Robertson's *Back Door to Richmond* (1987) and Herbert M. Schiller's *The Bermuda Hundred Campaign* (Dayton, Ohio, 1988) describe the Bermuda Hundred campaign of May, 1864. They are among a number of recent books that have focused in detail on specific episodes during the fighting around Petersburg. *The Battle of Old Men and Young Boys* (Lynchburg, Virginia, 1989), by William Glenn Robertson, covers Butler's 9 June thrust toward the city.

Thomas J. Howe's *Wasted Valor* (Lynchburg, Virginia, 1988) recounts the 15- 18 June opening assaults on the city. *The Battle of the Crater* (Lynchburg, Virginia, 1989), by Michael A. Cavanaugh and William Marvel, tells the story of the first battle of Deep Bottom and the battle of the Crater, fought in late July.

The Destruction of the Weldon Railroad (Lynchburg, Virginia, 1991), which I wrote, portrays the August battles around Petersburg: Second Deep Bottom, Globe Tavern and Second Reams Station.

Richard J. Sommers' "Richmond Redeemed" (Garden City, New York, 1981) analyzes the battles of Fort Harrison and Peebles Farm, fought during the first days of Grant's Fifth Offensive in late September and the first days of October.

The Battle of Five Forks, by Edwin C. Bearss and Christopher

Calkins (Lynchburg, Virginia, 1985), describes the battles of Lewis Farm, Dinwiddie Courthouse, White Oak Road and Five Forks, fought in the last days of March and the first day of April in 1865.

Many of the siege's other major episodes would bear book-length treatment, but as yet their historians have not appeared. No one has written a book about the struggles of late June, which include the battle of the Jerusalem Plank Road and the Wilson-Kautz Raid. "Richmond Redeemed" ends without describing the later battles of Grant's Fifth Offensive, first Darbytown Road on October 7 and Second Darbytown Road on 13 October. There is no book on the entire Fifth Offensive. No book exists on Fair Oaks and Burgess Mill, the 27 October battles of Grant's Sixth Offensive. The Apple Jack Raid of 7-12 December has likewise gone unchronicled. No one has written a book on February's battle of Hatcher's Run, March's battle of Fort Stedman or the final Federal assaults on 2 April, Battle Sunday. The number of major actions without book-length studies indicates the degree to which the Petersburg Campaign remains virgin territory for historians.

In the absence of specific studies, I drew on several books that proved of value throughout, and I acknowledge them here instead of listing them repeatedly: Douglas Southall Freeman's *R. E. Lee* (New York, 1934-5); Ulysses S. Grant's *Personal Memoirs* (New York, 1885); Andrew A. Humphreys' *The Virginia Campaign of 1864 and 1865* (New York, 1883); James G. Scott's and Edward A. Wyatt, IV's *Petersburg's Story: A History* (Petersburg, 1960); and Noah Andre Trudeau's *The Last Citadel* (Boston, 1991).

Indispensable to the understanding of any Civil War campaign is familiarity with *The War of the Rebellion: A Compilation of the Official Records of the Union and Confederate Armies* (Washington, D.C., 1880-1901), and particularly with the correspondence. There are 70 volumes of reports and correspondence in 128 parts, each part actually a volume in itself. Reports and correspondence concerning the pre-campaign planning are in Volume 33 (one part). Volume 36 (three parts) covers the Bermuda Hundred and Overland campaigns, including the 9 June attack on Petersburg. The reports and correspondence on the period from the crossing of the James River to the battle of the Crater are in Volume 40 (three parts). Volume 42 (three parts) contains the reports and correspondence for the period running from the August battles to the end of 1864. The last portion of the campaign is covered in Volume 46 (three parts). Volume 51 (two parts) contains additional correspondence for the entire period of the siege, particularly for the Confederates.

Volume IV of *Battles and Leaders of the Civil War*, edited by Robert U. Johnson and Clarence C. Buel (New York, 1888) contains a number of essential articles about the fighting around Petersburg: "The Defense of Drewry's Bluff" by P.G.T. Beauregard; "Butler's Attack on Drewry's Bluff" by William F. Smith; "Operations South of the James River," by August V. Kautz and Raleigh E. Colston; "Four Days of Battle at Petersburg," by P.G.T. Beauregard; "The Battle of the Petersburg Crater," by William H. Powell; "In The Crater," by Charles H. Houghton; "The Colored Troops at Petersburg," by Henry G. Thomas; "Actions on the Weldon Railroad," by Orlando B. Willcox; "Gordon's Attack at Fort Stedman," by George L. Kilmer; "The Recapture of Fort Stedman," by John F. Hartranft; "Closing Operations in the James River," by James R. Soley; "Five Forks and the Pursuit of Lee," by Horace Porter; and "General Warren at Five Forks and the Court of Inquiry."

Petersburg's own soldiers contributed most of *War Talks of Confederate Veterans* (Petersburg, 1892), edited by George S. Bernard. It includes *The Defense of Petersburg*, by Fletcher H. Archer, and *The Battle of the Crater*, by George S. Bernard.

Lee A. Wallace, Jr.'s *A Guide to Virginia Military Organizations 1861-1865* (Lynchburg, 1986) includes the history of Pegram's Battery. *The Sable Arm* (New York, 1956), by Dudley T. Cornish, provides information about *United States Colored Troops*. Glenn Tucker's *Hancock the Superb* (Dayton, Ohio, 1980) is a recent biography of Hancock. *William Mahone of Virginia* (Richmond, 1935), by Nelson M. Blake, chronicles Mahone's remarkable life. Manly W. Wellman's *Giant in Gray*

(Dayton, Ohio, 1988) is a reprint of the standard biography of Wade Hampton. "Grant's Railroad: Route Through Danger" (*Civil War Times Illustrated*, October, 1983), by Gordon C. Bennett, furnished information about the City Point & Army Line. Emerson G. Taylor's *Gouverneur Kemble Warren* (Boston, 1932) is the most recent published biography of Warren. I drew on the Memoir of James Eldred Phillips in the Virginia Historical Society for my conclusion about A.P. Hill's failure to intercept Warren during the Apple Jack Raid. Jeffry Wert's "George Crook: Sheridan's Second Fiddle" (*Civil War Times Illustrated*, December, 1983) provided special insight into the intensity of Sheridan's ambition. *The Generalship of Ulysses S. Grant*, by J.F.C. Fuller (London, 1929) discusses Lee's forest warfare tactics.

The Encyclopedia of Military History (New York, 1970), by R. Ernest Dupuy, helped put the Petersburg Campaign in historical perspective.

Touring Petersburg Campaign Sites

Petersburg National Battlefield Park

A proper tour of the this park should proceed from east to west, a course which generally follows the progress of the fighting.

From Parker's Battery on Bermuda Hundred, go to Route 10 and turn right. Proceed across the Appomattox River to Appomattox Street in Hopewell. Turn left on Appomattox Street, left again at Cedar Lane, and then right at Pecan Avenue to get to the City Point Unit of the park. This unit preserves the site of the Union supply base and Grant's headquarters.

Return to Route 10. Proceed directly across to West Broadway. Take this road to Route 36. Turn left on to Route 36 and proceed to the Visitor Center of the main unit of Petersburg National Battlefield Park. A walking trail leads to Battery 5 of the original Confederate defense line and the site where the "Dictator," a huge Union mortar, was located.

There is also a four-mile driving tour of the unit. This tour first goes past Battery 8 of the original Confederate defense line. This Battery was seized by *United States Colored Troops* on 15 June, 1864. Reversed and renamed Fort Friend by the Federals, it figured in the repulse of the Confederate attack on Fort Stedman on 25 March 1865.

Beyond is Battery 9 of the original Confederate defense line. *United States Colored Troops* captured this Battery on June 15, 1864.

Next comes the Harrison Creek line. The Confederates dug in along this stream on the night of 15 June 1864 after the Federals stormed the Dimmock line. The Southerners held this line for two days before retreating to the line they held until the end of the siege.

Farther along is Fort Stedman, the focus of the Confederate attack on 25 March 1865. A walking trail leads to Colquitt's Salient, where the Southern attack originated.

The driving tour proceeds next to Fort Haskell, south of Fort Stedman. Fort Haskell withstood the Confederate onslaught on 25 March 1865.

Beyond Fort Haskell is the Taylor Farm Site. Nearly 200 pieces of Federal artillery were concentrated along the ridge here for fire support during the battle of the Crater.

Next comes The Crater itself, the site of the abortive Union attack on 30 July 1864. A walking trail leads to points of interest around this site.

The driving tour exits the main unit of the park on to U. S. 301/460 (Crater Road). Turn left and proceed to the Flank Road, which follows the Union siege lines. Turn right on to the Flank Road and follow it to the Halifax Road (604), which runs along the old bed of the Weldon Railroad. Immediately west of the Halifax Road is the Fort Wadsworth unit of the Park. Fort Wadsworth was built by the Federals in late August and early September of 1864 to hold the Weldon Railroad.

Follow the Halifax Road south to Reams Station, where fighting took place on 29 June 1864 and 25 August 1864. There the Conservation Fund has recently acquired about 200 acres of the battlefield.

Returning to Fort Wadsworth, take 676 left to the Fort Keene unit of the park. Fort Keene was built in October of 1864 to hold the Federal gains of late September and early October.

676 leads west from Fort Keene to another unit of the park that begins at the Squirrel Level Road (613). Just west of this road is Fort Urmston. Like Fort Keene, Fort Urmston was built to protect the Northern gains of late September and early October, 1864. Beyond and to the left of Fort Urmston, a path leads to Fort Wheaton, formerly the Confederate Fort Archer captured 30 September 1864. Farther on is Fort Conahey, built to hold the Union gains of late September and early October, 1864. Just short of the Church Road (672) is Fort Fisher, completed by the Federals in March of 1865. West of the Church Road, a path leads to Fort Welch. The Federal *VI Corps* launched its successful assault of 2 April 1865 from between Forts Fisher and Welch. Farther along the path is the Union Fort Gregg.

Returning to the Church Road, take it north to 142 and turn right to go to the Confederate Fort Gregg. Here several hundred Southerners held off two Union divisions for two hours on the afternoon of 2 April 1865.

Go back to 142. Take it to the Church Road and bear right to Route 1, the Boydton Plank Road. Follow Route 1 to the Duncan Road (670) and turn left. As you proceed south on the Duncan Road, you will pass Tudor Hall, one of Dinwiddie County's most beautiful old houses, and acreage on which the 2 April breakthrough took place. The house and the acreage are being developed as a private park. After crossing Hatcher's Run at Armstrong's Mill, turn right on 613 and follow it by 50 acres recently acquired by the Association for the Preservation of Civil War Sites to preserve the 6 February 1865 battlefield.

Proceed under Interstate 85 to the Boydton Plank Road. Turn right and drive to the White Oak Road (613). Make a left turn on to the White Oak Road. At its junction with Claiborne Road (631) are 30 acres recently acquired by the Association for the Preservation of Civil War Sites. On this acreage are some earthworks of the extreme right of the Confederate siege lines, near where the battle of the White Oak Road took place on March 31, 1865.

The White Oak Road intersects with the Dinwiddie Court-house Road (627) and Scott's Road (645) at Five Forks, where the famous battle of 1 April 1865 occurred. The Conservation Fund recently acquired about 1100 acres of this battlefield and then donated the acreage to Petersburg National Battlefield Park.

Richmond National Battlefield Park

Richmond National Battlefield Park is one of two national battlefield parks that preserve battlefields of the Petersburg campaign. The preserved battlefields on the Peninsula and Bermuda Hundred are in Richmond National Battlefield Park.

This park's main visitor center is in Richmond, at Chimbo-razo, the former site of a huge Confederate hospital complex. To get to the park's preserved battlefields on the Peninsula, take Broad Street northwest from Chimborazo, which is at 32nd Street. Turn left at 25th Street. Turn left again at Route 5, the New Market Road. Take this road beyond Laburnum Avenue to the Battlefield Park Road. This road leads to Forts Gilmer, Gregg, and Johnson, the Fort Harrison Visitor Center, and Forts Harrison and Hoke. Forts Gilmer, Gregg, Johnson, Harrison and Hoke were parts of the Confederate defenses of Richmond. The capture of Fort Harrison by *United States Colored Troops* on September 29, 1864 forced a realignment of Richmond's southern defenses.

From Fort Hoke, the Hoke-Brady Road leads to Fort Beady. This Union fort was built in October of 1864 to neutralize Fort Darling across the river on Drewry's Bluff and to anchor the Federal line from Fort Harrison.

To get to the park's preserved battlefields on Bermuda Hundred from Chimborazo, take Broad Street northwest to Interstate 95 (near 14th Street). Follow Interstate 95 south to Exit 6 and the Willis Road. Go west on the Willis Road a short distance to U.S. 301. Turn right and ride about half a mile north to Bellwood Road (656). Turn right and follow the markers to Fort Darling on Drewry's Bluff. The fort figured in the fighting of May, 1864, that prevented Butler from investing Richmond from the south.

To get to the other battlefield preserved by Richmond National Battlefield Park on Bermuda Hundred, return to U. S. 301 and take it south to Route 10. Turn left and cross under Interstate 95. Turn right on to Ware Bottom Spring Road (898). Turn right again on to Bramblewood Road (617). After a short distance, you will come to Parker's Battery, part of the Confederate Howlett Line that bottled up Butler in Bermuda Hundred.

Orders of Battle

Abbreviations: Standard state abbreviations have been used. Unless otherwise noted a unit is always understood to be a regiment of infantry. Where capital letters are used companies or batteries are indicated; infantry regiments of both sides, and Confederate cavalry regiments, normally had companies A through K, omitting "J"; Union cavalry regiments normally had A-M, omitting "J"; but some regiments of both types had higher designated companies than the norm. Other abbreviations used are: Art., artillery; Btty., battery; Bn., battalion; Co., company; Hvy., Hvy.; Lt., light.

Order of Battle:
Opening of Petersburg Campaign

Armies of the United States, Lt. Gen. Ulysses S. Grant

Army of the Potomac, Maj. Gen. George G. Meade

General Headquarters
 Provost Guard, Brig. Gen.
  Marsena R. Patrick
  80th N.Y. (20th Militia)
  68th Pa.
  14th Pa.
  1st Mass. Cav., Cos. C and D
  3d Pa. Cav.

Volunteer Engineer Brigade,
 Brig. Gen. Henry W. Benham
 15th New York (5 cos.)
 50th New York
 Battalion U. S. Engineers
 Signal Corps
 Artillery, Brig. Gen. Henry J.
  Hunt

Artillery Park, Lt. Col. Freeman
McGilvery
*15th New York Hvy. Arty., Co.
F*
Guards And Orderlies
Independent Co. Oneida (New
York) *Cav.*

II *Army Corps*, Maj. Gen. Winfield S. Hancock
*50th New York Engineers (1st
Bn.)*

1st *Division*, Brig. Gen. Francis C. Barlow
1st Brigade, Brig. Gen. Nelson A.
Miles
28th Mass.
26th Mich.
5th N.H.
61st N.Y.
81st Pa.
40th Pa.
83d Pa.
2d N.Y. Hvy. Art.
MacDougall's Brigade, Col. Clin-
ton D. MacDougall
39th N.Y.
*52d N.Y./detachment 7thN.Y.
attached*
57th N.Y.
63d N.Y.
69th N.Y.
88th N.Y.
111th N.Y.
125th N.Y.
126th N.Y.
4th Brigade, Lt. Col. John Hast-
ings
2d Delaware (5 cos.)
64th N.Y.
66th N.Y.
53d Pa.
106th Pa.
145th Pa.
148th Pa.
7th N.Y. Hvy. Art.

2nd *Division*, Maj. Gen. John Gibbon
Provost Guard
2d Co. Minn. Sharpshooters
1st Brigade, Lt. Col. Francis E.
Pierce
19th Me.
19th Mass.
20th Mass./ detachment 15th
Mass. Attached
7th Mich.
1st Minn. (bn.)
59th N.Y. (bn.)
82d N.Y. (bn.)/detachment
42d N.Y. attached.
152d N.Y.
184th Pa.
36th Wis.
1st Co. Andrew (Mass.)
Sharpshooters
2d Brigade, Col. James P. McIvor
155th N.Y.
164th N.Y.
170th N.Y.
182d N.Y. (69th N.Y. National
Guard Art.)
8th N.Y. Hvy. Art.
3d Brigade, Col. Thomas A.
Smyth
14th Ct.
1st Del.
12th N.J.
10th N.Y. (bn.)
108th N.Y.
4th and 8th Ohio (bn.)
69th Pa.
72d Pa.
106th Pa.
7th West Virginia (bn.)

3d *Division*, Maj. Gen. David B. Birney
1st Brigade, Col. Henry J. Madill
20th Indiana
17th Me.
40th N.Y.
86th N.Y.
124th N.Y.

99th Pa.
110th Pa.
141st Pa.
2d U.S. Sharpshooters
4th N.Y. Hvy. Art., 1st Bn.
2d Brigade, Brig. Gen. Byron R. Pierce
5th Mich.
93d N.Y.
57th Pa.
63d Pa.
105th Pa.
1st Mass. Hvy. Art.
4th N.Y. Hvy. Art., 2d Bn.
1st U. S. Sharpshooters
3d Brigade, Brig. Gen. Gershom Mott
16th Mass.
5th N.J.
6th N.J.
7th N.J.
8th N.J.
11th N.J.
1st Me. Hvy. Art.
4th Brigade, Col. William R. Brewster
11th Mass. (bn.)
71st N.Y.
73d N.Y.
74th N.Y.
120th N.Y./72d N.Y. (three cos.) attached.
84th Pa.

Artillery Brigade, Maj. John G. Hazard
Me. Lt., 6th Btty. (F)
Mass. Lt., 10th Btty.
N.H. Lt., 1st Btty.
1st N.J. Lt., Co. B
N.J. Lt., 3d Btty.
1st N.Y. Lt., Co. G
4th N.Y. Hvy., 3d Bn.
4th N.Y. Hvy., Co. D
N.Y. Lt., 11th Btty.
N.Y. Lt., 12th Btty.
1st Pa. Lt., Co. F
1st R.I. Lt., Co. A

1st R.I. Lt., Co. B
4th U.S., Co. K
5th U.S., Cos. C and I

V Army Corps, Maj. Gen. Gouverneur K. Warren

1st Division, Brig. Gen. Charles Griffin

1st Brigade, Col. William S. Tilton
121st Pa.
142d Pa.
143d Pa.
149th Pa.
150th Pa.
187th Pa.
2d Brigade, Col. Jacob B. Sweitzer
22d Mass./2d Company Mass. Sharpshooters attached.
32d Mass.
4th Mich.
62d Pa.
91st Pa.
155th Pa.
21st Pa. Cav. (dismounted)
3d Brigade, Brig. Gen. Joseph J. Bartlett
20th Me.
18th Mass.
1st Mich.
16th Mich./Brady's Co. Mich. Sharpshooters attached.
44th N.Y.
83d Pa.
118th Pa.

2d Division, Brig. Gen. Romeyn B. Ayres

1st Brigade, Brig. Gen. Joseph Hayes
5th N.Y.
140th N.Y.
146th N.Y.
10th U.S.
12th U.S.
14th U.S.
17th U.S.
2d Brigade, Col. Nathan T. Dushane

1st Maryland
4th Maryland
7th Maryland
8th Maryland
Purcell (Maryland) Legion
3d Brigade, Col. J. Howard Kitch-
ing
6th N.Y. Hvy. Art.
15th N.Y. Hvy. Art.

3d Division, Brig. Gen. Samuel W. Crawford

1st Brigade, Col. Peter Lyle
16th Me.
13th Mass.
39th Mass.
104th N.Y.
90th Pa.
107th Pa.
2d Brigade, Brig. Gen. Henry Baxter
94th N.Y.
97th N.Y.
11th Pa.
88th Pa.
3d Brigade, Col. James Carle
190th Pa.
191st Pa.

4th Division, Brig. Gen. Lysander Cutler

Provost Guard
Independent Bn. Wis. Inf. (2
cos.)
1st Brigade, Col. Edward S. Bragg
7th Ind.
19th Ind.
24th Mich.
6th Wis.
7th Wis.
1st Bn. N.Y. Sharpshooters
2d Brigade, Col. J. William Hof-
mann
2d Del.
4th Del.
76th N.Y.
95th N.Y.
147th N.Y.
56th Pa.

157th Pa.

Artillery Brigade, Col. Charles S. Wainwright

Mass. Lt., 3d Btty. (C)
Mass. Lt., 5th Btty. (E)
Mass. Lt., 9th Btty.
1st N.Y. Lt., Co. B
1st N.Y. Lt., Co. C
1st N.Y. Lt., Co. D
1st N.Y. Lt., Co. E
1st N.Y. Lt., Co. H
1st N.Y. Lt., Co. L
N.Y. Lt., 15th Btty.
1st Pa. Lt., Co. B
4th U.S., Co. B
5th U.S., Co. D

VI Army Corps, Maj. Gen. Horatio G. Wright

Escort
8th Pa. Cav., Co. A
Engineers
50th N.Y., 2d Bn. (3 cos.)

1st Division, Brig. Gen. David A. Russell

1st Brigade, Col. William H. Penrose
4th N.J.
10th N.J.
15th N.J.
1st Del. Cav. (7
cos.—dismounted)
2d Brigade, Brig. Gen. Emory Up-
ton
121st N.Y.
95th Pa.
96th Pa.
2d Ct. Hvy. Art.
3d Brigade, Lt. Col. Gideon Clark
6th Me.
49th Pa.
119th Pa.
5th Wis.
4th Brigade, Col. Joseph E. Hamblin
65th N.Y.
67th N.Y.

122d N.Y.
23d Pa.
82d Pa.

2d Division, Brig. Gen. George W. Getty

1st Brigade, Brig. Gen. Frank
Wheaton
62d N.Y.
93d Pa.
98th Pa.
102d Pa.
139th Pa.

2d Brigade, Brig. Gen. Lewis A.
Grant
2d Vermont
3d Vermont
4th Vermont
5th Vermont
6th Vermont
11th Vermont

3d Brigade, Col. Daniel D. Bidwell
7th Me.
43d N.Y.
49th N.Y.
77th N.Y.
61st Pa.

4th Brigade, Col. Oliver Edwards
37th Mass./detachments 7th
and 10th Mass. and 2d R.I.
attached.

3d Division, Brig. Gen. James B. Ricketts

1st Brigade, Col. William S. Truex
14th N.J.
106th N.Y.
151st N.Y.
87th Pa.
10th Vt.

2d Brigade, Col. Benjamin F.
Smith
6th Maryland
110th Oh.
122d Oh.
126th Oh.
67th Pa.
138th Pa.
9th N.Y. Hvy. Art.

Artillery Brigade, Col. Charles H. Tompkins

Me. Lt., 4th Btty. (D)
Me. Lt., 5th Btty. (E)
Mass. Lt., 1st Btty. (A)
1st N.J. Lt., Co. A
N.Y. Lt., 1st Btty.
N.Y. Lt., 3d Btty.
9th N.Y. Hvy., 2d Bn.
1st Oh. Lt., Co. H
1st R.I. Lt., Co. C
1st R.I. Lt., Co. E
1st R.I. Lt., Co. G
5th U.S., Co. E
5th U.S., Co. M

IX Army Corps, Maj. Gen. Ambrose E. Burnside

Provost Guard
8th U.S.

1st Division, Brig. Gen. James H. Ledlie

1st Brigade, Col. Jacob P. Gould
3d Maryland (bn.)
21st Mass.
35th Mass.
56th Mass.
57th Mass.
59th Mass.
179th N.Y. (bn.)
100th Pa.

2d Brigade, Col. Ebenezer W.
Peirce
29th Mass.
14th N.Y. Hvy. Art.
2d Pa. Provisional Hvy. Art.

Artillery
Me. Lt., 2d Btty. (B)
Mass. Lt., 14th Btty.
N.Y. Lt., 27th Btty.

2d Division, Brig. Gen. Robert B. Potter

1st Brigade, Lt. Col. Henry Pleasants
6th Mass.
58th Mass.
2d N.Y. Mounted Rifles

45th Pa.
48th Pa.
7th R.I.
2d Brigade, Brig. Gen. Simon G.
Griffin
31st Me.
32d Me.
2d Md.
6th N.H.
9th N.H.
11th N.H.
17th Vt.
Acting Engineers
51st N.Y.
Artillery
Mass. Lt., 11th Btty.
N.Y. Lt., 19th Btty.

3d Division, Brig. Gen. Orlando B. Willcox

1st Brigade, Col. John F. Hartranft
8th Mich.
27th Mich./1st and 2d Cos.
Mich. Sharpshooters
attached.
109th N.Y.
51st Pa.
37th Wis.
38th Wis.
13th Oh. Cav. (dismounted
bn.)
2d Brigade, Col. William Humphrey
1st Mich. Sharpshooters
2d Mich.
20th Mich.
46th N.Y.
60th Oh./9th and 10th Cos.
Oh. Sharpshooters attached.
50th Pa.
24th N.Y. Cav. (dismounted)
Acting Engineers
17th Mich.
Artillery
Me. Lt., 7th Btty. (G)
N.Y. Lt., 34th Btty.

4th Division, Brig. Gen. Edward Ferrero

1st Brigade, Col. Joshua K. Sigfried
27th U.S. Colored Troops
30th U.S. Colored Troops
39th U.S. Colored Troops
43d U.S. Colored Troops
2d Brigade, Col. Henry G. Thomas
19th U.S. Colored Troops
23d U.S. Colored Troops
28th U.S. Colored Troops
29th U.S. Colored Troops
31st U.S. Colored Troops
Artillery
Pa. Lt., Co. D
Vt. Lt., 3d Btty.

Cavalry Corps, Maj. Gen. Philip H. Sheridan

1st Division, Brig. Gen. Alfred T. A. Torbert

1st Brigade, Brig. Gen. George A.
Custer
1st Mich.
5th Mich.
6th Mich.
7th Mich.
2d Brigade, Col. Thomas A. Devin
4th N.Y.
6th N.Y.
9th N.Y.
17th Pa.
Reserve Brigade, Brig. Gen.
Wesley Merritt
19th N.Y. (1st Dragoons)
6th Pa.
1st R.I. (8 cos.)
1st U.S.
2d U.S.
5th U.S./Cos. B, F, and K,
detailed as escort to Lt.
Gen. U. S. Grant.

2d Division, Brig. Gen. David McM. Gregg

1st Brigade, Brig. Gen. Henry E.
Davies, Jr.

1st Mass.
1st N.J.
10th N.Y.
6th Oh.
1st Pa.
2d Brigade, Col. J. Irvin Gregg
1st Me.
2d Pa.
4th Pa.
8th Pa.
13th Pa.
16th Pa.

3d Division, Brig. Gen. James H. Wilson
1st Brigade, Col. John B. McIntosh
1st Ct.
3d N.J.
2d N.Y.
5th N.Y.
2d Oh.

18th Pa.
2d Brigade, Col. George H. Chapman
3d Ind. (6 cos.)
1st N.H. (7 cos.)
8th N.Y.
22d N.Y.
1st Vt.
Horse Artillery Brigade, Capt. James M. Robertson
1st U.S., Cos. H and I
1st U.S., Co. K
2d U.S., Co. A
2d U.S., Co. B and L
2d U.S., Co. D
2d U.S., Co. M
3d U.S., Co. C
4th U.S., Cos. C and E

Department of Virginia and North Carolina, Maj. Gen. Benjamin F. Butler

Naval Brigade, Brig Gen. Charles K. Graham
13th N.Y. Hvy. Art., Co. I
13th N.Y. Hvy. Art., Co. K
13th N.Y. Hvy. Art., Co. L
3d Pa. Hvy. Art., Co. A
3d Pa. Hvy. Art., Co. B
3d Pa. Hvy. Art., Co. G
Engineers, Maj. Joseph Walker
1st N.Y.
Siege Artillery, Col. Henry L. Abbot
1st Ct. Hvy.
13th N.Y. Hvy., Cos. A and H
3d Pa. Hvy., Co. M
Unattached Troops
36th U.S. Colored Troops
38th U.S. Colored Troops
1st N.Y. Mounted Rifles
13th Co. Mass. Hvy. Art.
1st Pa. Lt. Art., Co. E
2d U. S. Colored Lt. Art., Co. B

Signal Corps, Capt. Lemuel B. Norton

X Army Corps, **Brig. Gen. William T. H. Brooks**
1st Division, Brig. Gen. Alfred H. Terry
1st Brigade, Col. Joshua B. Howell
39th Illinois
62d Oh.
67th Oh.
85th Pa.
2d Brigade, Col. Joseph R. Hawley
6th Ct.
7th Ct.
3d N.H.
7th N.H.
3d Brigade, Col. Harris M. Plaisted
10th Ct.
11th Me.
24th Mass.
100th N.Y.

1st Md. Cav. (dismounted)
Artillery, Capt. Loomis L. Langdon
  Ct. Lt., 1st Btty.
  N.J. Lt., 5th Btty.
  3d R.I. Hvy., Co. C
  1st U.S., Co. M

2d *Division*, Brig. Gen. John W. Turner

1st Brigade, Col. N. Martin Curtis
  3d N.Y.
  112th N.Y.
  117th N.Y.
  142d N.Y.
2d Brigade, Col. William B. Barton
  47th N.Y.
  48th N.Y.
  115th N.Y.
  76th Pa.
3d Brigade, Col. Louis Bell
  13th Ind.
  9th Me.
  4th N.H.
  69th N.Y.
  97th Pa.
Artillery, Capt. George T. Woodbury
  N.J. Lt., 4th Btty.
  Wis. Lt., 4th Btty.
  1st U.S., Co. D
  3d U.S., Co. E
  4th U.S., Co. D

3d *Division*, Brig. Gen. Orris S. Ferry

1st Brigade, Brig. Gen. Gilman Marston
  133d Oh.
  143d Oh.
  148th Oh.
  163d Oh.
2d Brigade, Col. James B. Armstrong
  130th Oh.
  132d Oh.
  134th Oh.
  138th Oh.
  142d Oh.

Artillery
  N.Y. Lt., 33d Bat.
Unattached Troops
  1st N.Y. Mounted Rifles
    (dismounted detachment)
  37th U.S. Colored Troops
  4th Mass. Cav. (8 cos.)

XVIII *Army Corps*, Maj. Gen. William F. Smith

1st *Division*, Brig. Gen. George J. Stannard

1st Brigade, Col. Edgar M. Cullen
  81st N.Y.
  96th N.Y.
  98th N.Y.
  139th N.Y.
2d Brigade, Brig. Gen. Hiram Burnham
  8th Ct.
  10th N.H.
  13th N.H.
  118th N.Y.
3d Brigade, Col. Guy V. Henry
  21st Ct.
  40th Mass.
  92d N.Y.
  58th Pa.
  188th Pa.

2d *Division*, Brig. Gen. John H. Martindale

1st Brigade, Col. Alexander Piper
  23d Mass.
  25th Mass.
  27th Mass.
  9th N.J.
  55th Pa.
  10th N.Y. Hvy. Art.
2d Brigade, Col. Griffin A. Stedman, Jr.
  11th Ct.
  8th Me.
  12th N.H.
  148th N.Y.
  19th Wis.
3d Brigade, Brig. Gen. Adelbert Ames

5th Md.
89th N.Y.
2d Pa. Hvy. Art.

3d Division, Brig. Gen. Edward W. Hinks

1st Brigade, Col. John H. Holman
1st U.S. Colored Troops
10th U.S. Colored Troops
1st U.S. Colored Cav.
(dismounted)
2d Brigade, Col. Samuel A. Duncan
4th U.S. Colored Troops
5th U.S. Colored Troops
6th U.S. Colored Troops
22d U.S. Colored Troops
2d U.S. Colored Cav.
(dismounted)
Artillery Brigade, Col. Henry S. Burton
3d N.Y. Lt., Co. E
3d N.Y. Lt., Co. K
3d N.Y. Lt., Co. M
N.Y. Lt., 7th Btty.
N.Y. Lt., 16th Btty.
1st R.I. Lt., Co. F
3d R.I., Co. C
1st U.S., Co. B
4th U.S., Co. L
5th U.S., Co. A
Unattached Troops
2d N.H.
79th N.Y.

Cavalry Division, Brig. Gen. August V. Kautz

1st Brigade, Col. Robert M. West
3d N.Y.
5th Pa.
2d Brigade, Col. Samuel M. Spear
1st D.C.
11th Pa.

Confederate Forces, 15 June, 1864

Army of Northern Virginia, Gen. Robert E. Lee

Provost Guard, Maj. D. B. Bridgford
1st Va. Bn.
39th Va. Bn. Cav.
Engineers, Col. T. M. R. Talcott
1st Confederate Engineers
2d Confederate Engineers

First Army Corps, Maj. Gen. Richard H. Anderson
Pickett's Division, Maj. Gen. George E. Pickett

Steuart's Brigade, Brig. Gen. George H. Steuart
9th Va.
14th Va.
38th Va.
53d Va.
57th Va.

Corse's Brigade, Brig. Gen. Montgomery D. Corse
15th Va.
17th Va.
29th Va.
30th Va.
32d Va.
Hunton's Brigade, Brig. Gen. Eppa Hunton
8th Va.
18th Va.
19th Va.
28th Va.
56th Va.
Terry's Brigade, Col. William R. Terry
1st Va.
3d Va.
7th Va.

11th Va.
24th Va.

Field's Division, Maj. Gen. Charles W. Field

Bratton's Brigade, Brig. Gen. John Bratton
1st S.C.
2d S.C. Rifles
5th S.C.
6th S.C.
Palmetto Sharpshooters

Anderson's Brigade, Brig. Gen. George T. Anderson
7th Ga.
8th Ga.
9th Ga.
11th Ga.
59th Ga.

Law's Brigade, Col. William F. Perry
4th Al.
15th Al.
44th Al.
47th Al.
48th Al.

Gregg's Brigade, Brig. Gen. John Gregg
3d Ark.
1st Tx.
4th Tx.
5th Tx.

Benning's Brigade, Col. Dudley M. DuBose
2d Ga.
15th Ga.
17th Ga.
20th Ga.

Kershaw's Division, Brig. Gen. Joseph B. Kershaw

Kershaw's Brigade, Col. John W. Henagan
2d S.C.
3d S.C.
7th S.C.
8th S.C.
15th S.C.
3d S.C. Bn.

Humphreys' Brigade, Brig. Gen. Benjamin G. Humphreys
13th Miss.
17th Miss.
18th Miss.
21st Miss.

Wofford's Brigade, Brig. Gen. William T. Wofford
16th Ga.
18th Ga.
64th Ga.
Cobb's (Ga.) Legion)
Phillips' (Ga.) Legion)
3d Ga. Bn. Sharpshooters

Bryan's Brigade, Col. James P. Simms
10th Ga.
50th Ga.
51st Ga.
53d Ga.

Third Army Corps, Lt. Gen. A. P. Hill

5th Al. Bn.

Anderson's Division, Brig. Gen. William Mahone

Sanders' Brigade, Col. John C. C. Sanders
8th Al.
9th Al.
10th Al.
11th Al.
14th Al.

Mahone's Brigade, Col. David A. Weisiger
6th Va.
12th Va.
16th Va.
41st Va.
61st Va.

Harris' Brigade, Brig. Gen. Nathaniel H. Harris
12th Miss.
16th Miss.
19th Miss.
48th Miss.

Wright's Brigade, Brig. Gen. Ambrose R. Wright
3d Ga.
22d Ga.
48th Ga.
2d Ga. Bn.
10th Ga. Bn.
Perry's Brigade, Brig. Gen. Joseph Finegan
2d Fla.
5th Fla.
8th Fla.
9th Fla.
10th Fla.
11th Fla.

Heth's Division, Maj. Gen. Henry Heth

Davis' Brigade, Brig. Gen. Joseph R. Davis
1st Confederate Bn.
2d Miss.
11th Miss.
26th Miss.
42d Miss.
55th N.C.
Cooke's Brigade, Brig. Gen. John R. Cooke
15th N.C.
27th N.C.
46th N.C.
48th N.C.
Kirkland's Brigade, Col. William MacRae
11th N.C.
26th N.C.
44th N.C.
47th N.C.
56th N.C.
Fry's Brigade, Col. Robert M. Mayo
13th Al.
2d Md. Bn.
1st Tenn.
7th Tenn.
14th Tenn.
40th Va.
47th Va.

55th Va.
22d Va. Bn.

Wilcox's Division, Maj. Gen. Cadmus M. Wilcox

Thomas' Brigade, Brig. Gen. Edward L. Thomas
14th Ga.
35th Ga.
45th Ga.
49th Ga.
Lane's Brigade, Brig. Gen. James H. Lane
7th N.C.
18th N.C.
28th N.C.
33d N.C.
37th N.C.
McGowan's Brigade, Brig. Gen. Samuel McGowan
1st S.C. (P. A.)
12th S.C.
13th S.C.
14th S.C.
Orr's Rifles
Scales' Brigade, Brig. Gen. Alfred M. Scales
13th N.C.
16th N.C.
22d N.C.
34th N.C.
38th N.C.

Cavalry Corps

Hampton's Division, Maj. Gen. Wade Hampton

Dunovant's Brigade, Brig. Gen. John Dunovant
3d S.C.
4th S.C.
5th S.C.
6th S.C.
Young's Brigade, Brig. Gen. Pierce M. B. Young
Cobb's (Ga.) Legion
Phillips (Ga.) Legion
Jeff. Davis (Miss.) Legion

Millen's (Ga.) Bn.
Love's (Al.) Bn.
7th Ga.
Rosser's Brigade, Brig. Gen.
Thomas L. Rosser
7th Va.
11th Va.
12th Va.
35th Va. Bn.

Fitzhugh Lee's Division, Maj. Gen. Fitzhugh Lee

Wickham's Brigade, Brig. Gen.
Williams C. Wickham
1st Va.
2d Va.
3d Va.
4th Va.
Lomax's Brigade, Brig. Gen.
Lunsford L. Lomax
5th Va.
6th Va.
15th Va.

W. H. F. Lee's Division, Maj. Gen. W. H. F. Lee

Barringer's Brigade, Brig. Gen.
Rufus Barringer
1st N.C.
2d N.C.
3d N.C.
5th N.C.
Chambliss' Brigade, Brig. Gen.
John R. Chambliss, Jr.
9th Va.
10th Va.
13th Va.

Artillery, Brig. Gen. William N. Pendleton

First Corps Art., Brig. Gen. E. Porter Alexander

Huger's Bn., Lieut. Col. Frank
Huger
Fickling's (Va.) Btty.
Moody's (La.) Btty.
Parker's (Va.) Btty.
J. D. Smith's (Va.) Btty.

Taylor's (Va.) Btty.
Woolfolk's (Va.) Btty.
Haskell's Bn., Maj. John C.
Haskell
Flanner's (N. C.) Btty.
Garden's (S. C.) Btty.
Lamkin's (Va.) Btty.
Ramsay's (N. C.) Btty.
Cabell's Bn., Col. Henry C. Cabell
Callaway's (Ga.) Btty.
Carlton's (Ga.) Btty.
McCarthy's (Va.) Btty.
Manly's (N.C.) Btty.
Gibbes' Bn., Maj. Wade H. Gibbes
Davidson's Btty.
Dickenson's Btty.
Otey's Btty.

Second Corps Art., Brig. Gen. Armistead L. Long

Carter's Bn., Lt. Col. Thomas H.
Carter
Morris (Va.) Art.
Orange Art.
King William Art.
Jeff. Davis (Al.) Art.
Cutshaw's Bn., Maj. Wilfred E.
Cutshaw
Charlottesville Art.
Staunton Art.
Courtney Art.
Brown's Bn., Lt. Col. Robert A.
Hardaway
Powhatan Art.
2d Co. Richmond Howitzers
3d Co. Richmond Howitzers
Rockbridge Art.
Salem Flying Art.

Third Corps Art., Col. R. Lindsay Walker

Cutts' Bn., Lt. Col. Allen S. Cutts
Ross' Btty.
Patterson's Btty.
Irwin Art.
Richardson's Bn., Lt. Col. Charles Richardson
Lewis Art.

Donaldsonville Art.
Norfolk Light Art.
Huger Art.
McIntosh's Bn., Lt. Col. David G.
McIntosh
Johnson's Btty.
Hardaway Art.
Danville Art.
2d Rockbridge Art.
Pegram's Bn., Lt. Col. William J.
Pegram
Pee Dee Art.
Fredericksburg Art.
Letcher Art.
Purcell Art.
Crenshaw's Btty.
Poague's Bn., Lt. Col. William T.
Poague
Madison Art.

Albemarle Art.
Brooks Art.
Charlotte Art.
Washington Art., Lieut. Col. Benjamin Eshelman
First Co.
Second Co.
Third Co.
Fourth Co.

Horse Art., Maj. R. Preston Chew
Breathed's Bn., Maj. James Breathed
Washington (S. C.) Art.
Johnston's (Va.) Btty.
2d Jeb Stuart (Va.) Horse Art.
Shoemaker's (Va.) Btty.
Thomson's (Va.) Btty.

Department of N.C. and Southern Va., Gen. P. G. T. Beauregard

Johnson's Division, Maj. Gen. Bushrod R. Johnson
Elliott's Brigade, Brig. Gen. Stephen Elliott
7th S.C.
8th S.C.
22nd S.C.
23rd S.C.
26th S.C.
Holcombe Legion (S. C. Infantry)
Gracie's Brigade, Brig. Gen. Archibald Gracie
41st Al.
43rd Al.
59th Al.
23rd Al. Bn.
Johnson's Brigade, Col. John S. Fulton
7th Tenn.
23rd Tenn.
25th Tenn.
44th Tenn.
63rd Tenn.

Moseley's (Art.) Bn., Maj. Edgar F. Moseley
Young's (Va.) Btty.
Miller's (N. C.) Btty.
Slaten's (Ga.) Btty.
Cumming's (N. C.) Btty.
Coit's (Art.) Bn., Maj. James C. Coit
Wright's (Va.) Btty.
Pegram's (Va.) Btty.
Bradford's (Miss.) Btty.
Kelly's (S. C.) Btty.

Hoke's Division, Maj. Gen. Robert F. Hoke
Clingman's Brigade, Brig. Gen. Thomas L. Clingman
8th N.C.
31st N.C.
51st N.C.
61st N.C.
Colquitt's Brigade, Brig. Gen. Alfred H. Colquitt
6th Ga.
19th Ga.

23d Ga.
27th Ga.
28th Ga.
Hagood's Brigade, Brig. Gen.
  Johnson Hagood
  11th S.C.
  21st S.C.
  25th S.C.
  27th S.C.
  7th S.C. Bn.
Martin's Brigade, Brig. Gen.
  James G. Martin
  17th N.C.
  42d N.C.
  50th N.C.
  66th N.C.
Read's (Art.) Bn., Maj. John P. W.
  Read
  Marshall's (Va.) Btty.
  Macon's (Va.) Btty.
  Sullivan's (Va.) Btty.
  Dickerson's (Va.) Btty.

First Military District, Brig.
Gen. Henry A. Wise
Wise's Brigade, Col. Powhatan
  R. Page
  26th Va.
  34th Va.
  46th Va.
  59th Va.
Dearing's (Cav.) Brigade, Brig.
  Gen. James Dearing
  7th Confederate
  62d Ga.
  4th N.C.
  6th N.C.
  Barham's Bn., Va. Cav.
  Petersburg Art.
Not Brigaded
  44th Va. Bn.
  Archer's Militia
  Hood's Bn.
  64th Ga.
Bogg's (Art.) Bn., Maj. Francis J.
  Boggs
  Martin's (Va.) Btty.
  Sturdivant's (Va.) Btty.

Department of Richmond, Lt. Gen. Richard S. Ewell

Ransom's Brigade, Brig. Gen.
  Matthew W. Ransom
  24th N.C.
  25th N.C.
  35th N.C.
  49th N.C.
  66th N.C.
Cav. Brigade, Brig. Gen. Martin
  W. Gary
  Hampton Legion
  7th S.C.
  24th Va.
Local Defense Troops and Reserves, Brig. Gen. George W.
  C. Lee

1st Bn., Local Defense Troops
2d Bn., Local Defense Troops
3d Bn., Local Defense Troops
4th Bn., Local Defense Troops
5th Bn., Local Defense Troops
6th Bn., Local Defense Troops
1st Regiment Reserves
Not Brigaded
  60th Al.
  25th Va. Bn. Infantry
  1st Bn. Cav., Local
  1st Battalion Cav., Local
    Defense

Art. Defenses, Lt. Col. John C. Pemberton

First Division (Inner Line), Lt.
  Col. John W. Atkinson

10th Va. Bn. Hvy. Art.
19th Va. Bn. Hvy. Art.

Second Division (Inner Line), Lt.
Col. James Howard
18th Va. Bn. Hvy. Art.
20th Va. Bn. Hvy. Art.
Unattached
La. Guard Art.
Light Art., Lt. Col. Charles E.
Lightfoot
Caroline (Va.) Art.
2d Nelson (Va.) Art.
Surry (Va.) Art.
Chaffin's Farm, Maj. Alexander
W. Stark

Mathews (Va.) Art.
McComas (Va.) Art.
Chaffin's Bluff, Lt. Col. J. M.
Maury
Goochland (Va.) Art.
James City (Va.) Art.
Pamunkey (Va.) Art.
Drewry's Bluff, Maj. F. W. Smith
Johnson (Va.) Art.
Neblett (Va.) Art.
Southside (Va.) Art.
United (Va.) Art.

Order of Battle:
1 April 1865

Armies of the U.S., Lt. Gen. Ulysses S. Grant

Escort
5th U.S. Cav., Cos. B, F and K

Headquarters Guard
4th U.S.

Army of the Potomac, Maj. Gen. George G. Meade

Provost Guard, Brig. Gen.
George N. Macy
1st Ind. Cav.
1st Mass. Cav., Cos. C and D
3d Pa. Cav.
11th U.S., 1st Bn.
14th U.S., 2d Bn.
Headquarters Guard
3d U.S.
Quartermaster's Guard
Independent Co. Oneida (N.Y.)
Cav.
Engineer Brigade, Brig. Gen.
Henry W. Benham
15th N.Y. (9 cos.)
50th N.Y.
Independent Brigade, Brig. Gen.
Charles H. T. Collis
1st Mass. Cav. (8 cos.)
61st Mass.
80th N.Y. (20th Militia)
68th Pa.

114th Pa.
Battalion U.S. Engineers, Maj.
Franklin Harwood
**Artillery, Brig. Gen. Henry J.
Hunt**
Siege Train, Brig. Gen. Henry W.
Abbot
1st Connecticut Hvy. Art.
Connecticut Lt., 3d Btty.
Artillery Reserve, Brig. Gen. William Hays
Maine Lt., 2d Btty. (B)
Maine Lt., 3d Btty. (C)
Maine Lt., 4th Btty. (D)
Maine Lt., 6th Btty. (F)
N.Y. Lt., 12th Btty.
1st Oh. Lt., Co. H
1st Pa. Lt., Co. F
1st R.I. Lt., Co. E
Vermont Lt., 3d Btty.

II Army Corps, Maj. Gen.
Andrew A. Humphreys
1st Division, Brig. Gen.
Nelson A. Miles
1st Brigade, Col. George W. Scott
26th Michigan
5th N.H. (bn.)
2d N.Y. Hvy. Art.
61st N.Y.
81st Pa.
140th Pa.
2d Brigade, Col. Robert Nugent
28th Mass. (5 cos.)
63d N.Y. (6 cos.)
69th N.Y.
88th N.Y. (5 cos.)
4th N.Y. Hvy. Art.
3d Brigade, Brig. Gen. Henry J.
Madill
7th N.Y.
39th N.Y.
52d N.Y.
111th N.Y.
125th N.Y.
126th N.Y. (bn.)
4th Brigade, Brig. Gen. John Ramsey
64th N.Y.
66th N.Y.
53d Pa.
116th Pa.
145th Pa.
148th Pa.
183d Pa.

2d Division, Brig. Gen.
William Hays
1st Brigade, Col. William A. Olmsted
19th Maine
19th Mass.
20th Mass.
7th Mich.
1st Minnesota (2 cos.)
59th N.Y. (bn.)
82d N.Y. (bn.)/detachment 4
2n N.Y. attaached.

152d N.Y.
184th Pa.
36th Wisconsin
2d Brigade, Col. James P. McIvor
8th N.Y. Hvy. Art.
155th N.Y.
164th N.Y.
170th N.Y.
182d N.Y. (69th N.Y. National
Guard Art.)
3d Brigade, Brig. Gen. Thomas A.
Smyth
14th Conn.
1st Delaware
12th N.J.
10th N.Y. (bn.)
108th N.Y.
4th Oh. (4 cos.)
69th Pa.
106th Pa. (3 cos.)
7th W.V. (4 cos.)
Unattached
2d Company Minnesota
Sharpshooters

3d Division, Maj. Gen.
Gershom Mott
1st Brigade, Brig. Gen. Regis de
Trobriand
20th Ind.
1st Me. Hvy. Art.
40th N.Y.
73d N.Y.
86th N.Y.
124th N.Y.
99th Pa.
110th Pa.
2d Brigade, Brig. Gen. Byron R.
Pierce
17th Me.
1st Mass. Hvy. Art.
5th Mich.
93d N.Y.
57th Pa.
105th Pa.
141st Pa.
3d Brigade, Brig. Gen. Robert
McAllister

11th Mass.
7th N.J.
8th N.J.
11th N.J.
120th N.Y.

Artillery Brigade, Lt. Col. John G. Hazard

Mass. Lt., 10th Btty.
1st N.H., Co. M
1st N.J. Lt., Co. B
N.Y. Lt., 11th Btty.
4th N.Y. Hvy., Co. C
4th N.Y. Hvy., Co. L
1st R.I. Lt., Co. B
4th U.S., Co. K

V Army Corps, Maj. Gen. Gouverneur K. Warren

Escort
4th Pa. Cav., Co. C
Provost Guard
104th N.Y.

1st Division, Maj. Gen. Charles Griffin

1st Brigade, Brig. Gen. Joshua L. Chamberlain
85th N.Y.
98th Pa.
2d Brigade, Brig. Gen. Edgar M. Gregory
187th N.Y.
188th N.Y.
189th N.Y.
3d Brigade, Maj. Gen. Joseph J. Bartlett
1st Me. Sharpshooters
20th Me.
32d Mass.
1st Mich.
16th Mich./Brady's and Jardine's companies Mich. Sharpshooters attached.
83d Pa.
91st Pa.
118th Pa.
155th Pa.

2d Division, Maj. Gen. Romeyn B. Ayres

1st Brigade, Brig. Gen. Frederick Winthrop
5th N.Y. (veteran)
15th N.Y. Hvy. Art.
140th N.Y.
146th N.Y.
2d Brigade, Brig. Gen. Andrew W. Denison
1st Md.
4th Md.
7th Md.
8th Md.
3d Brigade, Brig. Gen. James Gwyn
3d Delaware
4th Delaware
8th Delaware (3 cos.)
157th Pa. (4 cos.)
190th Pa.
191st Pa.
210th Pa.

3d Division, Brig. Gen. Samuel W. Crawford

1st Brigade, Col. John A. Kellogg
91st N.Y.
6th Wis.
7th Wis.
2d Brigade, Brig. Gen. Henry Baxter
16th Me.
39th Mass.
97th N.Y.
11th Pa.
107th Pa.
3d Brigade, Brig. Gen. Richard Coulter
94th N.Y.
95th N.Y.
147th N.Y.
56th Pa.
88th Pa.
121st Pa.
142d Pa.
Unattached
1st Bn. N.Y. Sharpshooters

Artillery Brigade, Brig. Gen. Charles S. Wainwright
1st N.Y. Lt., Co. B
1st N.Y. Lt., Co. D
1st N.Y. Lt., Co. H
15th N.Y. Hvy., Co. M
4th U.S., Co. B
5th U.S., Co. D and G

VI *Army Corps*, Maj. Gen. Horatio G. Wright
Escort
21st Pa. Cav., Co. E

1st *Division*, Maj. Gen. Frank Wheaton
1st Brigade, Brig. Gen. William H. Penrose
1st and 4th N.J. (bn.)
2d N.J. (2 cos.)
3d N.J. (1 cos.)
10th N.J.
15th N.J.
40th N.J.
2d Brigade, Brig. Gen. Joseph E. Hamblin
2d Conn. Hvy. Art.
65th N.Y.
121st N.Y.
95th Pa.
3d Brigade, Col. Oliver Edwards
37th Mass.
49th Pa.
82d Pa.
119th Pa.
2d R.I.
5th Wis.

2d *Division*, Maj. Gen. George W. Getty
1st Brigade, Brig. Gen. Frank Wheaton
62d N.Y.
93d Pa.
98th Pa.
102d Pa.
139th Pa.
2d Brigade, Maj. Gen. Lewis A. Grant

2d Vt.
3d Vt.
4th Vt.
5th Vt.
6th Vt.
1st Vt. Hvy. Art.
3d Brigade, Col. Thomas W. Hyde
1st Me. (veteran)
43d N.Y. (5 cos.)
49th N.Y. (5 cos.)
77th N.Y. (five cos.)
122d N.Y.
61st Pa.

3d *Division*, Brig. Gen. Truman Seymour
1st Brigade, Col. William S. Truex
14th N.J.
106th N.Y.
151st N.Y. (5 cos.)
87th Pa.
10th Vt.
2d Brigade, Brig. Gen. J. Warren Keifer
6th Md.
9th N.Y. Hvy. Art.
110th Oh.
122d Oh.
126th Oh.
67th Pa.
138th Pa.

Artillery Brigade, Maj. Andrew Cowan
1st N.J. Lt., Co. A
N.Y. Lt., 1st Btty.
N.Y. Lt., 3d Btty.
9th N.Y. Hvy., Co. L
1st R.I. Lt., Co. G
1st R.I. Lt., Co. H
5th U.S., Co. E
1st Vt. Hvy., Co. D

IX *Army Corps*, Maj. Gen. John G. Parke
Provost Guard
79th N.Y.

1st Division, Maj. Gen. Orlando B. Willcox

1st Brigade, Col. Samuel Harriman
8th Mich.
27th Mich.
109th N.Y.
51st Pa.
37th Wis.
38th Wis.

2d Brigade, Col. Ralph Ely
1st Mich. Sharpshooters
2d Mich.
20th Mich.
46th N.Y.
60th Oh.
50th Pa.

3d Brigade, Col. Gilbert P. Robinson
3d Md. (4 cos.)
29th Mass.
57th Mass.
59th Mass.
18th N.H.
14th N.Y. Hvy. Art.
100th Pa.

Acting Engineers
17th Mich.

2d Division, Maj. Gen. Robert B. Potter

1st Brigade, Brig. Gen. John I. Curtin
35th Mass.
36th Mass.
58th Mass.
39th N.J.
51st N.Y.
45th Pa.
48th Pa.
7th R.I.

2d Brigade, Brig. Gen. Simon G. Griffin
31st Me.
3d Md.
56th Mass.
6th N.H.
9th N.H.
11th N.H.
179th N.Y.
186th N.Y.
17th Vt.

3d Division, Brig. Gen. John F. Hartranft

1st Brigade, Lt. Col. William H. H. McCall
200th Pa.
208th Pa.
209th Pa.

2d Brigade, Col. Joseph A. Mathews
205th Pa.
207th Pa.
211th Pa.

Artillery Brigade, Brig. Gen. John C. Tidball
Me. Lt., 7th Btty. (G)
Mass. Lt., 5th Btty. (E)
Mass. Lt., 9th Btty.
Mass. Lt., 11th Btty.
Mass. Lt., 14th Btty.
N.J. Lt., 3d Btty.
1st N.Y. Lt., Co. C
1st N.Y. Lt., Co. E
1st N.Y. Lt., Co. G
1st N.Y. Lt., Co. L
N.Y. Lt., 19th Btty.
N.Y. Lt., 27th Btty.
N.Y. Lt., 34th Btty.
1st Pa. Lt., Co. B
Pa. Lt., Co. D
5th U.S., Cos. C and I

Cavalry
2d Pa.

Army of the Shenandoah, Maj. Gen. Philip H. Sheridan

Cavalry Corps, Maj. Gen. Wesley Merritt

1st Division, Brig. Gen. Thomas C. Devin

1st Brigade, Col. Peter Stagg
1st Mich.
5th Mich.
6th Mich.
7th Mich.

2d Brigade, Col. Charles L. Fitzhugh
6th N.Y.
9th N.Y.
19th N.Y.
17th Pa.
20th Pa.

3d (Reserve) Brigade, Brig. Gen. Alfred Gibbs
2d Mass.
6th Pa.
1st U.S.
5th U.S.
6th U.S.

Artillery
4th U.S., Cos. C and E

2d Division (Army of the Potomac), Maj. Gen. George Crook

1st Brigade, Brig. Gen. Henry E. Davies, Jr.
1st N.J.
10th N.Y.
24th N.Y.
1st Pa. (5 cos.)
2d U.S. Art., Co. A

2d Brigade, Col. J. Irvin Gregg
4th Pa.
8th Pa.
16th Pa.

21st Pa.
1st U.S. Art., Cos. H and I

3d Brigade, Brig. Gen. Charles H. Smith
1st Me.
2d N.Y. Mounted Rifles
6th Oh.
13th Oh.

3d Division, Maj. Gen. George A. Custer

1st Brigade, Col. Alexander C. M. Pennington
1st Conn.
3d N.J.
2d N.Y.
2d Oh.

2d Brigade, Col. William Wells
8th N.Y.
15th N.Y.
1st Vt.

3d Brigade, Col. Henry Capehart
1st N.Y. (Lincoln)
1st W.V.
2d W.V. (7 cos.)
3d W.V.

Cavalry Division (Army of the James) Brig. Gen. Ranald S. Mackenzie

1st Brigade, Col. Robert M. West
20th N.Y.
5th Pa.

2d Brigade, Col. Samuel P. Spear
1st District of Columbia (bn.)
1st Md.
11th Pa.

Artillery
Wis. Lt., 4th Btty.

Army of the James, Maj. Gen. Edward O. C. Ord

Headquarters Guard
3d Pa. Hvy. Art., Co. D
3d Pa. Hvy. Art., Co. I

Engineers
1st N.Y.
Pontoniers

3d Mass. Hvy. Art., Co. I
Unattached Cavalry
   4th Mass., Cos. I, L, and M
   5th Mass. (colored)
   7th N.Y. (1st Mounted Rifles)

Defenses of Bermuda Hundred, Maj. Gen. George L. Hartsuff
Infantry Division, Maj. Gen. Edward Ferrero

1st Brigade, Brig. Gen. Gilbert H.
   McKibbin
   41st N.Y.
   103d N.Y.
   2d Pa. Hvy. Art.
   104th Pa.
2d Brigade, Col. George C. Kibbe
   6th N.Y. Hvy. Art.
   10th N.Y. Hvy. Art.
Artillery
   N.Y. Lt., 33d Btty.
Artillery, Brig. Gen. Henry L. Abbot
   13th N.Y. Hvy., Cos. A and H
   N.Y. Lt., 7th Btty.
   3d Pa. Hvy., Co. E
   3d Pa. Hvy., Co. M
Separate Brigade, Brig. Gen.
   Joseph B. Carr
Fort Pocahontas, Va., Lt. Col.
   Ashbel W. Angel
   38th N.J. (4 cos.)
   20th N.Y. Cav., Co. D
   16th N.Y. Hvy. Art., Cos. E
     and H
   184th N.Y., Co. I
Harrison's Landing, Va., Col.
   Wardwell G. Robinson
   184th N.Y.
   1st U.S. Colored Cav., Co. I
Fort Powhatan, Va., Col. William
   J. Sewell
   38th N.J. (6 cos.)
   20th N.Y. Cav., Co. F
   3d Pa. Hvy. Art. (detachment)
   1st U.S. Colored Cav., Co. E

XXIV Army Corps, Maj. Gen. John Gibbon

Headquarters Guard, Capt.
   Charles E. Thomas
   4th Mass. Cav., Co. F
   4th Mass. Cav., Co. K

1st Division, Brig. Gen. Robert S. Foster

1st Brigade, Col. Thomas 0. Osborn
   39th Ill.
   62d Oh.
   67th Oh.
   85th Pa.
   199th Pa.
3d Brigade, Col. George B. Dandy
   10th Conn.
   11th Me.
   24th Mass.
   100th N.Y.
   206th Pa.
4th Brigade, Col. Harrison S.
   Fairchild
   8th Me.
   89th N.Y.
   148th N.Y.
   158th N.Y.
   56th Pa.

3d Division, Brig. Gen. Charles Devens

1st Brigade, Col. Edward H. Ri-
   pley
   11th Conn.
   13th N.H.
   81st N.Y.
   98th N.Y.
   130th N.Y.
   19th Wis.
2d Brigade, Col. Michael T. Dona-
   hue
   8th Conn.
   5th Md.
   10th N.H.
   12th N.H.
   96th N.Y.
   118th N.Y.

9th Vt.

3d Brigade, Col. Samuel H. Roberts

21st Conn.

40th Mass.

2d N.H.

58th Pa.

188th Pa.

Independent Division, Maj. Gen. John W. Turner

1st Brigade, Lt. Col. Andrew Potter

34th Mass.

116th Oh.

123d Oh.

2d Brigade, Col. William B. Curtis

23d Ill.

54th Pa.

12th W.V.

3d Brigade, Brig. Gen. Thomas M. Harris

10th W.V.

11th W.V.

15th W.V.

Artillery, Maj. Charles C. Abell

3d N.Y. Lt., Co. B

3d New York Lt., Co. H

3d N.Y. Lt., Co. K

3d N.Y. Lt., Co. M

N.Y. Lt., 17th Btty.

1st Pa. Lt., Co. A

1st R.I. Lt., Co. F

1st U.S., Co. B

4th U.S., Co. I.

5th U.S., Co. A

5th U.S., Co. F

XXV Army Corps, Maj. Gen. Godfrey Weitzel

Provost Guard

4th Mass. Cav., Cos. E and H

1st Division, Maj. Gen. August V. Kautz

1st Brigade, Brig. Gen. Alonzo G. Draper

22d U.S. Colored Troops

36th U.S. Colored Troops

38th U.S. Colored Troops

118th U.S. Colored Troops

2d Brigade, Brig Gen. Edward A. Wild

29th Conn. (colored)

9th U.S. Colored Troops

115th U.S. Colored Troops

117th U.S. Colored Troops

3d Brigade, Brig. Gen. Henry G. Thomas

19th U.S. Colored Troops

23d U.S. Colored Troops

43d U.S. Colored Troops

114th U.S. Colored Troops

Attached Brigade, Brig. Gen. Charles S. Russell

10th U.S. Colored Troops

28th U.S. Colored Troops

Cavalry

2d U.S. Colored

2d Division, Brig. Gen. William Birney

1st Brigade, Col. James Shaw, Jr.

7th U.S. Colored Troops

109th U.S. Colored Troops

116th U.S. Colored Troops

2d Brigade, Col. Ulysses Doubleday

8th U.S. Colored Troops

41st U.S. Colored Troops

45th U.S. Colored Troops

127th U.S. Colored Troops

3d Brigade, Col. William W. Woodward

29th U.S. Colored Troops

31st U.S. Colored Troops

Artillery Brigade, Capt. Loomis L. Langdon

Conn. Lt., 1st Btty.

N.J. Lt., 4th Btty.

N.J. Lt., 5th Btty.

1st Pa. Lt., Co. E

3d R.I., Co. C

1st U.S., Co. D

1st U.S., Co. M

4th U.S., Co. D

Confederate Forces

Army of Northern Va., Gen. Robert E. Lee

Provost Guard, Maj. D. B. Bridgford
- 1st Va. Bn.
- 44th Va. Bn. Cav., Co. B

Escort
- 39th Va. Bn.

Engineers, Col. T. M. R. Talcott
- 1st Confederate Engineers
- 2d Confederate Engineers

First Army Corps, Lt. Gen. James Longstreet

Pickett's Division, Maj. Gen. George E. Pickett

Steuart's Brigade, Brig. Gen. George H. Steuart
- 9th Va.
- 14th Va.
- 38th Va.
- 53d Va.
- 57th Va.

Corse's Brigade, Brig. Gen. Montgomery D. Corse
- 15th Va.
- 17th Va.
- 29th Va.
- 30th Va.
- 32d Va.

Hunton's Brigade, Brig. Gen. Eppa Hunton
- 8th Va.
- 18th Va.
- 19th Va.
- 28th Va.
- 56th Va.

Terry's Brigade, Brig. Gen. William R. Terry
- 1st Va.
- 3d Va.
- 7th Va.
- 11th Va.
- 24th Va.

Field's Division, Maj. Gen. Charles W. Field

Law's Brigade, Brig. Gen. William F. Perry
- 4th Al.
- 15th Al.
- 44th Al.
- 47th Al.
- 48th Al.

Anderson's Brigade, Brig. Gen. George T. Anderson
- 7th Ga.
- 8th Ga.
- 9th Ga.
- 11th Ga.
- 59th Ga.

Benning's Brigade, Brig. Gen. Henry L. Benning
- 2d Ga.
- 15th Ga.
- 17th Ga.
- 20th Ga.

Gregg's Brigade, Col. R. M. Powell
- 3d Ark.
- 1st Tx.
- 4th Tx.
- 5th Tx.

Bratton's Brigade, Brig. Gen. John Bratton
- 1st S.C.
- 5th S.C.
- 6th S.C.
- 2d S.C. Rifles
- Palmetto Sharpshooters

Kershaw's Division, Maj. Gen. Joseph B. Kershaw

DuBose's Brigade, Brig. Gen. Dudley M. DuBose
- 16th Ga.
- 18th Ga.
- 24th Ga.
- 3d Ga. Bn. Sharpshooters

Cobb's (Ga.) Legion
Phillips' (Ga.) Legion
Humphrey's Brigade, Brig. Gen.
Benjamin G. Humphreys
13th Miss.
17th Miss.
18th Miss.
21st Miss.
Simms' Brigade, Brig. Gen.
James P. Simms
10th Ga.
50th Ga.
51st Ga.
53d Ga.

Second Army Corps, Lt. Gen. John B. Gordon
Grimes' Division, Maj. Gen. Bryan Grimes
Battle's Brigade, Col. Edwin L.
Hobson
3d Al.
5th Al.
6th Al.
12th Al.
61st Al.
Grimes' Brigade, Col. D. G. Coward
32d N.C.
43d N.C.
45th N.C.
53d N.C.
2d N.C. Bn.
Cox's Brigade, Brig. Gen. William R. Cox
1st N.C.
2d N.C.
3d N.C.
4th N.C.
14th N.C.
30th N.C.
Cook's Brigade, Col. Edwin A.
Nash
4th Ga.
12th Ga.
21st Ga.
44th Ga.

Patterson s (Ga.) Bat.
Early's Division, Brig. Gen. James A. Walker
Johnston's Brigade, Col. John W.
Lea
5th N.C.
12th N.C.
20th N.C.
23d N.C.
1st N.C. Bn., Sharpshooters
Lewis' Brigade, Capt. John Beard
6th N.C.
21st N.C.
54th N.C.
57th N.C.
Walker's Brigade, Maj. Henry
Kyd Douglas
13th Va.
31st Va.
49th Va.
53d Va.
58th Va.
Gordon's Division, Brig. Gen. Clement A. Evans
Evans' Brigade, Col. John H.
Lowe
13th Ga.
26th Ga.
31st Ga.
38th Ga.
60th Ga.
61st Ga.
9th Ga. Bn. Art.
12th Ga. Bn. Art.
18th Ga. Bn. Infantry
Terry's Brigade, Col. Titus V.
Williams
2d Va.
4th Va.
5th Va.
10th Va.
21st Va.
23d Va.
25th Va.
27th Va.
33d Va.
37th Va.

42d Va.
44th Va.
48th Va.
York's Brigade, Col. Eugene
  Waggaman
1st La.
2d La.
5th La.
6th La.
7th La.
8th La.
9th La.
10th La.
14th La.
15th La.

Third Army Corps, Lt. Gen. A. P. Hill

Provost Guard
5th Al. Bn.

Mahone's Division, Maj. Gen. William Mahone

Forney's Brigade, Brig. Gen. William H. Forney
8th Al.
9th Al.
10th Al.
11th Al.
13th Al.
14th Al.
Weisiger's Brigade, Brig. Gen.
  David A. Weisiger
6th Va.
12th Va.
16th Va.
41st Va.
61st Va.
Harris' Brigade, Brig. Gen.
  Nathaniel H. Harris
12th Miss.
16th Miss.
19th Miss.
48th Miss.
Sorrel's Brigade, Col. George E.
  Tayloe
3d Ga.
22d Ga.

48th Ga.
64th Ga.
2d Ga. Bn.
10th Ga. Bn.
Finegan's Brigade, Col. David
  Lang
2d Fl.
5th Fl.
8th Fl.
9th Fl.
10th Fl.
11th Fl.

Heth's Division, Maj. Gen. Henry Heth

Davis' Brigade, Brig. Gen. Joseph
  R. Davis
1st Confederate Bn.
2d Miss.
11th Miss.
26th Miss.
42d Miss.
Cooke's Brigade, Brig. Gen. John
  R. Cooke
15th N.C.
27th N.C.
46th N.C.
48th N.C.
55th N.C.
MacRae's Brigade, Col. William
  MacRae
11th N.C.
26th N.C.
44th N.C.
47th N.C.
52d N.C.
McComb's Brigade, Brig. Gen.
  William McComb
2d Md. Bn.
1st Tn.
7th Tn.
14th Tn.
17th Tn.
23d Tn.
25th Tn.
44th Tn.
63d Tn.

Wilcox's Division, Maj. Gen. Cadmus M. Wilcox

Thomas' Brigade, Brig. Gen. Edward L. Thomas
14th Ga.
35th Ga.
45th Ga.
49th Ga.

Lane's Brigade, Brig. Gen. James H. Lane
18th N.C.
28th N.C.
33d N.C.
37th N.C.

McGowan's Brigade, Brig. Gen. Samuel McGowan
1st S.C. (P. A.)
12th S.C.
13th S.C.
14th S.C.
Orr's Rifles

Scales' Brigade, Col. Joseph H. Hyman
13th N.C.
16th N.C.
22d N.C.
34th N.C.
38th N.C.

Anderson's Corps, Lt. Gen. Richard H. Anderson

Johnson's Division, Maj. Gen. Bushrod R. Johnson

Wallace's Brigade, Brig. Gen. William H. Wallace
17th S.C.
18th S.C.
22nd S.C.
23rd S.C.
26th S.C.
Holcombe Legion (S. C. Infantry)

Moody's Brigade, Brig. Gen. Young M. Moody
41st Al.
43rd Al.
59th Al.

23rd Al. Bn.

Wise's Brigade, Col. John T. Goode
26th Va.
34th Va.
46th Va.
59th Va.

Ransom's Brigade, Brig. Gen. Matthew W. Ransom
24th N.C.
25th N.C.
35th N.C.
49th N.C.
56th N.C.

Cavalry Corps, Maj. Gen. Fitzhugh Lee

Fitzhugh Lee's Division, Brig. Gen. Thomas L. Munford

Munford's Brigade
1st Va.
2d Va.
3d Va.
4th Va.

Payne's Brigade, Brig. Gen. William H. Payne
5th Va.
6th Va.
15th Va.
36th Va. Bn.

Gary's Brigade, Brig. Gen. Martin W. Gary
7th Ga.
7th S.C.
Hampton (S.C.) Legion
24th Va.

W. H. F. Lee's Division, Maj. Gen. William H. F. Lee

Barringer's Brigade, Brig. Gen. Rufus Barringer
1st N.C.
2d N.C.
3d N.C.
5th N.C.

Beale's Brigade, Capt. Samuel H. Burt

9th Va.

10th Va.

13th Va.

14th Va.

Roberts' Brigade, Brig. Gen. William P. Roberts

4th N.C.

16th N.C. Bn.

Rosser's Division, Maj. Gen. Thomas L. Rosser

Dearing's Brigade, Brig. Gen. James Dearing

7th Va.

11th Va.

12th Va.

35th Va. Bn.

McCausland's Brigade

16th Va.

17th Va.

21st Va.

22d Va.

Artillery, Brig. Gen. William N. Pendleton

First Corps, Brig. Gen. E. Porter Alexander

Cabell's Bn., Maj. S. P. Hamilton

Anderson's (Va.) Bat.

Callaway's (Ga.) Bat.

Carlton s (Ga.) Bat.

Manly's (N. C.) Bat.

Huger's Bn., Maj. Tyler C. Jordan

Fickling's (S. C.) Bat.

Moody's (La.)Bat.

Parker's Va.) Bat.

J. D. Smith s (Va.) Bat.

Taylor's (Va.) Bat.

Woolfolk's (Va.) Bat.

Hardaway's Bn., Lt. Col. Robert A. Hardaway

Powhatan (Va.) Art.

3d Company Richmond Howitzers

Rockbridge (Va.) Art.

Salem Flying Art.

Haskell's Bn., Maj. John C. Haskell

Flanner's (N. C.) Bat.

Garden's (S. C.) Bat.

Lamkin's (Va.) Bat.

Ramsay's (N. C.) Bat.

Stark's Bn., Lt. Col. Alexander W. Stark

La. Guard Art.

Mathews (Va.) Art.

McComas (Va.) Art.

Johnson's Bn., Maj. Marmaduke Johnson

Clutter's (Va.) Art.

Fredericksburg Art.

Second Corps, Brig. Gen. Armistead L. Long

Nelson's Bn., Lt. Col. William Nelson

Amherst Art.

Milledge's (Ga.) Art.

Fluvanna Art.

Braxton's Bn., Lt. Col. Carter M. Braxton

Alleghany Art.

Lee Art.

Stafford Art.

Cutshaw's Bn., Maj. Wilfred E. Cutshaw

Orange Art.

Staunton Art.

2d Richmond Howitzers

Third Corps, Col. R. Lindsay Walker

McIntosh's Bn., Col. David G. McIntosh

1st Md. Bat.

4th Md. Bat.

Danville Art.

Hardaway Art.

2d Rockbridge Art.

Pegram's Bn., Col. William J. Pegram

Ellett's Art.

Letcher Art.

Pee Dee Art.

Purcell Art.

Poague's Bn., Lt. Col. William T. Poague

Madison Art.
Albemarle Art.
Brooks Art.
Charlotte Art.
Richardson's Bn., Lt. Col. Charles Richardson
Lewis Art.
Donaldsonville (La.) Art.
Norfolk Light Art.
Huger Art.
Lane's Bn., Maj. John Lane
Ross' Bat.
Patterson's Bat.
Irwin Art.
Owen's Bn., Maj. William M. Owen
Chamberlayne's Bat.
Dickenson's Art.
Walker's Bat.
Washington Art., Lt. Col. Benjamin Eshleman
1st Co.
2d Co.
3d Co.
4th Co.

Anderson's Corps, Col. Hilary P. Jones
Coit's Bn., Maj. James C. Coit
Wright's (Va.) Bat.
Pegram's (Va.) Bat.

Bradford's (Miss.) Bat.
Kelly's (S. C.) Bat.
Blount's Bn., Maj. Joseph G. Blount
Cumming's (N. C.) Bat.
Lowry's Bat.
Miller's (N. C.) Bat.
Slaten's (Ga.) Bat.
Stribling's Bn., Maj. Robert M. Stribling
Marshall's (Va.) Bat.
Macon's (Va.) Bat.
Sullivan's (Va.) Bat.
Dickerson's (Va.) Bat.
Sturdivant's Bn., Capt. N. A. Sturdivant
Martin's (Va.) Bat.
Sturdivant's (Va.) Bat.

Horse Artillery, Lt. Col. R. Preston Chew
Breathed's Bn., Maj. James Breathed
Johnston's (Va.) Bat.
Shoemaker's (Va.) Bat.
Thomson's (Va.) Bat.
Chew's Bn.
Petersburg Art.
2d Jeb Stuart (Va.) Horse Art.

Department of Richmond, Lt. Gen. Richard S. Ewell

G. W. C. Lee's Division, Maj. Gen. G. W. C. Lee
Barton's Brigade, Brig. Gen. Seth M. Barton
22d Va. Bn.
25th Va. Bn.
40th Va.
47th and 50th Va.
Moore's Brigade, Brig. Gen. Patrick T. Moore
3d Regiment Local Defense Troops
1st Va. Reserves

2d Va. Reserves
1st Va. Bn. Reserves
2d Va. Bn. Reserves
Artillery Brigade, Col. Stapleton Crutchfield
10th Va. Bn. Hvy. Art.
18th Va. Bn. Hvy. Art.
19th Va. Bn. Hvy. Art.
20th Va. Bn. Hvy. Art.
Garrison Chaffin's Bluff
Ninth Ga. Art. Bn.

**Light Art., Lt. Col. Charles E.
Lightfoot**
Caroline (Va.) Art.
2d Nelson (Va.) Art.
Surry (Va.) Art.
**Chaffin's Bluff, Lt. Col. J. M.
Maury**
Goochland (Va.) Art.
James City (Va.) Art.

Pamunkey (Va.) Art.
**Drewry's Bluff, Maj. F. W.
Smith**
Johnson (Va.) Art.
Neblett (Va.) Art.
Southside (Va.) Art.
United (Va.) Art.

Department of North Carolina and Southern Virginia

**First Military District, Brig.
Gen. Henry A. Wise**
Petersburg, Maj. W. H. Ker
3d Bn. Va. Reserves
44th Va. Bn.

Hood's Bn. Operatives
Second-Class Militia
Independent Signal Corps

Index